FOR THE KINGDOM AND THE POWER

The Big Money Swindle That Spread Hate Across America

Dale W. Laackman

First Edition

S. **Woodhouse** Books

Chicago ▪ Milwaukee

For the Kingdom and the Power:
The Big Money Swindle That Spread Hate Across America
Dale W. Laackman

First Edition-May 2014

S. **Woodhouse** Books
S. Woodhouse Books, an imprint of Everything Goes Media
www.swoodhousebooks.com
www.everythinggoesmedia.com

Publisher's Cataloging-In-Publication Data
(Prepared by The Donohue Group, Inc.)

Laackman, Dale W.
   For the kingdom and the power : the big money swindle that spread hate across America / Dale W. Laackman. -- 1st ed.

   p. : ill., facsims. ; cm.

   Includes bibliographical references and index.
   Issued also as an ebook.
   ISBN: 978-1-893121-98-0 (hardcover)
   ISBN: 978-1-893121-43-0 (trade pbk.)

1. Tyler, Mary Elizabeth Bessie, 1881-1924. 2. Clarke, Edward Young, Jr., 1877- 3. Ku Klux Klan (1915-)--Membership--History. 4. Swindlers and swindling--United States. 5. Advertising executives--United States. I. Title.

HS2330.K63 L33 2014
322.4/20973
2013951206

18 17 16 15 14   10 9 8 7 6 5 4 3 2 1

For Natalie, Andrew, and Christopher

CONTENTS

INTRODUCTION

This is not a Klan book.

There have been many books written about the history and the activities of the Ku Klux Klan. Its violent, clandestine past has been well chronicled.

This is a book about selling, about marketing, about public relations, and about journalism.

The product just happens to be the Klan.

This is a story of two brilliant marketing executives who, in the early days of the twentieth century, used their collective genius to spread hate across America.

The year 1920 saw a combustible mix of socioeconomic conditions, events, and personalities that may never occur again. Edward Young Clarke Jr. and Elizabeth "Bessie" Tyler understood their opportunity and seized it. Their reward was unbelievable treasure. Their place in history lies solidly in the halls of infamy.

Their legacy is not a proud one. They could have sold any product. Instead, they chose profit over principle. Their methods and strategies were groundbreaking, the plan was all encompassing, their execution was seamless and decisive.

This is a cautionary tale. Communications professionals have an obligation to conduct their business responsibly. Their power to persuade is considerable. The public needs to be wary of both message and motive.

I am reminded of a powerful image I first saw as a young advertising major in college. Assigned reading for my Intro to Advertising course was *The Hidden Persuaders* by Vance Packard. The cover illustration on my paperback edition showed a barbed fish hook buried in a gleaming fresh, red apple.

The message was clear.

PROLOGUE

Thursday, November 25, 1915. Thanksgiving Day in Atlanta, Georgia.

As days go, it had been fairly typical for late autumn in the heart of the American South. The United States Weather Bureau recorded a high temperature of sixty-three, and the low would reach forty-three degrees. There was no precipitation reported.[1]

The bold heading on the front page of the November 25 *Atlanta Constitution* read "Husband slays wife and then shoots self after attending play at theatre."

Another article announced "Baghdad almost in grip of British Forces." The ancient Babylonian capital was a part of the Central Power's Ottoman Empire. At war's end Britain and Gertrude Bell would create the new nation of Iraq.

World War I was in its second year. Earlier in the year, the British ship *Lusitania* had been sunk by a German U-boat, killing 128 Americans. Woodrow Wilson strove to remain neutral. The United States would not send troops to France for nearly two more years.

There was the little matter of Pancho Villa. United States–Mexico relations were strained and tension was high. The Mexican revolutionary general bristled at America aiding the effort to defeat him. The *Constitution* article on Thanksgiving Day filed from Nogales, Arizona, told of U.S. troops massing against Villa's men on the Mexican border. In three months, on March 9, 1916, Villa would stage one of the most daring invasions of American soil. At 4:20 that morning he raided and burned the city of Columbus, New Mexico, killing eighteen U.S. citizens. General John J. Pershing and 6,000 troops would be dispatched to find and capture Villa. Pershing would never defeat the elusive general.

November 25, 1915, was Andrew Carnegie's eightieth birthday. By the time of his death, at eighty-four, the steel magnate would give away over $350 million, much of it to build libraries across the country.

The Sports page previewed Georgia Tech's year-ending football game at Grant Field against archrival Alabama Polytechnic Institute. In 1960 Alabama Poly's name would be officially changed to Auburn University.

The Civil War had ended just fifty years earlier, and Reconstruction had kept hated federal troops in the South until only thirty-eight years prior to 1915. Confederate veterans still walked the streets, now in their seventies and eighties. Memories of Sherman's burning of Atlanta and march through Georgia were still fresh in the minds of many Georgians. Yet Atlantans still celebrated the national Thanksgiving holiday proclaimed in 1863 by the Republican, Union commander in chief, Abraham Lincoln.

A notice in the *Constitution* announced Thanksgiving Dinner at the Winecoff Hotel from Noon to 6:30 p.m. "Roast young, Georgia turkey, chestnut dressing, cranberry sauce, candied sweet potatoes, fancy appetizers, and desserts. Good food—Good service—Good music." All for the princely sum of $1.

Advertisements in the November 25 edition give a snapshot of life in 1915 Atlanta. Dr. E. G. Griffith's Gate City Dental on Alabama Street featured crown and bridge work for $4, painless extractions for $.50, teeth filled for $1, and a complete set of teeth for $5.

Davison-Paxon-Stokes announced a sale of Paradise Plumage—feather trimming for women's hats—a bunch of ten for $1.95 (regularly $3.50).

A. O. & Roy Donettoo offered a $75 complete funeral with twenty-five separate items.

At the Georgian movie theatre you could see "the graceful actor Hobart Henley in *The Phantom Fortune*, a Broadway Universal Feature." At the Grand, Dustin Farnum starred in *The Gentleman from Indiana*.[2]

However, the events of the day were of little concern to William Joseph Simmons.

For months he had planned an excursion and ceremony that would not be reported in the November 25 *Atlanta Constitution*. Yet the consequences of this event would resonate in print—and history—for many years to come.

On October 16, Simmons and thirty-three other men had applied for a charter from the State of Georgia and Fulton County, Georgia. The charter was for a fraternal, patriotic, secret, not-for-profit organization. In 1915 there were dozens of similar private clubs operating in the state of Georgia. Fully four years before the enactment of Prohibition, Georgia was a dry state, though the Georgia legislature had provided that members of such clubs could keep liquor in their lockers and drink it on the premises. These organizations had come to be known as "bottle clubs."

As was the custom with fraternal orders, most had elaborate initiations, secret handshakes, intricate hierarchies, and lavish uniforms. Simmons's organization was no different. He had been a member of at least a dozen fraternal societies. What was different was the name affixed to the charter—The Knights of the Ku Klux Klan.[3]

On that Thanksgiving evening, Simmons had rented a travel bus and he and fifteen others headed for Stone Mountain at twilight.

Stone Mountain today is one of the most popular tourist destinations in Georgia, described as the world's largest exposed piece of granite. Skeptics will say larger examples exist, and that Stone Mountain is a quartz monzonite dome, therefore not technically granite.[4] Only sixteen miles east of Atlanta, it affords views from atop of up to thirty miles on a clear day.

The mountain reaches a height of 825 feet above the ground surface and is nearly five miles in circumference at the base. Its post–Civil War history boasts a quarry that supplied building materials for the gold depository at Fort Knox, the foundation of the Lincoln Memorial, the Imperial Hotel in Tokyo, and the Panama Canal.[5]

Visitors today can golf, camp, and hike at the Stone Mountain theme park. They can also take a cable car ride to the summit, view laser and fireworks shows, and boat on Stone Mountain Lake.[6]

That is has the world's largest bas relief carving imbedded in its north face, the brainchild of the United Daughters of the Confederacy in 1912, is the mountain's claim to fame. Funds were raised, and a young sculptor was commissioned to design a memorial to Confederate war heroes. Gutzon Borglum envisioned a massive carving featuring General Robert E. Lee.

By 1924 creative differences forced Borglum off the project. He went on to another large sculpture, Mount Rushmore in the Badlands of South Dakota. The Stone Mountain project continued under Augustus Lukeman and now featured Lee, Confederate President Jefferson Davis, and General Thomas "Stonewall" Jackson.

The Confederate memorial was ultimately completed in 1970 and measures 90 feet by 190 feet. The surface covers an area of three acres, is the size of three football fields.

The dedication ceremony in 1970 was attended by a standing United States vice president, Spiro Agnew—an odd decision for a monument to leaders of a rebellion against the federal government. The mountain had become a symbol of slavery and segregation, so much so that it was mentioned in Martin Luther King Jr.'s "I Have a Dream" speech on August 28, 1963, when he said, ". . . Let Freedom ring from Stone Mountain of Georgia . . ." Certainly Dr. King had in mind Joseph Simmons and his fifteen adherents.[7]

On that chilly November evening in 1915 there were no miniature golf courses or laser shows. Simmons could not take a cable car ride to the top or gaze upon the Confederate heroes. All that lay ahead of him was a cold rock dome with a steep trail to the summit.

William Simmons's choice of Stone Mountain was certainly dramatic and, possibly, symbolic. Lashed atop his rental bus was a tall pine cross the group solemnly carried to the crest of this barren slab of rock. Simmons's followers dutifully covered the cross with excelsior and soaked it with kerosene. They gathered sixteen boulders, presumably one each for those present, and formed a crude altar upon which rested an American flag and an unsheathed sword.

Bathed in the blaze of the fiery cross, the sixteen dedicated themselves to American principles, the tenets of Protestant Christianity, and the eternal maintenance of white supremacy. Simmons described his new order as "The World's Greatest Secret, Social Patriotic, Fraternal, Beneficiary Order. . . . A High Class Order for Men of Intelligence and Character."

Simmons read a passage from the Bible. Romans 12 drips with the necessary platitudes associated with fraternal and beneficial organization. It is not known if Simmons read the entire chapter that night, but these verses sum the tone intended:

Recompense to no man evil for evil. Provide things honest in the sight of all men. If it is possible, as much as lieth in you, live peaceably with all men. . . . Be not overcome of evil, but overcome evil with good.
—Romans 12, Verses 17–18, 21, King James Version

With that, the Invisible Empire was born.

Few Atlantans took notice of the orange glow in the distance.[8]

Within four years, Simmons's Klan would be near extinction with only a few thousand loosely organized members. Yet, just five years later in 1924, thousands of Klansmen would boldly march down Pennsylvania Avenue in Washington, D.C., active Klan chapters would operate in all forty-eight states, the Klan would be powerful enough to influence state and national elections, and the ranks would swell to four to six million—nearly one in every three eligible men in America.

This uniquely American drama was played out by a fascinating cast of characters—a charismatic true believer, an amoral flim-flam man, a tough-as-nails single mother, an idealistic whistle blower, and a poetic crusader. It is a tale of violence and terror, of spectacle and sex, of hatred and hypocrisy. And behind-the scenes, it is also a story of misguided genius and unbridled greed.

CHAPTER 1
True Believer

"Man is made by his belief. As he believes, so he is."
—Johann Wolfgang von Goethe

"Belief creates the actual fact."
—William James

"The thing always happens that you really believe in; and the belief in a thing makes it happen."
—Frank Lloyd Wright

William Joseph Simmons was a good Calvinist.

Calvinists believe in original sin, sometimes called total depravity. All men are born sinful. There's nothing you can do about it. They also believe in unconditional election, a condition also known as predestination. Some men are predestined into everlasting life. They are called the elect. Romans 8 tells Protestants that God already knows the outcome of the choices men make, and God causes everything to work together for the good of those who love God and are called according to his purpose.

William Simmons knew God had a very important plan for his life.

He was born on May 6, 1880, in Harpersville, Shelby County, Alabama, to a country doctor named Calvin Henry Simmons and his wife, Lavonia David Simmons. Little is known about Simmons's early life, including his formal education. By his own assertion he intended to follow in his father's footsteps and enter the medical profession. Simmons claimed to have completed some pre-medical training at Johns Hopkins University in Baltimore, though researchers have not been able to find his name in the records there.[1]

Since medicine was not in the cards, Simmons next considered a career in the Army. Throughout American history a tried-and-true path to success came through the military. Heroes have long been revered in American society. As Simmons approached his eighteenth birthday, the United States was a nation at peace. That was about to change.

In the late 1890s America was itching to enter the colonial arena. European powers had long held lands in South America, Africa, and the Far East. American industrialists longed to operate in a mercantilist system that would provide raw materials and markets. It all began innocently enough. The United States began to focus on human rights abuses by the Spanish government in nearby Cuba. President William McKinley hoped for a diplomatic solution, but public favor for the war was fanned by a journalistic corps intent on military action and newspaper sales.

> How long are the Spaniards to drench Cuba with the blood and tears of her people? . . . How long shall old men and women and children be murdered by the score, the innocent victim of Spanish rage against the patriot armies they cannot conquer? . . . How long shall the United States sit idle and indifferent?
>
> ———New York World, 1897[2]

On February 15, 1898, the U.S. Navy battleship *Maine* was blown up in the harbor of Havana, resulting in the death of 266 American sailors. To this day it is not certain if the damage was done externally by Spanish forces, or internally by some accident. Americans were positive of the former.

A hesitant President McKinley received a declaration of war on April 23, 1898. Secretary of State John Hay would call the following ten-week conflict a "Splendid Little War."

The Navy was prepared for war. The Army was not. With only 28,000 active troops, whose last significant action had come against the Plains Indians, a call went out for 50,000 additional men. A nation hungry for adventure responded with over 200,000, both volunteers and mobilized state National Guard units.[3]

William Joseph Simmons was one who answered the call. The 1st Alabama Volunteer Infantry was organizing in Mobile in May 1898. Freshly turned eighteen, Simmons was there. Patrick McSherry's *A Brief History of the 1st Alabama Volunteer Infantry* provides an interesting saga.

Forty-eight officers and 941 enlisted men comprised the unit under the command of Col. E. L. Higdan. "Simmons, William J." is found on the roster as a private in Company B, the Wheeler Rifles out of Florence, Alabama. The Alabama Volunteers trained quickly and intensely. Eventually they were stationed in Miami, Florida.

There was glory to be found in battle. No one knew that as well as the extremely ambitious Theodore Roosevelt. An architect of the Navy's preparedness as undersecretary of the Navy, Roosevelt resigned and assembled a volunteer unit known as the Rough Riders. By the middle of June, Roosevelt was in Tampa ready to embark for Cuba. On July 1 he led the assault on San Juan Hill that would eventually propel him to the presidency.

The 1st Alabama was not quite so fortunate. They reached their embarkation point, Camp Cuba Libre in Jacksonville, on August 13, 1898, the day the Spanish and the United States agreed to an armistice. Since there was no longer a need for their services, the regiment requested to be relieved from service. The soldiers returned to Birmingham, Alabama, and were given pay and a thirty-day furlough. According to McSherry, money and time off proved a recipe for disaster. There were several "bloody affairs," including drunken fights, bayonet wounds, and one private shooting another to death. The men of the 1st Alabama were officially mustered out on October 31, 1898, in Birmingham. During its existence, the 1st Alabama recorded the deaths of one officer and fifteen enlisted men, all of disease. A total of thirty-two soldiers were listed as deserters. McSherry concluded that the regiment proved more dangerous to themselves and to other American citizens than the military forces of Spain.[4] For young William Simmons, the experience apparently dulled any expectations of a military career.

As it turns out, a talent William Simmons did possess was with the spoken word. He was a spellbinding speaker. Soon he gravitated to the Protestant ministry, where sermon giving is central to worship. For approximately ten years Simmons was in the employ of the Methodist Episcopal Church, South (MEC,S). The denomination was an offshoot of the Methodist Episcopal Church.[5]

English theologian John Wesley founded Methodism in the eighteenth century. He was appalled by slavery, and when the Methodist Episcopal Church was founded in 1784, it officially opposed the institution. However, there were congregations in the American South controlled by wealthy plantation owners. A controversy arose in the early 1840s concerning a Methodist bishop, the Rev. James Osgood Andrew in Georgia. The Reverend Andrew owned two slaves. The Church Conference voted to remove Andrew from his office unless he freed his slaves. The dispute led Methodists in the South to break off and form the Methodist Episcopal Church, South in 1844.[6] At the conclusion of the Civil War, freed blacks left the church to begin their own Methodist denomination, leaving the MEC,S exclusively white.[7]

William Simmons worked as a circuit minister. Due to the rural nature of the South, preachers often had to travel from small church to small church. These communities could not financially support a full-time pastor. MEC,S records show that in 1892 5,368 men were employed as traveling preachers.[8] Simmons spent his time traveling the circuit to tent revivals and camp meetings. As a hellfire-and-brimstone orator he gained a reputation as a powerful evangelist. However, in 1912, Simmons was relieved of duty by the Alabama Methodist Conference for overspending allowances and running his churches into debt.[9]

It was during his decade in the ministry that Simmons learned he was predestined by God to perform a great mission. He received an epiphany, a spiritual event that was a sudden flash of recognition. Later he would describe that summer evening. Sitting at his window, he had suddenly seen a row of white-robed figures on horseback riding across the sky. Behind them was a rough outline of a map of the United States. He fell at once to his knees in prayer. Documenting it afterwards, he wrote, "Ere long, I clearly conceived the embryonic medium of its supply. I then and there solemnly dedicated my life and consecrated my all, to the task of maturing that medium."[10]

William Simmons was no stranger to the Ku Klux Klan. Dr. Calvin Henry Simmons had been a member of the original Klan. At his father's knee he heard many tales of the Klan's activities. His family had had African American help and they, too, told the young boy of terror-filled days following the Civil War.[11]

The history of the first Klan is, in essence, a history of post–Civil War Reconstruction. In December 1865 six young men in Pulaski, Tennessee, decided to form a social club. The war had ended in April of that year. The six had been officers in the Confederate Army and were looking for something to do to cure their newfound boredom. A number of the six had been college men, familiar with the southern collegiate fraternity, Kuklos Adelphon. The name translates to "circle of brothers." They simply added *clan* after the word Kuklos to name the club, later changing the *c* to *k* for alliterative convenience. Initially, their sport was to dress up in robes and play the part of ghosts of Confederate dead. The targets of their pranks were superstitious former slaves. The club gained new members but remained primarily relevant in central Tennessee.[12]

Washington, D.C., dictated the next move. Abraham Lincoln had formulated a benevolent process for readmitting the rebellious Southern states back into the Union. Lincoln's untimely death at Ford's Theatre had passed the task to his vice president, Andrew Johnson. Under the plan, ten percent of each state's 1860 electorate was required to abolish slavery, repeal secession ordinances, and settle any Confederate war debts. Blanket amnesty was given to any ex-Confederate who swore an oath of loyalty to the United States. By November 1865 all states, with the exception of Texas, had come to terms. Newly elected congressmen were ready to return to Capitol Hill. However, these Southern states began enacting "Black Codes," which virtually returned black citizens to a status near slavery. This open defiance of civil rights infuriated the Radical Republicans faction led by Thaddeus Stevens and Charles Sumner, whose sole ambition was to punish the once rebellious states. In a quick series of legislative moves, Congress passed America's first Civil Rights Bill and the Fourteenth Amendment to the Constitution, guaranteeing freed men full citizenship. Finally, in March 1867, Congress passed the first of several Reconstruction Acts. The new Southern state governments were dissolved and the former Confederacy was partitioned into military districts ruled by Union generals. New elections were held and blacks were empowered to vote for the first time in Southern history. For Southern whites, the world had turned upside down.[13]

It was time for the Klan to act. In April 1867 leaders held a meeting in Nashville's Maxwell House Hotel to organize and bind isolated groups together. The social situation in the South had changed significantly, and their goal was to restore that antebellum society of white supremacy. The Klan claimed to be "lovers of law and order, peace and justice." They would be just the opposite.

The conference elected as their first grand wizard Confederate hero Nathan Bedford Forrest. Forrest represented a solid choice for leading a terrorist organization bent on the suppression of blacks. He was a self-made millionaire who gained his fortune as a planter, real estate investor, and slave trader. Enlisting as a private at the onset of hostilities, Forrest quickly rose to the rank of lieutenant general, commanding an elite cavalry unit. His most infamous act during the war was the massacre of more than 250 black prisoners of war at Fort Pillow, Tennessee.[14]

With that, a reign of terror ensued. In his *The Ku Klux Klan: History, Organization, Language, and Activities of America's Most Notorious Secret Society*, Michael Newton describes some of the violence:

> *Murders were common, and floggings more so: one victim was left crippled after he received 900 lashes on a midnight raid. In Alabama Congress documented 109 murders committed by Grand Dragon John Morgan's knights, and that number was no doubt conservative. Klansmen burned Greene County's courthouse, followed shortly by three schools for blacks. In Eutaw, Klan rioters killed four blacks and wounded fifty in October 1870. Georgia was worse under Grand Dragon (later Governor and U.S. Senator) John Gordon. In a three month period from August to October 1868, Klansmen killed thirty-one persons, shot forty-three more, stabbed five, and whipped at least fifty-five, including eight floggings of 300 to 500 lashes apiece.* [15]

Much of the Klan violence was politically inspired. Both Northern carpetbaggers and freed blacks tended to vote Republican. Southern whites were overwhelmingly Democrats. Republicans, black and white, were constantly at risk. Klan threats made a significant difference in election outcomes. During the spring primary in 1868 in Oglethorpe County, Georgia, Republicans had received more than 1,100 votes. In the November election, the number had slipped to 116. In Columbia County, the numbers fell from 1,122 to a single vote.

Again, it was time for the federal government to intervene. The Fifteenth Amendment was passed, giving the vote to all former slaves. In 1870 and 1871 Congress passed the "Force Acts." These laws made it a federal offense to influence voters, to prevent citizens from voting, and to deprive one's civil rights, including life. Finally, in April 1871 a bill called the Ku Klux Act defined Klan violence as rebellion against the United States, allowing the president to declare martial law.[16] U.S. President Grant sent in the 7th Cavalry to arrest and prosecute Klan terrorists. George Armstrong Custer was called in from the Indian Territories and stationed in Elizabethtown, Kentucky. (Klan activity in Elizabethtown was minimal so Custer spent most of his time breeding horses and collecting hunting dogs.) The Army intervention was effective, and organized Klan activity ceased to exist in the South.[17] Imperial Wizard Forrest decreed a dissolution of the order. Organized violence was no longer necessary. However, the residual effect of terror remained. Most blacks again understood their place in Southern society. The Klan would lie dormant for forty-three years.

The disputed presidential election of 1876 sealed the fate for blacks for the South for a long time to come. The Compromise of 1877 secured twenty vital and contested electoral votes for Republican Rutherford B. Hayes. The price was the removal of federal troops in the South. In 1877 the U.S. Army marched out of the former Confederacy, and Reconstruction was over.

It took little time for whites to act. Black Codes returned as Jim Crow Laws and whites regained control of state legislatures. Whites separated themselves from blacks in virtually every aspect of daily life. The antebellum socioeconomic system had been restored. Slavery was no longer legal, but it was replicated through legislative and economic control. In

1896 the Supreme Court decision known as *Plessy v. Ferguson* formally validated segregation as long as it was "separate but equal." Of course, it was never equal.

If God had chosen William Joseph Simmons to revive the Ku Klux Klan, he selected a man ill prepared for the task. Simmons was a talented speaker, but as his Methodist experience had indicated, not necessarily a gifted organizer and businessman. He needed training and found it not in the formal arena of academia, but in the hard knocks, grass-roots world of early twentieth-century fraternal organizations.

The period following the Civil War could be called the "Golden Age of Fraternalism." Charles Metz, writing in 1927, stated there were 800 different fraternal organizations operating in the United States. He went on to estimate that 30,000,000 to 60,000,000 people in the U.S. (1920 Census) held membership in some fraternal group.[18] Most of these organizations had their beginnings in the late 1800s and the early 1900s.

The following is a representative sampling of major fraternal organizations in nineteenth-century America.

The American Protective Society (1887)—2,000,000 members in 1900. Opposed Roman Catholicism. Used a patriotism theme.

Fraternal Order of Eagles (1891)—Local units are called aeries. Many presidents and celebrities have been members.

Benevolent and Protective Order of Elks (1867)—Men only. Prominent members include FDR, Truman, and JFK.

Ancient Order of Foresters (1832)—Ritual based on Robin Hood and his Merry Men.

Free Masons (1720)—Model for most fraternal groups. Influential in formation of early American government.

Knights of Columbus (1882)—Catholic males eighteen and older. Answer to Free Masonry. Symbol is the Maltese Cross.

Knights of Pythias (1864)—Based on the story of Damon and Pythias. 1,000,000 members in 1920.

Junior Order of United American Mechanics of the U.S. of North America (1853)—200,000 members in 1900. Opposed to anything non-American, including the Catholic Church.

Loyal Order of the Moose (1888)—Still 1.3 million members in 1980.

Independent Order of Odd Fellows (1819)—3.4 million members in 1915.

Patrons of Husbandry (1867)—Known as the Grange. Championed farmers' rights. First to admit women.

Improved Order of Red Men (1847)—Claimed origins with The Sons of Liberty. 520,000 members in 1921 in forty-six States.

Woodmen of the World (1890)—Membership surpassed 750,000 in 1915.[19]

Albert Stevens, in his *The Cyclopedia of Fraternities,* posited that at the beginning of the twentieth century the number of fraternal memberships equaled the number of adult males in the country. This took into account the fact that many men held multiple memberships. In 1831 famed French observer Alexis de Tocqueville wrote in his *Democracy in America,* "Americans of all ages, all conditions, and all dispositions constantly form associations."[20] Historian Arthur M. Schlesinger Sr. called America a "nation of joiners." William Simmons was, therefore, under this definition, a very typical American of his time. He claimed to hold membership at one time or another in twelve to fifteen fraternal organizations.

Alvin Schmidt provides an analysis of this cultural phenomenon in his encyclopedia of American fraternal organizations. These societies can be classified, in almost all cases, in one of two ways. There are secret orders, and there are benefit societies. Secret orders are all about ritual and secrecy. They are characterized by elaborate ceremonies, ordered rankings, and extensive paraphernalia. Many are restrictive in their membership. Benefit societies are primarily engaged in providing financial security for their members, usually in the form of insurance. While secret orders generally do not exhibit beneficial traits, there are many examples of benefit orders with secret tendencies.[21]

There are many reasons for the spectacular growth of fraternal organizations in the late nineteenth and early twentieth centuries. First and foremost, they provided a feeling of importance to the common man. There was a sense of belonging. Most societies did not discriminate economically. Importantly, fraternal organizations also helped to socially integrate millions of immigrants to America. Between 1860 and 1920, forty million people left their homelands to come to America. Fraternal orders offered fellowship to these new arrivals. Many were ethnically oriented and often conducted meetings in native languages. These were orders like the Czechoslovak Society of America (1854), the Polish National Alliance (1880), the Ukrainian National Association (1894), and the Sons of Italy (1905). The benefit societies provided much-needed economic security. Insurance and death benefits were offered at a fraction of the cost in the general marketplace. Finally, belonging to a fraternal order allowed a certain social prestige for the member. There were occasions when they could be seen in public with their uniforms, medals, and colorful regalia.[22]

This was, generally, a rural movement at the turn of the century. In small towns it was easy to be noticed for one's fraternal associations. People were more anonymous in major urban areas. America was just then tilting toward an urban majority for the first time. After the 1920s, fraternal organization membership began a steady decline. As a rural phenomenon this was also a primarily Protestant one. The Catholic population was centered in the larger cities. Consequently, there was only one major Catholic order, the Knights of Columbus.

William Simmons would belong to many of these organizations, but one would become prominent in his career and in his future aspirations.

The Woodmen of the World (WOW) was founded in 1890 by Joseph Cullen Root in Omaha, Nebraska.[23] Root took the name from a sermon he had heard in church. The pastor spoke about pioneer woodsmen clearing away the forest to provide for their families. Root envisioned a society that would clear away problems of financial security for its members, making it technically a benefit order. The Woodmen of the World provides insurance for its members. Still rising above the Omaha skyline is the thirty-story Woodmen Tower constructed in 1969. Today the order is comprised of some 2,000 lodges and over 750,000 members. WOW offers youth programs, camping experiences, disaster relief assistance, and support for the orphaned children of members. Until the 1920s members were buried under tombstones shaped like tree stumps.

This benefit order also happened to have a secretive nature. In looking at photographs from the early 1900s, you will see stern-faced men in military-type uniforms, all clutching symbolic axes. One unit has a goat mascot. There are dozens of fancy medals and gold WOW pocket coins. A look at the new-member initiation ceremony from that time tells a great deal about the organization. Everything was written down, to the smallest detail. A military component ordered members to "Present axes; Carry axes; Return axes." Members entered under crossed axes. There was a carefully ordered series of secret signs, countersigns, and salutes, and the ceremonious drinking of pure water. The leaders sat behind stumps on the stage. There was a social song and an opening ode.

At one point in the ceremony, the adviser lieutenant says:

> *Consul Commander, The Sovereigns will silently and reverently bow their heads and in self-communion vow to throw aside vexations, cares, and troubles of the outside world and concentrate their thoughts upon the business of the hour, . . . that avarice, selfishness, and hatred may be banished from the Forests of Woodcraft.*

Potential new members, their heads covered in what they called a "hoodwink," paid their fee and took the Woodmen oath.[24]

William Joseph Simmons was intimately versed in all things associated with the Woodmen of the World. He rose quickly through the ranks, becoming a colonel at the youngest age then recorded by the order. His command included five regiments. WOW then hired Simmons for recruiting and insurance sales duties. Within two years he was free of debt and earning between $10,000 and $15,000 a year, a handsome salary in 1913. His new assignment, Atlanta, Georgia.[25]

It was at this point in Simmons's life that the first of three meaningful events occurred. First, he was injured in an automobile accident and forced to convalesce for a number of months.

Simmons took the time to organize his revival of the Ku Klux Klan. Borrowing heavily from the original Klan Prescript, Simmons wrote a fifty-four-page pamphlet he named "The Kloran." In it he dreamed up ranks, titles, passwords, and codes, most beginning with the letters "Kl."[26] Klankraft (similar to Woodcraft) was the essence of the Klan. A klavern was a local branch or a meeting place. A klonvocation was a general meeting or convention. The klaliff was the vice president and the person who presided over the klonvocation. The kligrapp was the organization's secretary. Kleagles were Klan organizers and recruiters.

The Kloran was the holy book of the order, and Simmons warned members to keep its secrets away from any person in the outside world. Simmons, however, was also concerned with his financial interest in the organization, and he copyrighted the Kloran on January 6, 1917, duly depositing two copies with the Library of Congress. From that day forward the secrets of the Klan were available in the nation's capital for anyone who wished to view them.[27]

Michael Newton describes the new Klan's basic philosophy. "The Simmons Klan would stand for an uncompromising standard of pure Americanism untrammeled by alien influences and free from the entanglements of foreign alliances . . . Simmons described Klannishness as real fraternity practically applied, supporting the soul of chivalry and virtue's impenetrable shield. Simmons's Knights would shield the sanctity of the home and the chastity of womanhood, while vowing to forever maintain white supremacy."[28]

The second event that would eventually lead to the Thanksgiving Day stand on Stone Mountain was the sad and sensational case of Leo Frank.

On the morning of April 26, 1913, thirteen-year-old Mary Phagan arose, setting in motion the series of events that would come to reveal a simmering stew of hatred and fear hiding beneath the surface of American society. It was a Saturday, and more importantly, Confederate

Memorial Day. The Marietta, Georgia, girl planned to attend the festive parade in nearby Atlanta. After eating a breakfast of cabbage and wheat biscuits, Mary dressed herself in her finest clothes—stockings and garters, a store-bought violet dress, gray pumps, ribbons in her hair, and a blue straw hat. She was a very attractive young woman with blue eyes, high cheek bones, a rosy smile, and a busty figure. Steve Oney in *And the Dead Shall Rise* says of young Mary, "She was exceedingly well-developed for her age, she had undoubtedly already tortured many a boy. There was simply something about her—a tilt to the chin, a dare in the gaze—that projected those flirtatious wiles that Southern girls often employ with devastating effect."[29] She then boarded the English Avenue trolley and headed to downtown Atlanta.

The Phagans were not a wealthy family. Originally from Marietta, they had moved to Alabama to farm. Mary's father, William, died there of the measles in 1899, a few months before her birth. Mary's widowed mother, Fannie, moved her family back to Georgia. Fannie eventually remarried but they barely scratched out an existence in the grimy, industrial tenement suburbs of Atlanta. Like many girls in their situation, Mary had left school to help out at home. Her first job, at age ten, was in a textile mill. At eleven her employer was a paper manufacturer. In 1911 Mary began work at her present employer, the National Pencil Factory, where she was paid ten cents an hour to run a knurling machine that inserted rubber erasers into the metal tips of pencils. Child labor had reached a crisis level throughout America, and Georgia was the only state that allowed ten-year-olds to work eleven hours a day in mills and factories.[30]

Mary Phagan never attended the Confederate Memorial Day Parade in Atlanta. On her way to the festivities, she decided to pick up her pay at the National Pencil Factory. At around 3 a.m. Sunday morning Atlanta Police received a call. At 3:30 they discovered Mary's body. She had been savagely raped and murdered.[31]

The police first centered their investigation on a black night watchman, but eventually began to suspect the twenty-nine-year-old factory superintendent, Leo Frank. Frank was a Cornell-educated Jew who was rising rapidly in Jewish Atlanta society.[32] The white, Protestant South blamed much of its misfortune on wealthy industrialists. That Frank was Jewish and northern only served to exacerbate the situation. A black janitor implicated Frank, and he was indicted for the murder.

A sensational trial ensued, enlivened by Atlanta newspapers vying for readership. Mobs surrounded the courthouse daily, listening to every word through open windows. The court of public opinion had already convicted Frank. Both the prosecution and the defense presented their cases. The jury deliberated for less than four hours. Frank and his defense team were not allowed to be present for the reading of the decision for fear of mob reaction. The verdict was guilty and Frank was sentenced to death.

A series of appeals ensued, reaching in the end the Supreme Court. An overturn of the decision was denied and an execution date of June 20, 1915, set.[33]

One man came to Leo Frank's defense. Out-going lame duck Georgia Governor John M. Slaton began investigating the case, perhaps more carefully than the judge and jury had. Slaton came to the conclusion that some doubt existed in Frank's guilt. On the day before the scheduled execution, Slaton commuted the sentence to life imprisonment and sent Frank to the Georgia prison at Milledgeville. It was an unpopular decision. Slaton and his family left Georgia and the governor was hung in effigy by angry mobs.[34]

Almost immediately, a group of Marietta men known as the "Friends of Mary Phagan" began planning an intricate operation. On the afternoon of August 16, 1915, they began the 150-mile journey from Marietta to Milledgeville. At midnight they turned off their headlights and approached the prison. The passengers covered their faces with crude masks. The men cut telephone wires and handcuffed the warden. It was reported that prison guards, many sympathetic to the cause, offered no resistance to the night invaders. Leo Frank was taken from his cell and placed in an automobile for the seven-hour drive back to Marietta.[35]

At dawn, Leo Frank was hung from a tree two miles outside Marietta, Georgia. News of the event spread quickly. Men, women, and children hurried to the grove to look at the dead body of Mary Phagan's accused killer. Photos taken that morning are both bizarre and macabre, as citizens posed with the hanging body.[36]

Frank was finally cut down and transported to Atlanta before the mob could burn his body. In Atlanta people demanded to see Frank's corpse.

His remains were then spirited to New York, where he was laid to rest in Queens.

As a result of the Leo Frank incident, The B'nai B'rith established the Anti-Defamation League in 1913. In 1982, sixty-nine years after Mary Phagan's death, Leo Frank's office boy, Alonzo Mann, gave information that cast doubt on Frank's guilt. In 1986 the state of Georgia officially pardoned Leo Frank.

Three months after the lynching of Leo Frank, a number of the men who ascended Stone Mountain with William Simmons were former members of the Friends of Mary Phagan. They were among the first recruits to the new Ku Klux Klan.[37]

The final circumstance arrived in the form of a cultural milestone—from Hollywood, California.

> *"Since Griffith, there has been no major improvement in the art of film direction."*
>
> —Frank Capra

> *"People used to flatter me by saying that D. W. Griffith and I were rivals. Griffith had no rivals. He was the teacher of us all."*
>
> —-Cecil B. DeMille

> *"He (Griffith) was instrumental in transforming movies from the nickelodeon novelty to an art form. And he originated and formalized much of the syntax of moviemaking now taken for granted."*
>
> —Stanley Kubrick

Capra, the director of *It's a Wonderful Life* and *Mr. Smith Goes to Washington*, DeMille, the director of film epics such as *The Ten Commandments*, and Kubrick, the acclaimed director of *A Clockwork Orange*, were talking about the man who unashamedly titled his autobiography, *The Man Who Invented Hollywood*.

David Wark Griffith did not intend to aid William Joseph Simmons in his launch of the modern Ku Klux Klan. He just wanted to be an actor.

D. W., as he came to be known, was born on a farm near Crestwood, Kentucky, on January 22, 1875. The Griffith home was a 264-acre plot known as Lofty Green. He was the sixth child of Jacob Wark Griffith and Mary Oglesby Griffith. Born in 1819, the elder Griffith was a virtual history textbook of the middle of the American nineteenth century. At age twenty-one he apprenticed himself to two doctors. After setting up a medical practice, he soon volunteered as a surgeon in the Mexican War, seeing action at Buena Vista and Saltillo. After the war, he married Mary but was soon on his way to the gold fields of California. Jacob returned penniless, but he soon gained a reputation for oratory and served a term in the Kentucky state legislature.[38]

When the Civil War broke out, Jacob went off to fight for the Confederacy. Kentucky was not a secessionist state, but the Griffiths were slave holders and many in Shelby County fought to maintain their economic system.[39] Jacob fought nearly the entire war. He was wounded at least twice and quickly advanced through the ranks to become a cavalry lieutenant colonel.[40]

Jacob Griffith returned from the war to a farm in debt. According to Richard Schickel, "For Jacob Griffith did little with the twenty years of life left to him when the war ended, other than to produce three more children (David in 1875). And drink. And give orations and tell tall tales. And play the fiddle at home and at country dances. And gamble."[41] On March 31, 1885, David's tenth year, Jacob Wark Griffith died at the age of sixty-six. In 1889 the family left the heavily mortgaged farm and moved to the teeming metropolis of Louisville.[42]

It was in Louisville that young D. W. was first exposed to the world of theater. At age sixteen he began touring as an actor in southern Indiana.[43] In 1897 he left Louisville for the New York stage, for uncertainty, and for the life of a starving artist.

Meanwhile, in 1893, Thomas Alva Edison created fifteen seconds of history in a black tar-paper building in West Orange, New Jersey. Using new, flexible celluloid stock, he filmed his assistant, Fred Ott, sneezing. It was the first motion picture. Soon people were viewing short, simple features in Kinetoscope parlors and nickelodeon galleries. They were intimate, one to one, viewing experiences. Then Edison created the

Vitascope projector in 1896. It was the first movie projector, and now many people could view a film together. The movie theater had been invented.[44] Frank Capra explains this new phenomena in his forward to Griffith's autobiography.

> *Film art was to be the first new art created by man since the Greeks had formalized the theatre twenty five centuries earlier . . . The story of man previously told with paint and canvas, with sculptured marble, with song and music, with written words in books, with spoken words behind footlights, that same story could now be told in a spectacular new medium. And not in cheap amusement parlors, but in one hundred thousand movie theatres throughout the world.*[45]

D. W. Griffith soon realized that his talent was not in front of the camera, but behind it. He went to work for the Biograph Film Company, first as an actor, but primarily as a director.[46]

Griffith's first directorial effort was *The Adventures of Dollie* in 1908.[47] By the time he left Biograph in 1913, D. W. Griffith had directed nearly 450 films. Of those 450 films, Edward Wagenknecht estimates eleven were two-reelers and one was a four-reeler. All the rest were one-reelers.[48] A "reel" in silent film days ran approximately thirteen to fifteen minutes in length. Biograph was focused on the bottom line. Short films meant high output and low budgets. Griffith learned his trade well. He was innovative and groundbreaking. Still, he chafed at Biograph's restrictions. He needed more time to be a better storyteller. He worked very hard at getting *Judith of Bethulia*, a four-reeler, produced in 1913. It was a critical triumph, but Biograph wanted to return to their time-worn formula. European directors were turning out six-reelers and Griffith wanted the same freedom. He left Biograph and began looking for a long-form property.[49]

He found it in a play from his earlier theater days. In 1906, Griffith had acted the lead in a production called *The Clansmen* on the New York stage. This openly Southern view of the Reconstruction era by Thomas Dixon had been a best-selling novel before being adapted for the stage. The New York press hated the play, but rural America loved it.

The Clansmen had the elements Griffith needed for his expansive feature-length film. First and foremost, there was the Civil War. In later life, Griffith would tell a biographer that his first memory was Jacob Wark Griffith's Confederate saber.[50] The elder Griffith would don his old uniform and thrust at imagined enemies for the amusement of his children. D. W. saw great battles to recreate and film. The history of the South was his history.

Secondly, the play had a great rescue scene at the end of the story. Members of the original Klan gallantly ride to save white women from threatening black Union soldiers. Griffith was perfecting an editing technique he called "switchback" or "parallel" cross cutting. The camera would switch back and forth from rescuer to rescued, building tension and anxiety. The story would also allow the director to use his other technical innovations: the close-up, the fade, masks, split screens, vignettes, and the use of an original music score.

Dixon wanted $10,000 for the film rights. Griffith didn't have the money, instead offering a percentage of box office receipts. Dixon relented. His choice netted him an eventual $1,000,000 windfall.[51]

Griffith would make a film like no other made to that point. *The Birth of a Nation* (the title was changed after previews) occupied twelve reels—nearly 190 minutes. The final budget was $100,000, more than double that of any previous movie. There are spectacular battle scenes, immense sets, and a cast of thousands. Most of all Griffith was a great storyteller. Audiences went on an emotional roller-coaster ride with the Stoneman and Cameron families.

In northern cities, there was a critical backlash to the story. According to Wagenknecht, "When Griffith was attacked for alleged racism in *The Birth of a Nation*, he seemed both surprised and hurt, and there is considerable evidence to support the view that he was sincere in this. Certainly, he has nowhere committed himself to Dixon's extremist views."[52] Griffith wasn't a propagandist. He was a filmmaker. He told, brilliantly, a story of his South.

After the March 3, 1915, New York premiere, audiences flocked to see the film. It would go on to gross more than $18,000,000.

Atlanta eagerly awaited its *Birth of a Nation* opening. Ten days after

Simmons's theatrical Stone Mountain ceremony, the film opened on December 6, 1915, at the Atlanta Theatre. Simmons had persuaded the *Atlanta Journal* to run an ad for his new society next to the ads for *The Birth of a Nation*.

Ward Greene, a film reviewer for the *Journal*, filed this story in the December 7 edition:

> *It swept the audience at the Atlanta Theatre Monday night like a tidal wave. A youth in the gallery leaped to his feet and yelled and yelled. A little boy downstairs pounded the man's back in front of him and shrieked. The man did not know it. He was a middle-aged, hard lipped citizen; but his face twitched and his throat gulped up and down. Here a young girl kept dabbing at her eyes and there an old lady just sat and let the tears stream down her face unchecked. For Birth of a Nation is the awakener of every feeling. Your heart pulses with patriotism when those boys in gray march to battle with banners whipping and the band playing Dixie; you are wringing with compassion for the mother and her girls desolate at home; you are shocked by the clamor of mighty armies flung hell bent into conflict; your throat chokes for a boy who dies with a smile on his face beside the body of his chum, the enemy. Then "the South's best friend" crumples under the assassin's bullet and the land of the Lost Cause lies like a ragged wound under a black poison that pours out upon it. Loathing, disgust, hate envelope you, hot blood cries for vengeance. Until out of the night blazes the fiery cross that once burned high above old Scotland's hills and the legions of the Invisible Empire roar down to the rescue and that's when you are lifted by the hair and go crazy![63]*

Excited theatergoers exited onto Peachtree Street to another sensational sight. Simmons's Klansmen were there in full robes and on horseback, firing rifles into the air. It was a spectacular and auspicious beginning for the Klan.

Ninety-two new members enlisted over the next two weeks. The numbers grew steadily, but slowly, in the ensuing years. Kenneth Jackson maintains that in the early years Simmons intended the secret society be no more than a genuine fraternal lodge. Publicity was nearly nonexistent. There were more B'nai B'rith members in Atlanta than there were Klansmen. There was some sporadic recruiting, plus the occasional cross burning and torchlight parade. Jonathan B. Frost had other ideas.[54]

Frost was an associate of Simmons in his Woodmen of the World days. He also edited a magazine that championed white supremacy. When Simmons organized the Klan, Frost was among the charter members. He was what Simmons was not. Simmons was a spellbinding speaker with little business sense. Frost was a hard-nosed businessman who saw great profit potential in the Klan. Ever the idealist, Simmons rejected Frost's plans. Frost responded by embezzling Klan funds and fleeing the state to begin his own secret order. Simmons successfully sued to retain sole rights to Klan rituals and regalia. He had been wise to copyright the material years earlier.

The legal battle left Simmons in financial disarray. When expenses often exceeded income Simmons attempted to meet the deficit with his own money, including placing a mortgage on his home. He later talked about those difficult days: "There were times during those five early years before the public knew of the Klan, when I walked the streets with my shoes worn through because I had no money."[55] The Invisible Empire had shrunk to two to three thousand members spread throughout Georgia and Alabama. Order was nonexistent, and they were more and more prone to violence.

William Joseph Simmons's vision of knights riding across the sky was dimming as the 1920s were dawning. The modern Ku Klux Klan was dying.

CHAPTER 2
Flim-Flam Man

"Every crowd has a silver lining."

—P. T. Barnum

"Ya got trouble, right here in River City."

—Harold Hill, The Music Man

In an early scene from Meredith Wilson's classic musical *The Music Man*, a traveling salesman seated on a train barreling through the Iowa landscape asks the man seated next to him, "How far you going, friend?" Wilson's quintessential con man, Harold Hill, replies, "Wherever the people are as green as the money."[1]

A former employee of Edward Young Clarke, Edgar I. Fuller, once said of him, "E. Y. Clarke was a modern disciple of Barnum. It was never his purpose to offer the people anything in a simple, direct, honest way."[2] Clarke liked being called "E. Y.," just as his idol was called "P. T."

Phineas Taylor Barnum was perhaps the greatest showman and promoter in American history. He was also a businessman, author, publisher, philanthropist, and politician. Notably, "I am a showman by profession . . . and all the gilding shall make nothing else of me" is what he said of himself. His desire was to make money. Barnum is the man erroneously credited with saying, "There's a sucker born every minute." He may not have uttered the phrase, but he certainly lived it and believed it.[3]

Barnum was born on July 5, 1810, in Bethel, Connecticut, the son of storekeeper Philo Barnum.[4] The young man proved to be adept at arithmetic, but no fan of physical work. The life of a storekeeper did not offer a quick way to riches, and P. T. became involved in real estate speculation and set up a statewide lottery network.[5]

When lotteries were outlawed in Connecticut in 1834, P. T. moved to New York City, seeking fame and fortune. His first foray into the entertainment world involved the purchase of a blind and partially paralyzed slave woman named Joice Heth. Barnum claimed she had been George Washington's nurse and that she was over 160 years old. Heth died in 1836, no more than eighty.[6] He then established his Barnum's American Museum, which featured curiosities including albinos, giants, midgets, jugglers, magicians, exotic women, and an animal menagerie.[7] In 1844 and 1845 Barnum toured Europe with the dwarf Tom Thumb, performing before Queen Victoria and the Czar of Russia.[8]

This was the launching pad to a career that would include theatrical promotion and the eventual "Greatest Show on Earth," The Ringling Brothers Barnum and Bailey Circus. Barnum once said, "I don't believe in duping the public, but I believe in first attracting and then pleasing them." Barnum is considered one of the first great pioneers in the field of advertising, famously quipping, "Without promotion something terrible happens . . . Nothing!" As a businessman, he was always aware of his market: "Nobody ever lost a dollar by underestimating the taste of the American public."

E. Y. Clarke Jr. was born on September 29, 1877, in Atlanta, Georgia, the son of Edward Young Clarke Sr. and Nora V. Clarke. The young man was born into a family of position and wealth in the New South following the Civil War. His father, born in 1841, had served as a Confederate colonel, and to attain such a rank in his early twenties would indicate that he came from a wealthy and influential Southern family.

After the war many members of the South's gentility found themselves in economic distress. Plantations and businesses were often ransacked and ravished by the invading Union troops. Additionally, the Confederate dollars Southerners held in great quantity proved to be worthless. Still, the elder Clarke had survived the conflict with some financial resources. Two years after the 1868 founding of the *Atlanta Constitution*, Clarke purchased the paper and made himself managing editor.[9]

There is a saying that the acorn doesn't fall far from the tree. Young

Edward learned his craft at his father's knee. Newspaper owners and editors in the late nineteenth century were tireless promoters. In the days before the invention of motion pictures, radio, and television, newspapers were a powerful instrument of communication. They existed to transmit news and to right societal wrongs, but they also published to profit. These journalistic pioneers were ever on the hunt for increased readership and advertising dollars. As such, they often became tireless boosters for the economic development of their regions. Population growth and investment translated into healthy bottom lines.[10]

The early 1870s ushered in a new journalistic genre that captivated the world's newspaper readers. It could be best described as the time of the reporter/adventurer. There were still many areas of the world unexplored by white Western civilization, and these intrepid reporters were the eyes and ears of their readers. The man most identified with this trend was Henry Morton Stanley.

The Welsh-born Stanley came to New Orleans as an eighteen-year-old in 1859.[11] He fought as a Confederate and was captured during the Battle of Shiloh in 1862. At Camp Douglas in Chicago he changed his allegiance to the Union Army, a practice known as becoming a "Galvanized Yankee."[12] At the conclusion of the war, Stanley embarked on a career as a journalist. His articles dispatched from expeditions in the Ottoman Empire and in India soon drew interest from James Gordon Bennett, the founder of the *New York Herald*. Stanley became the paper's overseas correspondent, and in 1869 he drew the assignment that would make him famous. He was told to locate the Scottish missionary David Livingstone, who had been missing for years in the deepest reaches of the African continent.[13] With a nearly unlimited budget, Stanley embarked from Zanzibar with an expedition consisting of no fewer than 200 native porters.[14] For six months they traveled through dense tropical forests, suffering through disease and desertion. Finally, in November 1871, Stanley found Livingston near Lake Tanganyika in present-day Tanzania and reportedly uttered the famous phrase, "Dr. Livingstone, I presume." Readers around the world had followed the harrowing adventure, reveling in Stanley's descriptive prose.[15]

While Stanley began a second expedition, this time to trace the course of the Congo River in 1874, two inventive Georgia newspapermen began their own quest. Charles R. Pendleton of the *Valdosta* (GA) *Times* and George W. Haines of the *Jesup* (GA) *Georgian* decided to explore the last undeveloped part of Georgia, the Okefenokee Swamp.[16]

Straddling the Georgia–Florida border, the swampland encompasses more than 438,000 acres (660 square miles) of wilderness carved 250,000 years ago by Pleistocene Age glaciers. It is the largest peat-based backwater swamp in North America.[17] The peat deposits reach depths of fifteen feet and are so unstable that the trees seem to tremble with any movement. In fact, Okefenokee is the Hitchiti Indian word for "Trembling Earth."[18]

Pendleton and Haines were seen as modern-day disciples of Lewis and Clark—manly, brave men devoted to the scientific exploration and development of the desolate and dangerous Okefenokee. In May 1875, the two enterprising explorers began their journey. The May 8 *Valdosta Times* reported that Pendleton, "is sloshing his way through mud, water, bamboo, mosquitoes, alligators, snakes, and—Gosh, our blood runs cold when we think of it!"[19] This first expedition ended in only two weeks. Heavy rain hampered every movement, and they soon ran out of provisions. However, their stories had been reprinted in several Georgia papers, including the *Atlanta Constitution*, prompting a second attempt in the drier month of August. This time the *Constitution* was a sponsor. Atlanta readership soared with each installment from the intrepid adventurers. A third expedition was immediately planned, this one exclusively funded by the *Atlanta Constitution*. Twenty-two men, including Pendleton and Haines, would enter the ominous swamp. One would be Edward Clarke Sr.

In military terms, Clarke would report to his readers, "Our tents are pitched on Billy's Island. They make quite a martial appearance, stretching in a line fronting the mighty swamp, our pretty little flag floating jauntily from its staff at the centre tent."[20] Clarke loved the romance of the moment. He said the troupe was "fully armed with the necessary implements of warfare against undergrowth and beast." The expedition was fully invested in science, geology, and surveying. So much so that Clarke lamented, "Pendleton and myself will find it no easy task to keep up with the adventure part of the programme."[21]

After his valorous incursion into the wilderness of the Okefenokee, Clarke had other matters to attend to. The September 7, 1876, *Atlanta*

Constitution happily announced the marriage of Edward Young Clarke Sr. to Miss Nora Harrison. "On account of the large number of friends of both parties and their high social position, the event created no little interest in our community." One of the wedding gifts was a magnificent style 14 grand piano made by the world renowned Wm. Knabe & Co., given to Nora by the Georgia Press Association. Another was a complete toilet set of fine china presented by the employees of the *Constitution* office. Edward was a member of the Atlanta social elite.[22]

Just over a year later, baby Edward Young Clarke Jr. arrived in the world. Observers would describe the adult E. Y. as an unimposing man with bushy black hair, a long face, and black horn-rimmed glasses. He had a nervous intensity that was often mistaken for drive and intellectualism.[23]

Edward Jr. had much in common with William Joseph Simmons, a man who would play prominently in his future. E. Y.'s first career path also led to the ministry, in this case with the Presbyterian Church. Like Simmons, he believed in predestination, and he, too, survived an automobile accident. Edward would also vacate the ministry and eventually become a solicitor and sales manager for the Woodmen of the World.

Edward's first post-pulpit job, though, would be with the *Atlanta Constitution*. Although his father had sold the newspaper, he still wielded considerable influence. In 1902 Edward landed a job as a reporter and quickly became religious editor because of his ministerial background. (E. Y.'s younger brother, Francis, also joined the paper, working his way up to managing editor before retiring in 1937.)[24]

On December 6, 1903, the *Constitution* published another wedding announcement.

SOCIAL

Clarke-Cartledge

Miss May Cartledge and Mr. Edward Young Clarke Jr., two of the most popular young people in Atlanta were married yesterday at 11 o'clock at 27 East Harris Street, the home of the bride by Dr. C.P Bridewell. Only the immediate family connections were present.[25]

According to the notice, the marriage was a surprise to all, and the young couple wanted a quiet, unpretentious ceremony. May worked as a pharmacist at the Grady Hospital, "probably the only woman in the state in her occupation." The wedding was likely one of the few moments in Edward's life not accompanied by bombast and flamboyance.

Edward settled in to married life and his profession as a newspaperman. In 1908, when May was thirty-three and Edward was thirty-one, the couple had a son named Samuel. It appears to have marked a turning point.

Perhaps the responsibility of being both husband and father began to wear thin for Edward. It is possible he chafed at a job that grew tedious and limiting. An honest day's work for an honest dollar was not enough for him anymore. In 1909, after seven years with the *Constitution,* he resigned his post and looked for ways to make money quickly. Over the next five years he indulged in a variety of money-making schemes, often resorting to chicanery, fraud, and deceit to accomplish his goals.

Edgar Fuller described his former associate in unflattering terms: "All of his (Clarke's) methods were subterranean and devious, all of his offerings were cloaked with promises that he never meant to keep, and with benefits that he could not bestow. Clarke was imbued with the idea that deception and misrepresentation were the quickest and most profitable ways to the purse of the American people."[26] Journalist Robert L. Duffus wrote in 1923 that Clarke "learned how easily people can be induced to part with their money in what is represented as a good cause."[27] Clarke, it should be noted, was not altogether successful. Neither he nor the people who trusted him made many gains.

But, in 1914, Edward did find success, and legitimacy, when he took a job with the fledgling Georgia Chamber of Commerce.

The national Chamber of Commerce movement had its genesis with the muckraking writers of the early 1900s. The American population was flowing from the farm to the city at the turn of the century. With the growth came problems of overcrowding, inadequate infrastructure, and municipal corruption. In 1904 reporter/editor Lincoln Steffans wrote his powerful "The Shame of the Cities" in *McClure's Magazine.* The article illustrated examples of corruption in city government, seeking to bring about political reform in urban America. Harold and Edgar

Buttenheim took up the cause, setting up the American City Bureau, and began publishing *The American City* magazine.[28] In 1911 President William Howard Taft in a message to Congress called for a central organization that would coordinate the activities of state and local municipal organizations. In April 1922, 700 delegates from around the country met to form the U.S. Chamber of Commerce.

In Georgia, E. Y Clarke Sr. had been a pioneer in this arena. Since selling the *Constitution* he had been a tireless crusader for the city of Atlanta. When he died in 1910 at the age of sixty-eight, his obituary trumpeted his many accomplishments: "Mr. Clarke was a constructive influence in Atlanta's early career, and subsequently, when the fledgling city had gained a foothold and was striding forward toward the expanding destiny of today. His going marks the sure and saddening disappearance of the old band of pioneers who participated in the fierce civic battles of the early days, and whose self-sacrificing endeavors were instrumental in paving the way for the metropolis of our time."[29]

Edward Jr.'s job with the Chamber was to promote cities, and he was a natural. He soon gained the nickname "the healer of sick towns" and moved up in the hierarchy of the organization. His specialty was booming communities that were not progressing as rapidly as they wished to. In 1915 he received an assignment that would shape the rest of his life.

In 1914 Georgia agriculture endured a disastrous year because of a major drought. When 1915 produced a bumper crop, Atlanta decided to sponsor a fair, "in celebration of the return of prosperity in the harvest season."[30] It was to be the most spectacular event ever seen in Georgia's capital. Edward was chosen as general manager of the Georgia Harvest Festival. This would be Clarke's homage to Barnum. This would be his "Greatest Show on Earth."

The festival would run for six days in November, from Monday the 15th until Sunday the 20th. Edward announced to the press that the Georgia Harvest Festival would "present the most dazzling line of events ever attempted within the space of one week in any city in the south, and tells the story of why the people of the state are stirred as never before in their history over an occasion of its kind."[31] It was a daunting undertaking.

Edward had all of downtown Atlanta decorated in red, white, and blue bunting. Each morning there were free vaudeville shows on Marietta Street, which included trained dog and pony acts, Russian dancers, a baby elephant, and the famous "Cloud Swing," said to be the most sensational act ever performed. On Tuesday through Friday, Lakewood Park was filled with more than $250,000 worth of cattle on exhibit. In addition there were Boy's Corn and Girl's Canning club exhibits. Daily Better Babies shows were held in the auditorium from 9 a.m. to 6 p.m. It was the largest Better Babies show ever staged in the South. Feature motion pictures were shown at every movie house in the city, with titles changed daily. The organizers claimed it constituted the most features shown in the same week of any city in the country. Carnival City featured fifteen of the finest shows ever seen, all under the management of Con T. Kennedy, the best carnival showman in the world. Included were a balloon ascension, a tight-wire performer walking between the roofs of two downtown fourteen-story buildings, and auto driver O. K. Hagen at the wheel of his 60-horsepower Metz racer. Finally, there would be morning and afternoon band concerts held at the new stand erected at the foot of the Henry W. Grady Monument on Marietta Street.

There were special daily events. Monday saw the crowning of the Harvest Festival Queen, followed by the pomp and splendor of the Queen's Ball. Regina Rambo of Marietta gathered 136,800 votes to win coronation honors.

Tuesday saw a massive civic parade that took more than two hours to pass the reviewing stand. Included in the procession were women suffragettes and 300 beautiful children pushing decorated perambulators. In the evening there was the Atlanta Society Costume Ball.

Wednesday featured the Decorated Floral Automobile Parade with maids of honor from 100 Georgia cities riding in wonderfully decorated cars. At noon fairgoers watched an Aerial Exhibition conducted by Captain J. H. Worden in his Bleriot war aeroplane. That night saw the fraternal order parade consisting of over 10,000 men from across the state.

Thursday brought more parades and dinners.

On Friday Captain Worden returned to drop an actual bomb, destroying a fort that had been constructed at the center of Piedmont Park's race track. At 2 p.m. Edward staged the spectacular "Fighting the Flames" exhibition at Ponce de Leon. A three-story frame hotel, constructed for the occasion, was set afire and "hair-breadth escapes of dancers were made from the roof."[32]

On the final day, E. Y. presented a Masked Ball in the auditorium. At midnight whistles blew and bells rang throughout the city. The Georgia Harvest Festival had come to an end. The *Atlanta Journal* called the Festival "the most successful event Atlanta had ever staged," and praised Edward, "for the highly efficient way in which all events were handled."[33]

Five days later, William Joseph Simmons and his fifteen disciples climbed to the top of Stone Mountain.

Edward Young Clarke felt like he was on top of the world. Little did he know the festival experience would effectively alter the course of his life.

CHAPTER 3
On Her Own

"She has a positive genius for executive direction. Her courage is a thing to admire."

—Louis D. Wade

"Her experience in catering to men's appetites and vices had given her an insight into their frailties. She knew how to handle them all."

—Edgar I. Fuller

"I am woman, hear me roar."

—Helen Reddy, "I Am Woman"

Bessie Tyler should have fallen through the cracks, relegated to the endless list of the nameless and faceless ignored by history.

Born Mary Elizabeth Cornett on July 10, 1881, to Benjamin M. and Frances "Fannie" Crawford Cornett, "Bessie" was the oldest of six children. She had three brothers—Rodolphus, John Wesley, and Lenard. Her sisters were Elesby and Anna.

The Cornetts lived on a small farm on the north edge of Atlanta. The U.S. Census listed the address as Militia District 469, Cooks (east part), Fulton, Georgia, enumeration district 0028, household ID-114.[1] Two-thirds of Americans still lived in rural areas. It wouldn't be until the early twentieth century that urban dwellers would outnumber those on the farm.

The South was slowly beginning to recover from the ravages of the Civil War and Reconstruction. Atlanta, burned by Sherman's forces at the end of the war, was rising like a phoenix from the ashes. The city's population had grown from 9,554 in 1860 to nearly 60,000 by 1881. In 1887 Atlanta converted from gas to electric street lamps. In 1890 more than forty miles of water pipes were laid, serving 3,800 residential and commercial subscribers. However, by 1890 not everything had been modernized. Two-thirds of the city's privies were still served by Atlanta's twelve night-soil carts.[2]

We don't know a great deal about Mary Elizabeth Cornett's early life. Record keeping in the late nineteenth-century rural South was spotty if it existed at all. Birth certificates were seldom recorded. Often a family would note the arrival of a new member on a piece of paper placed in the family Bible.

Bessie most certainly received some schooling. The Reconstruction-era Republican legislature mandated a free public education in 1866 for Georgians, funding to be derived from poll and liquor taxes. Decrees aside, little happened until the Home Rule Act of 1870 and the leadership of State School Commissioner Gustavus J. Orr.[3]

It was free and it was public, but the education was seldom equal or adequate. The schools were segregated and many could afford to operate only three to four months a year. That was okay for farm families, who needed their children to help with planting in the spring and harvest in the fall. Most schoolhouses consisted of a single room with one teacher attending to the educational needs of students ranging from kindergarten to eighth grade. At one time there were more than 7,000 of these schools in Georgia. In the 1898 Annual Report of the Department of Education for Georgia, school attendance on a given day averaged around fifty percent. The monthly salary for white teachers was $40 and $22 for blacks. The courses of study were: Orthography (the art of spelling according to established usage), Reading, Writing, English Grammar, Geography, Arithmetic, and History. By 1900 over two-thirds of America's schools still fell under the one-room model.[4]

Bessie did attend school, but for poor, Southern white girls the real education began at home. The vocation young ladies were destined to fill was that of wife and mother, often the younger the better. In this case Bessie followed the "barefoot and pregnant" stereotype perfectly.

On May 13, 1897, at age fifteen years and 307 days, Mary Elizabeth Cornett was married to Andrew Manning of neighboring Coweta County.[5] Eight days short of her sixteenth birthday she gave birth to a daughter, Minnie Dorris Manning, on July 2, 1897. She was a young mother facing a future of child bearing and child rearing. In a male-dominated society she was conceivably a second-class citizen in her own marriage. She was about to fall through the cracks.

But she didn't.

Tracing the events following Bessie's marriage to Manning is like assembling a rummage-sale jigsaw puzzle with a number of lost pieces.

We know a great deal about other famous figures of the nineteenth century. Volumes have been written about Abraham Lincoln and Mark Twain. They wrote letters and gave speeches. Friends and associates published memoirs. They were very public people. Each had poor, rural beginnings. Lincoln succeeded in spite of the absolute poverty of a log cabin upbringing in Kentucky, Indiana, and Illinois to become one of America's greatest presidents. Twain survived the rough and tumble life along the Mississippi. At the turn of the century he was arguably the most famous American in the world. This kind of upward mobility was possible in America. Horatio Algers's "Rags to Riches" novels proclaimed the rewards possible through hard work and perseverance, but it was a path to success almost exclusively available to men.

There were distinguished celebrity women in the 1800s, however, they began with distinct advantages. Florence Nightingale was born to a rich, upper-class English family, and she received a spectacular education. Louisa May Alcott was the daughter of a prominent educator whose circle of friends included Henry David Thoreau. She learned from the likes of Ralph Waldo Emerson and Nathaniel Hawthorne. Marie Curie's educator parents sent her from Poland to Paris to study. Impressionist painter Mary Cassatt had a stockbroker father and a mother raised in a family of bankers.

Mary Elizabeth Cornett Manning didn't fit any success formula. She was not a man, and she did not come from money or privilege. She did not write about herself and very few people wrote about her. She is a bit of a mystery woman. With virtually no chance for fame and fortune,

Bessie became both rich and powerful. And she did it on her own.

Records are sketchy as to exactly what happened next. Author Wyn Wade in his book, *The Fiery Cross: The Ku Klux Klan in America*, claims Bessie became a widow shortly after Minnie's birth.[6] There is no record of Andrew Manning's death, but U.S. Census Records in 1900 show Bessie again living with her parents north of Atlanta. Strangely, there is no record of Minnie living in the household with her mother.[7]

Again there are missing jigsaw puzzle pieces. The next mention we find of Mary Elizabeth Cornett Manning is in 1906. She had married again, this time to a man named Owen C. Carroll. The date of their marriage is not clear. The 1906 reference was the occasion of a Cherokee Claim.

In 1905 a U.S. Claims Court had found in favor of the Eastern Cherokee nation. In the 1830s and 1840s the United States had forcibly removed them from their land in Georgia and other parts of the Southeast to land in the Indian Territory of Oklahoma. The Cherokee had not received payment for the land and filed a case for the purpose of receiving reparations. The sum of $1,000,000 had been set aside, and the U.S. Court of Claims was given the responsibility of determining suitable recipients.

Bessie and Owen Carroll applied for a piece of the Cherokee Claim, claiming Bessie's fifth-generation Cherokee heritage. The application gave the following rationale: Bessie's father, Benjamin, had been born in Cherokee County, Georgia. He was the son of Mary Elizabeth Helton, who was the daughter of Calvin Helton, who was the son of Abraham Helton. Bessie claimed that Abraham Helton was a full-blooded Eastern Cherokee, making her fifth-generation and eligible for a portion of the government award.[8]

Mary Elizabeth Cornett Carroll's claim was rejected. Of over 90,000 applicants 30,820 were approved, each receiving approximately $33. Even if she had been accepted, that award would not have guaranteed financial security.

There are more missing pieces. The next time Bessie surfaced she was Mary Elizabeth Cornett Manning Carroll Tyler. Sometime after 1906 she was either widowed again or divorced from Owen Carroll. Bessie then married a third time to a Mr. Tyler about whom very little is known. His only apparent contribution is the name by which Bessie is best recognized. Tyler is never mentioned in literature and nothing has been found on his birth, marriage, divorce, death, or even his first name. It seems Bessie shed husbands as quickly as she acquired them.

Bessie's mastery over men is at the same time fascinating and perplexing. She was not a classically beautiful woman. There are, perhaps, a half dozen extant photographs of her. In them we see a large woman weighing at least two hundred pounds, full-faced and buxom, with auburn hair and blue eyes.[9] In all of the photos there is an air of confidence and strength that probably initially disturbed and then attracted some men. This was still at the end of the Victorian era when women were expected to be shy, demure, and secondary in status to their men. Few worked outside the home, and when they did it was in menial jobs paying far less than their male counterparts. The divorce rate was low as women tended to stay in unhappy marriages.

Whatever stigma was attached to divorce didn't seem to bother Bessie. She had been married three times by her early thirties. It is possible she manipulated men to pull herself out of poverty, using matrimony as a social mobility ladder.

The date of Bessie's next appearance was July 17, 1913, a photo and article in the *Atlanta Constitution*. Thirty-two-year-old Bessie is shown, waist up, in an ornate frame, wearing a dark dress and dark hat with an enormous brim. Her head is tilted upward and her eyes look past the camera. Her pose is confident and dignified.

Bessie's appearance in the paper had to do with a sensational story that was the talk of Atlanta. A wealthy man named Joshua B. Crawford had died and there was a bitter fight over his will. It seems that after marrying Mary Belle Crawford, Joshua had rewritten his will making his new wife the sole heir of his $250,000 estate. This was a sizable amount of money in 1913. In 2014 dollars, the inheritance would total nearly $5,000,000.

Family members previously in the will, including Bessie and her mother, were contesting. Fannie Cornett was a Crawford before marriage and was Joshua Crawford's niece. The contention was that the new Mrs. Crawford, Mary Belle, had murdered her husband or had paid someone to do the deed. Apparently the *Atlanta Constitution* sought out anyone involved in the case. In the article Bessie feigned nonchalance and ignorance in the matter, saying that she wouldn't have known great uncle Joshua if he walked past her in the street. She may very well have had great interest in the story, hoping to receive a share of the money at some point.[10] She had certainly tried for a piece of the Cherokee claim with Owen Carroll.

The interesting part of the article comes at the very end. Bessie told the reporter that she was taking a course in medicine at the Southern College of Medicine and Surgery, and that she expected to become a regularly licensed physician within the next three years. This is an unexpected statement from a largely uneducated woman who came from an impoverished background.[11]

In fact, it would be the only course she took in medical school. As with most things in Bessie's life, the brief foray into medicine was done for a reason. Years later, when Bessie granted an interview to a reporter for the *New York World*, she said, "I was interested in hygiene work for babies—sort of a better babies movement. I had taken enough of a medical course to fit myself for the work of visiting among the tenements and advising mothers about their babies."[12]

> *"Better babies mean better mothers and fathers, better homes, better cities, a better nation, a better world."*
> —Woman's Home Companion, 1913[13]

> *"The splendidly sensible Better Babies movement is spreading rapidly, is based upon sound scientific principles, and ought to arrest the attention, and command the active support, of every man and woman in the land . . . and is bringing to parenthood and childhood a dignity of recognition sorely lacking hitherto."*
> —The Farmer's Wife, 1914[14]

Bessie had padded her resume in order to join the ranks of a cultural phenomenon of early twentieth-century America.

It appears Bessie had latched on to the fashionable Better Babies contests that were spreading across rural America in 1913 and 1914. It is doubtful that she participated on a volunteer basis. Bessie was always looking for ways to make money. She is often mentioned in literature as an organizer and fundraiser for the movement.

Mary DeGarmo was the first to stage a Better Baby contest at the 1908 Louisiana State Fair in Shreveport. She was a former classroom teacher who put into practice ideas about health and intelligence standards. At the beginning of the twentieth century there were growing concerns over high rates of infant mortality in the United States. There was a move to establish benchmarks for normal childhood development and to implement new findings from health care professionals. This was one aspect of the bigger social efficiency movement that sought to standardize most elements of daily life.

DeGarmo and pediatrician Dr. Jacob Bodenheimer developed grading sheets for contestants, with standardized measurements for physical traits and intelligence. Every child started at 1,000 points and then had points deducted for areas falling below designated norms. Parents flocked to the events, hoping their child would be deemed most perfect.[15]

Another adherent to the Better Babies philosophy was Mary T. Watts, president of the Iowa Congress of Mothers. The natural place to hold contests was at large public gatherings like state fairs. Watts was able to convince organizers of the 1912 Iowa State Fair to allow a tent to be erected in which physicians would evaluate babies in the same way judges did livestock. She said, "If a hog is worth saving, why not a baby? . . . If there is a standard for calves and colts, why not for babies. In order that each mother may strive toward (that standard) for her child."[16]

How can the judges measure
All this human treasure?
Which in looks is wealthiest,
Cutest, plumpest, healthiest?
In each mother's eyes,
Hers deserves the prize.
Howling ones and yammerers,
Posing for the cameras,
What do babies care
If they're cute or fair?
Weary little winners,
Crying for their dinners!
　　—Adelaide W. Neall, "Babies on Parade"
　　　　Saturday Evening Post, 1932[17]

The Better Babies movement was a showy, seemingly harmless, man-ifestation of a larger and more insidious feeling in the early 1900s in America. As more and more immigrants flowed into the United States from southern and eastern Europe and from Asia, establishment whites feared a dilution of the American population base. World-renowned plant breeder Luther Burbank openly opposed immigration from these areas, claiming the new Americans constituted a "large portion of in-ferior representatives." David Starr Jordan, author of *Blood of the Na-tions*, wrote in 1902 about the superiority of the British Anglo-Saxon race. Burbank and Jordan were proponents of Eugenics, a social move-ment that believed America's strength lay with Nordic, Germanic, and Anglo-Saxon peoples who possessed superior genetic makeup. To keep the American population pure, they supported strict immigration and anti-miscegenation laws as well as forcible sterilization of the poor, dis-abled, and immoral. Some went so far as to advocate euthanasia in cer-tain instances.[18] This all, of course, presages the actions of WWII Nazis in Germany.

The winning standards for Better Baby contests were decidedly those of the mainstream, established white majority, and the contests drew large crowds of parents hoping their child would be deemed "perfect." Festival organizers like Edward Young Clarke also welcomed the events because the increased attendance in turn "attracted all manner of pro-moters, advertisers, food manufacturers, etc., whose purposes are com-mercial and selfish."[19]

The Better Babies people gave Bessie the task of organizing the con-tests for the Georgia Harvest Festival. By all accounts, she did her job very well. Atlanta newspapers were filled with articles on Better Babies activities both before and during the festival. Such contests often fea-tured attractive prizes, elaborate awards ceremonies, catchy slogans, and media coverage. Her Perambulator Parade held in the auditorium on Tuesday the 16th was a highlight of the week. Three hundred adorable tots handled brightly decorated baby carriages as they took dolls and stuffed animals for a stroll.

Fairgoers and the press took notice of Bessie's efforts. So did the man-ager of the Georgia Harvest Festival. The intersection of these two tra-jectories would have a profound effect on the history of America.

CHAPTER 4
An Association

"When a match has equal partners then I fear not."
—Aeschylus

"If we are together nothing is impossible. If we are divided all will fall."
—Winston Churchill

"A friendship founded on business is a good deal better than a business founded on friendship."
—John D. Rockefeller

It is not known specifically where and when Edward and Bessie met at the Georgia Harvest Festival, but they certainly did meet. And they saw a lot they liked in each other. Edward was a flashy, smooth operator filled with big ideas. Bessie was a tough, practical, and sometimes ruthless survivor. They were both excellent promoters and marketers. Together, they saw huge potential in the burgeoning Atlanta marketplace.

Shortly after the festival they took offices in the Flatiron Building in downtown Atlanta and formed the Southern Publicity Association.

The seed money for this venture came from Bessie. Edgar Fuller, a later associate, would say of her:

> *Mrs. Tyler was an extraordinary woman. She was untaught,*
> *but endowed with unusual mentality. She was ambitious,*

*but continued in associations that were degrading. She was
identified with a number of places in the city of Atlanta and
frequently changed her residence because of the objections
and complaints lodged with the police department about the
conduct of her establishments.*[1]

She had learned to manipulate men, and had used that knowledge to
survive on her own. Bessie lived in the notorious Pryor Street section of
downtown Atlanta,[2] and the so-called "Queen of Pryor Street" was the
proprietress of a brothel.[3]

The timing of this new partnership could not have been more propi-
tious. Edward was the front man, and he was riding a wave of popularity from the success of the Harvest Festival. In his capacity as general
manager he had interacted with every business and organization in the
city. Additionally, the Clarke name still carried appreciable weight. Atlanta was growing rapidly, and there was substantial need for promotion
expertise.

The public relations industry in America was still surfacing in the
early days of the twentieth century. However, the concept of getting
other people to believe things and do things—and it being an art, a
talent—had been around for centuries. One of the earliest PR practitio-
ners was Julius Caesar. The Roman general's campaign autobiography,
Gallic Wars, promoted himself to the people of the empire as a great
leader. Thomas Paine's pamphlets "Common Sense" and "The Crisis"
galvanized the revolutionary fervor of colonial Americans in the late
eighteenth century. P. T. Barnum, of course, was a master at convincing audiences they needed to view his spectacles. Even William Seward,
Lincoln's secretary of state, learned how to get his message conveyed: "I
speak to the newspapers. They have a large audience and can repeat a
thousand times what I want to impress on the public."[4]

The actual profession of public relations probably originated with Ivy
Lee.

Ivy Ledbetter Lee was born in Georgia in 1877, the same year as Edward. He was the son of the Rev. James Wideman Lee, one of the most
prominent Methodist ministers in the South. Lee being the pastor of
Atlanta's Trinity Methodist Church, the Lees would have been mem-

bers of the city's high society. It is very possible they would have mingled with the family of newspaper publisher Edward Young Clarke Sr.[5]

The two young Atlantans took ironic career paths. Edward would first gravitate to the Methodist ministry, while Ivy would begin his career as a newspaper reporter. After graduation from Princeton, Ivy worked for the *New York American*, the *New York Times*, and the *New York World*. By 1903 he left journalism to become a publicity manager for the Citizen's Union.[6] In 1905 Lee partnered with George Parker, establishing one of America's first public relations firms, Parker and Lee. A year later Ivy published his *Declaration of Principles*, a philosophy that public relations professionals had a responsibility that extended beyond the obligations to the client. In 1906 he was representing a railroad company involved in a train wreck in Atlantic City. During that appointment, Lee issued what is considered to be the first press release. He convinced his client to openly give information to newspapers before they could hear it from other sources.

In 1912 he was hired full time by the Pennsylvania Railroad as an executive, one of the first VP-level corporate public relations positions.[7]

Undoubtedly, Ivy Lee's most famous client was John D. Rockefeller Jr. In 1914 Lee was called on to make the best of a bad situation in an early case of "spin doctoring." There had been a long and violent strike at a Rockefeller-owned coal mine in Ludlow, Colorado. On April 20, 1914, the Colorado National Guard attacked a tent city of strikers with machine gun fire and then set the tents ablaze. Three strikers were shot to death. Four women and eleven children had hidden in a pit beneath a tent and died in the fire. Lee sent a release saying the deaths were due to an overturned stove. An outraged Upton Sinclair dubbed him "Poison Ivy."

Perhaps that sting help mold Ivy's philosophy for he is famous for saying: "Tell the truth because sooner or later the public will find out anyway. And if the public doesn't like what you are doing, change your policies and bring them into line with what people want."[8] Lee also advised George Westinghouse, Charles Lindbergh, Walter Chrysler, and other elite names in his career.

The other major influence in the early days of public relations was the Creel Committee. Formed by Woodrow Wilson and headed by newspaperman George Creel, its purpose was to persuade the American people to support the U.S. effort in WWI.[9] Creel's Committee on Public Information (CPI) used every weapon at its disposal—newsprint, posters, radio, telegraph, cable, and movies—to accomplish their mission. A new technique was the use of "four-minute men." Over 70,000 speakers were sent to social events across the country to give short speeches in support of the war effort. Four minutes was thought to be the attention span of the average American. The CPI was a sophisticated communications machine.[10]

The Southern Publicity Association was born in this era of experimentation and innovation in the PR field.

One contact Edward had certainly made during his Chamber of Commerce days was Isaac Anderson Allen. The highly successful businessman was president of both the Atlanta Chamber and of the Atlanta Convention Bureau. Allen spearheaded a number of U.S. World War I bond campaigns.

The Southern Publicity Association was soon distinguished themselves as experts in fundraising and at membership drives. The Atlanta chapter of the Red Cross became a client prior to 1920 and SPA helped them raise money for the families of American soldiers and for the victims of the Great Atlanta Fire of 1917. Both the Atlanta YMCA and YWCA were also clients, and Edward and Bessie worked with the local Salvation Army as well.[11]

With clients of this stature, Clarke and Tyler were clearly very good at their jobs. They were known to deliver. History records at least one unhappy customer. The Theodore Roosevelt Memorial Fund sued the Southern Publicity Association for over $1,000 it claimed Edward had embezzled and another $4,000 he had been unable to account for. Nothing remains documenting how this issue was resolved.[12]

A notable addition joined the Southern Publicity Association staff in its early years. His name was John Quincy Jett. J. Q., as he was known—he also liked initials—was a fraternal organizer and sometime bootlegger from the tiny town of Ellijay in northern Georgia. J. Q. first appears in this story upon his marriage to Bessie's eighteen-year-old daughter, Minnie Dorris Manning, in 1916. Jett would play a pivotal role in Edward and Bessie's future.

The most prominent client in the Southern Publicity Association stable was the Anti-Saloon League. It is very possible the business came their way through Edward's wife, May. A 1919 roster of the Georgia Anti-Saloon League Headquarters Committee lists a Dr. E. C. Cartledge as its secretary. Edward Cornelius Cartledge was the older brother of May Cartledge Clarke. The Emory School of Medicine and Atlanta Medical College trained physician was a prominent Atlanta doctor and an avowed temperance man. As such, E. C. was active in the league and rose to a leadership role. It may be no coincidence that the Anti-Saloon League's Georgia offices were also in the Flatiron Building.[13]

This was no small client. The Anti-Saloon League was the leading organization in twentieth-century America lobbying for the prohibition of alcohol. It is considered the largest and most powerful single-issue group in American history. The league borrowed its methods from successful business organizations and developed many of the modern techniques of public relations. It aggressively lobbied all levels of government—local, state, and national—for legislation to prohibit the manufacture or import of spirits, beer, and wine.[14]

As the Georgia PR arm of the Anti-Saloon League, Edward and Bessie learned their craft from the best in the business. The national league had pioneered the use of printed materials for mass mailings and for leaflet distribution. Its publishing arm, the American Issue Publishing Company, printed and mailed over forty tons of material per month from its Westerville, Ohio, presses.[15] League leaders Howard Hyde Russell and Wayne Wheeler were innovative geniuses in the art of persuasion and in the use of the power of modern communications.

Clarke and Tyler were also innovators. Edward is credited with a new distribution method employed to support an Anti-Saloon fundraising drive. He hired an airplane—still a new and risky mode of transportation—for the purpose of distributing leaflets over Atlanta. Bessie did the actual dropping. There is a photo of her in the cockpit wearing an aviator's hat and goggles. They took their cue in this from the Allies in World War I, who had dropped propaganda over German lines.[16]

The Southern Publicity Association, by all outward appearances, was a dynamic and successful concern in the years prior to 1920. But there were dangers looming on the horizon.

The professional relationship between Edward and Bessie had become very personal. They had become partners in bed as well as in business. According to many sources, their affair was not a well-kept secret, and apparently May had become aware of the liaisons. On October 18, 1919, she filed for divorce charging that Edward had deserted her and their son.

About two weeks later, on October 29, 1919, there came a fateful knock on the door of Bessie's infamous home at 185 Pryor Street. It was nearly midnight. May stood outside accompanied by her brother and a police officer. When they gained entry they discovered Edward and Bessie together, scantily dressed, in bed. The police found bottles of whiskey in the room. The two were arrested, charged with disorderly conduct and possession of alcohol, and taken to police court in their pajamas.

Unable to make bail, the two spent the night in jail. Clarke gave his name as "Jim Slaton." Bessie used "Mrs. Carroll," her name from her second marriage. The next morning they were charged under their real names. Edward's brother, Francis, made bail. On the 31st Edward and Bessie pled guilty and paid $5 fines for the disorderly conduct charge. J. Q. Jett took the fall for the alcohol charge, claiming ownership of the whiskey. He paid a $25 fine.[17]

May now had a great deal of leverage. She and Edward negotiated a monetary settlement. They did not divorce, but were formally separated.

The incident had financial implications for the Southern Publicity Association as well. An embarrassing arrest was not good for an agency with high-profile clients. An affair spoke to the questionable morality of the principals in the concern. Finally, the spurned woman, May, was the sister of a high-ranking official with the Southern Publicity Association's largest client.

Continued work with the Anti-Saloon League was already tenuous. The Eighteenth Amendment to the Constitution had been ratified nine months earlier outlawing the manufacture and sale of alcohol in the United States. Two days prior to Bessie and Edward's arrest, Congress had passed the Volstead Act, which outlined enforcement of Prohibition.

As America dried up, so did the Southern Publicity Association's work with the Anti-Saloon League. The war's end in November 1918 had already ended the need for bond drives. Bessie and Edward's remaining clients were low-paying not-for-profits.

As 1919 was drawing to a close, the future of Clarke and Tyler's Southern Publicity Association was very bleak indeed.

CHAPTER 5
Contract with the Devil

"I really do think that any deep crisis is an opportunity to make your life extraordinary in some way."

—Martha Beck

"Ability is nothing without opportunity."

—Napoleon Bonaparte

"Deal with the Devil if the Devil has a constituency—and don't complain about the heat."

—C. J. Cherryh

William Joseph Simmons was in a tight spot. His Ku Klux Klan was in a state of disarray. His membership rolls had dwindled to a few thousand, and he had very little control over them. Simmons's financial situation was dire. He had seen no income from dues for some time and had been forced to vacate his second-floor offices over an oculist shop. The Imperial Wizard was now working out of his home—a home he had mortgaged in a search for more working capital.[1]

Simmons had created his order as a secret society, purposely shying away from publicity, but desperate times demanded desperate measures. With the last of his money, he placed a quarter-page ad in the *Atlanta Constitution* in an effort to attract new members.

The ad featured a robed Klansman rearing his horse with dramatic flair under the words, "The Most Sublime Lineage in History." The body copy extolled the Klan, "This order is not a mere social, fraternal organization but it is the embodiment of a GREAT CAUSE that strongly appeals to sober manhood." Simmons included a post office box number to write to for information.

J. Q. Jett had made two contributions to this tale to date. First, he had become Bessie's son-in-law by marrying Minnie Dorris. Then he took a fall for his employers by claiming ownership of the whiskey found in Bessie's Pryor Street home during their arrest. This next action, however, was the one that would impact an entire nation.

John Quincy Jett was yet another character in this story attracted to fraternal organizations. He belonged to a number of societies and had worked as an organizer for some. The ad in the *Constitution* caught his eye—probably the heroic, robed figure on horseback. J. Q. wrote to the post office box and Simmons arranged a meeting. When times were tough, the Imperial Wizard himself was available for a sales call. J. Q. signed up on the spot.

After attending several meetings and hearing Simmons speak, J. Q. became a believer "that the only thing that would save America and the white people of the world was the Ku Klux Klan." At the same time, he was also aware of the financial difficulties of his employer, the Southern Publicity Association. J. Q. saw enormous potential for both groups.[2]

Jett reasoned that the successful and innovative fundraising and membership techniques used by Edward and Bessie could be easily applied to spreading the Klan. Convincing Clarke and Tyler proved to be a tougher sell. They were certainly aware of the Ku Klux Klan and its reputation for being anti-Catholic, anti-Semitic, anti-black, and violent. The two were not particularly broadminded, but they were practical. Taking on the Klan as a client was a dangerous professional gamble.

J. Q., however, was very persuasive. It was decided that Edward would also join the Klan in order to research the organization from the inside. He saw something he liked. Bessie would later say:

We found that Colonel Simmons was having a hard time

getting along. He couldn't pay his rent. The receipts were not sufficient to take care of his personal needs. He was a minister and a clean living and thinking man, and he had his heart and soul for the success of the Ku Klux Klan. After we investigated it from every angle, we decided to go into it with Colonel Simmons and give it the impetus that it could best get from publicity.[3]

Bessie and Edward had done membership drives before. If they were to venture forward on this one, the payoff would need to be big. There was a high risk-to-reward ratio involved. They did have their experience in the fraternal world on their side. Edward had worked for the Woodmen of the World and Bessie was a member of the Daughters of America, an auxiliary of the Junior Order of United American Mechanics. Both were organizations bearing philosophical similarities to the Klan.[4] Besides, the atmosphere in America in 1920 was ripe for fraternal society organizers, and Bessie and Edward believed there was a significant market for a group cloaked in secrecy and preaching white supremacy.

Clarke and Tyler prepared a contract and set a meeting with the Imperial Wizard. Because women had no status within the Klan, it is probable that only Clarke met with Simmons on June 7, 1920. The document signed that day would have enormous implications for the history of the American twentieth century. It began with proper legal language:

STATE OF GEORGIA, COUNTY OF FULTON

This agreement, made and entered into on this the 7th day of June, A.D. 1920, by and between the Knights of the Ku-Klux-Klan, a corporation of said county, acting by its imperial wizard (president), W.J. Simmons, party of the first part, and Edward Young Clarke, of said county, party of the second part.

The next portion of the contract addressed Edward's new and significant role in the Klan.

Witnesseth, that the said party of the second part here-

> to having, by virtue of this agreement, been appointed imperial kleagle (general superintendent of the organization Department) of said first party.

This was not to be a standard agency/client relationship. Edward would have a place on the executive committee of the Klan. Next came an important item:

> Therefore, it is agreed by the said parties hereto that this contract shall continue so long as it is mutually agreeable; that it shall remain of force and may be canceled by either party hereto without previous notice of any intention to do so.

For his protection, Simmons had inserted an "out" clause. The agreement with Clarke and Tyler could be ended without warning or cause.

This new Propagation Department was empowered to employ "such assistant organizers as he (Clarke) would deem necessary in order to properly carry out the plans for the propagation and extension of said corporation." They would be subject to Simmons's approval and were to be in good and regular standing.

Then came the financial agreement.

> It is agreed that the said second party shall receive as in full compensation and expenses of himself and his duly appointed and commissioned subordinate organizers the sum of $8 dollars for each and every new member brought into the said corporation by himself and his assistant subordinate organizers, and in addition to the $8 dollars he shall receive $2 for each new member added to all klans organized by himself or is subordinate organizers within a period of six months after the date of the charter of all such klans organized by himself and his subordinate organizers.[5]

The initiation fee for joining the Klan was $10, so Edward and Bessie would receive an eighty percent commission on each new member. Out of that figure would come all expenses incurred in running the Propagation Department. The remaining $2 was to be deposited into the Klan

General Fund. Edward had convinced Simmons that it would take a great deal of money to organize and maintain their operation. He said, "Colonel, it's going to take a lot of money to create an organizational force. We have no machinery of that nature, and I've got to find men. We'll have to spend a lot of time finding men, and this machinery must be constructed and it'll cost something."[6]

With that, Edward and Simmons affixed their signatures and the Propagation Department came into being.

Why would Simmons agree to such an arrangement? He really had no other choice and nothing to lose. It was simple math. One hundred percent of nothing was still nothing. Twenty percent of something was much better, and he did not have to invest any cash to get it. He did not have the capital, expertise, or organizational skills to do the job himself.

Edward and Bessie immediately put their plan into action. It did, of course, take seed money in the early stages. Again, Bessie opened her pursed and anted up $14,000 of her own money.[7]

They decided their campaign would not be regional, but instead national. They felt the Nativist appeal of the Klan extended beyond the South.

They began by dividing the United States into nine domains. The states within each were referred to as realms. The organization was as follows:

The Domain of the Southeast—Georgia, Tennessee, Virginia, Alabama, Mississippi, North and South Carolina. Headquarters were in Atlanta.

The Western Domain—Arizona, Arkansas, Texas, Oklahoma, Louisiana, New Mexico, Colorado, Utah, Wyoming, and Montana. Headquarters in Houston.

The Domain of the East—New York. Headquarters in New York City.

The Domain of the Great Lakes—Wisconsin, Illinois, Indiana, Kentucky, Ohio, Minnesota, and Michigan. Headquarters in Chicago.

Domain of the Mississippi Valley—Nebraska, Missouri, Kansas, Iowa, Minnesota, and North and South Dakota. Headquarters in St. Louis. (Minnesota was in both domains.)

Domain of the Pacific Coast—California, Washington, Nevada, Oregon, and Idaho. Headquarters in Los Angeles.

The Atlantic Domain—Pennsylvania, New Jersey, Delaware, and Maryland. Headquarters in Philadelphia.

The New England Domain—Maine, New Hampshire, Vermont, Massachusetts, and Connecticut. Headquarters in Boston.

The Capitol Domain—District of Columbia.[8]

Each domain was ruled by a grand goblin. Reporting to him in each realm was a king kleagle. The individual salesmen in the field were called kleagles. Bessie and Edward recruited these men from the ranks of other fraternal organizations. They were experienced in the world of rituals, oaths, and ceremonies. Each would become a member of the Klan in order to officially administer the oath and initiate inductees. These kleagles would then organize and run provisional klans in their sales districts until given a formal charter.

The work was purely on a commission basis, and Bessie and Edward were able to attract a strong sales force because of a generous and immediate sales package.

When a kleagle signed up a new member and collected $10, he immediately pocketed $4 and then sent the remaining $6 on to his king kleagle. The king kleagle took $1 and sent the $5 to the grand goblin at the domain office who in turn retained 50 cents. There was now $4.50 remaining and that was sent to Clarke and Tyler in Atlanta. Two dollars was to go to the Klan general treasury and the balance, $2.50, belonged to Edward and Bessie.

This was selling in its simplest form. The reward was instantaneous and the red tape minimal. There was no approval needed from management on the merits of a potential member. The kleagle made that call, and if an eligible man had $10 there were few questions asked. Bessie and Edward had developed an early form of single-level marketing. It was direct, one-to-one sales.[9]

This should not be confused with multi-level marketing, which is sometimes called a pyramid scheme. In that model salespeople are allowed to recruit others to sell, receiving a percentage of their sales. The Klan kleagles only received commissions on their own sales.

In many typical single-level systems, the salesperson purchases product from the parent company and then sells directly to the customer. Classic examples include beauty products, vacuum cleaners, and cutlery. In the Klan's case, there was no tangible product to transfer. The product was an idea. No capital outlay required for an idea.

The incentive for middle management—grand goblins and king kleagles—was in conscribing more kleagles into the field in new territories. They were expected to forward weekly reports to Atlanta, detailing both sales results and future plans. Their other motivation was keeping their job by driving sales.

Edward and Bessie's investment was minimal. They provided printed materials to the field—selling points, ritual material to be used in initiations, and receipts known as klecktokens. When a new inductee paid his $10 he was given one of these forms indicating the money was a donation. Simmons's Klan was chartered in Georgia as a not-for-profit and did not want to pay tax.

With that, Edward and Bessie sent the sales force into the field, casting their nets and hoping for a good catch.

CHAPTER 6
Fertile Ground

"They (the Sales Leaders) implement a prospect-centered approach to selling. The successful sales professional is clearly focused on the needs, issues, and concerns of the prospect."
—Zig Ziglar, 7 Traits of Sales Leaders

"Prospects buy for their reasons, not yours."
—Zig Ziglar, super salesman,
motivational speaker, and author

Memberships arrived at the offices of the Southern Publicity Association—not as a trickle, but as a torrent. Many applications came from the Southern states. That was to be expected. The message of the Klan was a natural for whites who had grown up in a culture that imposed slavery, servitude, and repression onto a whole group of people. All Bessie and Edward had to do was provide the organization that Colonel Simmons had failed to establish.

The white South's objective was to maintain dominion over the black population. Even though successive constitutional amendments had abolished slavery, granted citizenship, and bestowed voting rights, little had changed for African Americans. Plantation slaves often remained on the land they had worked, now as sharecroppers. The economic system was designed to bind the new citizens in a perpetual cycle of debt and poverty. White landowners could change the percentage of the crop owed them at their whim. Storeowners and bankers could and would demand usurious interest rates for food, seed, tools, and the other staples of life. Blacks seemed never able to catch up, much less break even.

There was more than an economic stranglehold keeping blacks down in the South. The strategy also extended to politics and voting. Because blacks had little money, poll taxes were instituted to discourage voting. Because few blacks could read, literacy tests were devised to further bar the former slaves from the polling place. The white South remembered the harrowing days of Reconstruction when blacks were elected to offices in state legislatures and even Congress. That could never be allowed to happen again.

Another method for keeping the black population in check was legislative. States began enacting so-called Jim Crow laws, named after a buffoon-like, black-faced character in Southern minstrel shows. Some examples from different states include:

No colored barber shall serve as a barber to white girls or women. (Georgia)

There are to be separate facilities for the care and support of blind people of the colored race. (Louisiana)

It is unlawful for a Negro and a white to play a game of pool or billiards together. (Alabama)

Separate telephone booths are required for white and colored persons. (Oklahoma)

It is unlawful for a white amateur baseball team to play baseball within two blocks of a field devoted to Negro baseball. (Georgia)

Cohabitation by a Negro man and a white woman, not married to each other, who share in the nighttime the same room are subject to imprisonment up to twelve months or fined up to $500. (Florida)[1]

There were even unwritten norms of etiquette. Blacks were to be introduced to whites, never whites to blacks. A black male could not shake hands with a white male. If you are black, never comment on the appearance of a white female. Never accuse a white of lying. Never curse or laugh at a white person.[2]

All of this was legitimized by a United States government unwilling to enforce the spirit and the word of the Constitution. In the landmark 1896 Supreme Court case *Plessy v. Ferguson,* the court upheld an 1890 Louisiana statute mandating racially segregated, but equal, railroad carriages. Speaking for the majority, Justice Henry Billings said "separate but equal laws did not imply the inferiority of one race to another," ruling that the equal protection clause of the Fourteenth Amendment dealt with political and not social equality.[3]

Of course separate never meant equal in the white man's South.

If economic, political, legislative, and cultural means were not sufficient, there was one remaining and highly effective method to keep blacks in place. Fear. Instilling fear in African Americans through threatened and actual violence. And the Klan was custom made for this purpose. It provided a structure and methods for organized and anonymous hate. In the hands of skilled marketers like Edward and Bessie, membership flourished in the South.

However, an influx of new Klan memberships was coming from places outside the South. Bessie and Edward had begun to mine the North and East, markets newly receptive to their hateful proselytizing on account of the Great Migration. The marketplace had expanded, and Bessie and Edward were prepared.

When the Emancipation Proclamation was signed by Abraham Lincoln in 1863, less than five percent of the African-American population lived in the Northeastern or Midwestern United States. In 1900, about ninety percent still lived in the Southern states.[4]

And then it began. It was a leaderless and unorganized movement. Before it was over, nearly half of blacks in America left their homes in the South, never to return.

They made the monumental decision for many reasons. They left, of course, to escape the hopelessness of life in the South. The 1890s ushered in numerous Jim Crow laws, legalizing discrimination and hate. The Supreme Court in *Plessey* had upheld a culture of inequity and despair. The government in Washington showed no signs of challenging a system designed to subjugate an entire class of American citizens. That decade also saw a spike in lynchings and other racially motivated murders. The South was a desperate and dangerous place.

The North held hope. The Industrial Revolution of the late nineteenth century had created a nearly unquenchable appetite for labor. The jobs and the pay available to blacks were not equal to whites', but they were better and they held hope for a better future.

A 1917 poem published in the influential black daily, the *Chicago Defender*, summed up the emotions of the travelers:

> *From Florida's stormy bank I go.*
> *I've bid the South "Good-by,"*
> *No longer shall they treat me so,*
> *And knock me in the eye.*
> *The Northern States is where I'm bound.*
> *My cross is more than double.*
> *If the chief executive can be found,*
> *I'll tell him all my trouble.*
>
> *Arise! Ye Darkies now a-slave.*
> *Your chance at last has come.*
> *Hold up your head with courage brave,*
> *'Cause times are changing some.*
> *God is punctual to his Word,*
> *Faithful to his dating,*
> *Humble prayers is what he heard*
> *After years of faithful waiting.*
>
> *Hasten on, my dark brother,*
> *Duck the Jim Crow laws.*
> *No "Crackers" North to slap your mothers*
> *Or knock you in the jaw.*
> *No "Crackers" there to seduce your sister,*
> *Nor hang you to a limb,*
> *And you're no obligated to call them mister,*
> *Nor show your teeth to them.*[5]
> —*Chicago Defender*, January 13, 1917 (excerpted)

Many historians delineate the Great Migration into two distinct phases. During the first, from 1900 to 1940, approximately 1.6 million migrants moved northward, mostly to major Northern and Midwestern cities. The second Great Migration, from 1940 to 1970, saw nearly five million leave the South, with a wider variety of destinations, including California.[6]

Between 1910 and 1930 the African-American population grew by forty percent in northern states, mostly in major cities like Chicago, Detroit, New York, and Cleveland. It was a relocation that dwarfed that of the California Gold Rush in the 1850s and the migration forced by Dust Bowl of the 1930s.

For people who had no effective personal means of transportation, the railroad provided a conduit to the North. Cities at the end of rail lines saw spectacular population growth. Chicago, for example, appealed to African Americans in Louisiana, Tennessee, Alabama, and Mississippi. The Illinois Central line ran directly from New Orleans to Chicago. Between 1916 and 1919 alone 50,000 to 70,000 black migrants flowed into Chicago. In total it is estimated that 400,000 people left the South during the two-year period of 1916 through 1918. In 1910 the African-American population of Detroit numbered 6,000. By 1929 the figure had ballooned to 120,000.[7]

There were problems that went along with the promises of the new Promised Land. White landlords charged the Southern arrivals with excessive rents for substandard housing. Additional friction arose between African Americans and the already established European immigrants over jobs; blacks were making substantial inroads, particularly in the steel, automobile, shipbuilding, and meat packing industries. Between 1910 and 1920 the number of blacks employed in industrial jobs nearly doubled from 500,000 to 910,000. During these years labor was in demand, and the union movement made great advances in pay and working conditions.[8] Blacks happily rode the coat tails of organized labor.

The Great Migration scared white America, and no one embodied the black threat in America more than Jack Johnson.

Geoffrey C. Ward, in his book *Unforgivable Blackness*, describes Johnson:

> *At a time when whites ran everything in America, he took*
> *orders from no one and resolved to live always as if color did*
> *not exist. . . . Most whites (and some Negroes as well) saw*
> *him as a perpetual threat. Profligate, arrogant, amoral, a*
> *dark menace, and a danger to the natural order of things.*[9]

Young Jack was born in Galveston, Texas, on March 31, 1878. He was the second child, and first son, of former slaves Henry and Tina Johnson who worked multiple jobs in order to raise their six children. From them, Jack learned to read and write. He also attended five or six years of school before going to work as a dockworker in Galveston.[10] He would later develop an interest in opera (his favorite was *Il Trovatore*) and in history (he was an admirer of Napoleon Bonaparte). He also loved driving cars fast—very fast. Once he got pulled over and was given a $50 ticket. Johnson gave the officer a $100 bill. The policeman protested that he could not make change on that amount. Johnson told him not to worry since he was going to make the return trip at the same speed.[11]

What he did best, however, was box. He was skillful and scientific, dealing blows while avoiding punishment. He allowed his opponents to make mistakes and then made them pay with punishing counterpunches. Because he was black, the white press labeled this style as cowardly. White World Champion "Gentleman" Jim Corbett employed many of the same techniques and was praised as "the cleverest man in boxing."[12]

By 1902, at age twenty-four, Johnson had won fifty fights against both black and white fighters. All that remained was a title fight for the World Heavyweight Championship. But that opportunity was not forthcoming. That mantle was reserved exclusively for whites. The legends of boxing had always been white, and often Irish. Bare-knuckled John L. Sullivan was legendary, and the aforementioned Corbett was godlike to the white boxing community. The reigning champion was an imposing, undefeated boxer named James J. Jeffries. Jeffries refused to fight a black man and eventually retired to his farm in California.

Even though Jeffries was no longer in his sights, Johnson began to stalk the new champion, Canadian Tommy Burns. For two years, Johnson followed Burns around the world and used the press to taunt him into a match. Finally, Burns agreed to a December 26, 1908, bout in Sydney, Australia.

Twenty thousand fans came to see their white hero destroy the brash, black giant. For fourteen rounds Johnson jabbed, feinted, counter-punched, and carried on a conversation with Burns and spectators in the ringside seats. Burns was clearly overmatched and Johnson punished the champion. In the fourteenth, the end was clearly at hand. Movie cameras had documented every moment of the fight. This was an early manifestation of pay per view; the big boxing matches were seen in movie theaters across the country. When Burns was ready to finally fall, the cameras were ordered shut down. The police rushed into the ring to stop the fight. Neither spectator, nor moviegoer, was going to see the white champion knocked out by the grinning black hulk.[13]

News of Johnson's victory in Australia resounded in both the black and white communities. No less a celebrity than famous author and fight fan Jack London called out for a "Great White Hope" to arise and take the title away from Johnson. In 1909 Johnson fought a succession of so-called Great White Hopes, each falling before his flashing fists. White America seethed with each defeat. What bothered them more was Johnson himself. He did not follow those unwritten codes of col-ored behavior. He was outspoken, demonstrative, and downright cocky. He spent lavishly on clothes, fast cars, and women. And those women were white, flaunting one of the biggest taboos in white America.

Boxing fans knew the man they wanted. Pressure increased on the retired champ to come out of retirement and restore the world to its proper alignment. London formally issued the challenge: "One thing now remains. Jim Jeffries must now emerge from his alfalfa farm and remove that golden smile from Jack Johnson's face. Jeff, it's up to you. The white man must be rescued."[14] In 1910 the undefeated, gentleman farmer agreed to "The Fight of the Century." Jim Jeffries said, "I feel obligated to the sporting public at least to make an effort to reclaim the heavyweight championship for the white race. . . . I should step into the ring again and demonstrate that a white man is king of them all."[15] He hadn't fought in six years and his weight had ballooned to nearly 300 pounds, but whites felt sure he was up to the task.

In his prime Jeffries was a brute of a man. He stood nearly six-feet, two-inches tall and tipped the scales at 225 pounds. It was said he could run a 100-yard dash in just over ten seconds and high jump over six feet. There was nothing subtle about his boxing style. He fought out of a crouch and was able to absorb incredible punishment, wearing down his opponent while waiting to unleash his lethal, left hook knockout punch.[16]

Jeffries became the World Heavyweight Champion on June 9, 1899, with a victory over the reigning titleholder, Bob Fitzsimmons. He defended his title seven times until his retirement in 1904, with a record of nineteen wins without a defeat. Fourteen of the victories were via knockout.

Jeffries knew his style was a poor match against the consummate boxing skills of Jack Johnson, but the two camps hammered out a compelling agreement on prize money. The winner would receive sixty percent and the loser forty percent. Billed as "The Fight of the Century," interest ran high across the nation and the world, and, win or lose, both men would cash in handsomely.

Enormous sums of money were bet on Jeffries and the pressure on him grew daily. An entire race expected him to win. Jeffries managed to get his weight down to 230 pounds, but at age thirty-five he was not "The Grizzly Bear" of his youth.

Promoter Tex Rickard set the fight for July 4, 1910, in Reno, Nevada. Nevada was one of the few states where prize fighting was legal in the United States. The fight was set for forty-five rounds, and the temperature was expected to reach 110 degrees. Neither of these factors favored the aging Jeffries. Nearly 20,000 overwhelmingly white fans filled the seats of a newly erected stadium.

A breathless world awaited word from the Nevada desert. More than three hundred reporters descended on the town. Telegraph operators prepared to feed a hungry world. Novelist turned journalist Rex Beach described Reno as "the precise magnetic center of the civilized world."

The Fight of the Century was no contest from the beginning. Jeffries charged out of his corner like a bull, but Johnson deftly turned aside every advance. The champion played with his lumbering opponent while carrying on a confident dialogue with Jeffries's corner and anyone who could hear him at ringside. The punishment doled out on Jeffries was frightening. At the end of the fourteenth round the retiree's nose was broken and his eyes were nearly swollen shut. He was exhausted and covered with blood. In the fifteenth Johnson sensed an opportunity to finish the fight. With a succession of punches Johnson sent Jeffries to the canvas. The crowd gasped. He had never been knocked down before. Jeffries struggled to his feet, but a quick series of punches saw Jeffries collapse once more. His corner quickly threw in the towel and referee/ promoter Rickard announced Johnson the winner. Jeffries would later say to a reporter, "I could never have whipped Jack Johnson at my best. I couldn't have reached him in a thousand years."[17]

As news of the fight raced along telegraph wires, black America rejoiced wildly, and white America seethed with anger. William Waring Cuney summed up the feelings of a beleaguered black race in his poem, "My Lord What a Morning":

> *O, My Lord*
> *What a morning,*
> *O My Lord,*
> *What a feeling,*
> *When Jack Johnson*
> *Turned Jim Jeffries'*
> *Snow-White Face*
> *To the ceiling.*[18]

The *Los Angeles Times* issued a stern editorial warning.

> *Do not point your nose too high. Do not swell your chest too much. Do not boast too loudly. Do not be puffed up. Let not your ambition be inordinate or take a wrong direction. Remember you have done nothing at all. You are just the same member of society you were last week. You are not on a higher plane, deserve no new consideration, and will get none. . . . No man will think a bit higher of you because your complexion is the same as that of the victor in Reno.*[19]

The morning after the fight Jack Johnson and his entourage drove into Reno to collect his winnings. The total was $121,000, a stunning number for one day's work. Using an inflation calculator that figure amounts to $2.7 million in 2014 dollars. (That would have Jeffries limping back to Southern California with approximately $80,000 per the pre-flight arrangement.)

Johnson and company then boarded the *Overland Limited* for Chicago. Before long the champion began to hear of trouble erupting around the country. The *New York Tribune* reported, "Rioting broke out like prickly heat all over the country between whites sore and angry that Jeffries had lost the big fight at Reno and Negroes jubilant that Johnson had won." Whites confronted blacks in Norfolk, Philadelphia, Roanoke, Los Angeles, Columbus, and Chattanooga. In Manhattan a mob set fire to a building filled with blacks and then tried to block its windows and doors. In Houston a white man slit the throat of a black passenger on a streetcar because he cheered for Johnson. In Wheeling, West Virginia, a black man was hung because he drove a handsome automobile like Jack Johnson's. At least eleven and maybe as many as twenty-six people died and hundreds were hurt, almost all of them black. It was a foreboding sign of what was possible in America. White superiority would not be threatened or challenged. And, any threat would be met with violence. It was white fear backed by muscle.[20] There would be more.

The years following Simmons's 1915 revival of the Klan created a perfect storm of potential for the marketing minds of Edward and Bessie. As America prepared for an eventual entry into WWI, the Selective Service Act would mobilize four million mostly white men into the Army. Nearly two million would reach Europe before war's end. At the same time the inpouring of immigrants began to dry up. In the early 1900s large numbers of workers had been coming from eastern and southern Europe. Many of those nations were now enemies, and others were threatened by unrestrictive German U-boat warfare in the north Atlantic. These circumstances resulted in jobs for African Americans, and plenty of them.

When the war ended in November 1918 the life of the new northern black would change dramatically again. The American Expeditionary Force demobilized, disembarked from Europe, and returned to civilian life. The job pool exploded at the same time the U.S. economy contracted, a common predicament after wars as industry retools from wartime to peacetime production.

A year before the fateful 1920 contract that named the Southern Publicity Association as the official Klan membership arm, a series of events gave final evidence of growing and dangerous anti-black sentiment in America. The Red Summer of 1919 told Bessie and Edward everything they needed to know about the pulse of the nation on race relations.

The *Red* in the name refers to two things. One had to do with the Bolshevik Revolution in Russia. With the war over in Europe, anti-German sentiment was quickly replaced by a fear of ideas and people from Eastern Europe. In this early American "Red Scare," any radical or even progressive thought was seen as un-American, subversive, and dangerously socialistic by mainstream America. Included in this fearful stew was anything encouraging of racial equality. One hundred percent Americanism left little room for anyone else. Inflation was rampant, and unemployment was sky rocketing. Tensions ran high and violence lurked near the surface. Blacks and whites battled over jobs and the new pressures of urban life.

Red is also the color of blood, and during the summer and early fall of 1919 bloody race riots broke out in over two dozen American cities. On May 10 the first outbreaks occurred in Charleston, South Carolina, and in Sylvester, Georgia. In late September and early October the violence ended in Omaha, Nebraska, and Elaine, Arkansas. All corners of the United States were represented—Pennsylvania, Texas, New York, Arizona, Maryland, Louisiana, Connecticut, and Washington, D.C. Before the summer of violence ended, hundreds were dead and wounded and thousands were left homeless.

There was a difference in 1919 from the days following the Johnson-Jeffries fight. In 1910 targeted blacks ran from white mobs. In Ward's *Unforgivable Blackness* he tells of the New Orleans experience of ten-year-old paper boy, and future jazz trumpeter, Louis Armstrong. The boy was told to run for his life, that the white boys were sore and were going to take it out on African Americans. Nearby a jubilant black marching band celebrating Johnson's win had to flee a deadly shower of bricks.

Nine years later, in 1919, the mood was different. Blacks resisted. The war had improved the lives of those who stayed home. Labor was at a premium, and factories had run at capacity to feed the war effort. The labor union movement made meaningful gains. Jobs and pay improved for blacks as well as whites. During the two-year period between 1916 and 1918 more than one million workers joined unions, boosting American Federation of Labor (AFL) membership to 3.2 million.

Whites were not the only ones coming down the gangways of homecoming troopships. Over 200,000 African Americans had fought with the American Expeditionary Forces (AEF) in France, many with hopes of bettering their lives through military service. The Army was fully segregated, and black units never mixed with white units. As whites and blacks did not fight side by side in this U.S. Army, blacks were often assigned instead to supporting roles, as construction workers and cooks.

Ironically, the opportunity for equality came not from the Americans, but from the French. After nearly four years of savage warfare, the French army was in desperate need of men. American general John Pershing committed four regiments to fight under French command. The first was the all-black 369th "Harlem Hellfighters." Fighting side by side with their French counterparts, the 369th distinguished themselves as one of the most highly decorated units of the war. One hundred seventy-one African Americans received the French Legion of Honor for their heroism in battle. And at war's end over 600 African Americans had been commissioned as officers in the U.S. Army, a rank denied them before the war. Knowing the contributions they had made, the men assumed they would be welcomed home as heroes, and felt they had made important strides in race relations.

Instead, returning black soldiers suffered terrible prejudice. Whites feared the veterans would demand the equality the French had extended them. They also feared black men with military training and combat experience. In the first year after the war, angry white mobs lynched seventy black veterans, many still in uniform.

Of the nearly thirty riots during the Red Summer of 1919, three stand out as prime examples—Washington, D.C., Chicago, and Elaine, Arkansas.

A violent race riot breaking out in the nation's capital seems incongruent with its history and what it represents. This was, after all, where Lincoln had signed the Emancipation Proclamation. It was also where

Congress had proposed the Thirteenth, Fourteenth, and Fifteenth Amendments to the Constitution outlawing slavery, making former slaves citizens, and giving African-American men the vote. But Washington was also a very Southern city, its location brokered shortly after the signing of the Constitution to placate Southern concerns over Northern interests in the new nation. And, in 1919, the White House was occupied by a man who was Southern by birth.

Woodrow Wilson is generally considered by Americans to be one of our finest presidents. If a word-association test were conducted with a random sampling of citizens, the name Wilson would produce responses like "brilliant," "principled," "peacemaker," and "idealist." Author James W. Loewen goes as far to say, "If a fifth face were to be chiseled into Mount Rushmore, many Americans would propose that it should be Wilson's."[21]

Wilson, indeed, had an unusual background for America's top office. In any biographical sketch of Wilson, one will find that, first and foremost, he was an academic. His most noteworthy pre-election accomplishment was his advancement to the president's chair at prestigious Princeton University. As an author, he penned a number of widely read volumes on American history. In Wilson's first term (1912–1916) he was known as "the man who kept us out of war." In his second term, America entered World War I and he became the man who "saved the world for Democracy." At the Versailles Peace Conference he stepped to the front with his Fourteen Points proposal. Wilson is also famous as the designer of the League of Nations, a body whose sole purpose was to prevent future wars.

There is a lesser-known side to the man. Loewen's bestseller, *Lies My Teacher Told Me*, attempts to provide needed balance to the way history is taught in American schools. He maintains "what we did not learn about Woodrow Wilson is even more remarkable."[22]

Wilson had been president of Princeton, but it was the only major northern university that refused to admit blacks. Once in Washington, he systematically carried out a program bent on segregating the federal government. Republican predecessors had routinely appointed blacks to important government jobs, particularly in cities and states with significant black populations. Wilson designated whites for those positions, fought civil rights legislation, and ordered D.C. black and white federal workers segregated from each other. According to Loewen, Wilson was an outspoken racist who often told "darky" stories in cabinet meetings.[23] He did nothing to interfere with the South's onerous Jim Crow laws and took the lead in upholding the segregation policies of the Army in World War I.

Wilson had also been a classmate of Thomas Dixon, the author and playwright whose *The Clansmen* would be made into the blockbuster film *The Birth of a Nation*. Director D. W. Griffith even used an excerpt from Wilson's two volume *A History of the American People* in an opening title of the silent masterpiece. He said of the Reconstruction South:

> *The white men were roused by a mere instinct of self preservation . . . . until at last there had sprung into existence a great Ku Klux Klan, a veritable empire of the South, to protect the Southern country.*

Dixon persuaded his old classmate to screen *The Birth of a Nation* in the White House. After seeing the film, Wilson was reported to have said, "It is like writing history with lightning. My only regret is that it is all so true."[24]

America's leader had set a tone for the District of Columbia in the summer of 1919.

It started on a steamy Saturday night, July 19, 1919. Rumors began to spread that a black suspect, questioned in an attempted sexual assault on a white woman, had been released by the Washington Police. The local bars were filled with angry drunken whites spoiling for a fight. Most were unemployed and many were in uniform. Their numbers swelled, and they headed for a predominantly poor black section in the southwest part of the city. Along the way they picked up clubs, lead pipes, and pieces of lumber. Two unsuspecting black men, Charles Linton Ralls and George Montgomery, were attacked and severely beaten. The local police offered no help; in fact, they arrested more blacks than whites. The wave of violence would continue for four days. Nine people were killed and thirty more would eventually die from their wounds. More than 150 men, women, and children were clubbed, beaten, and shot by mobs of both races. Blacks were even beaten in front of the White House.

When the *Washington Post* published a misunderstood front-page article calling for all available servicemen to report to Pennsylvania Avenue and Seventh Street at 9 p.m. for a "cleanup" operation, blacks realized local authorities would be of no help to them. As the white mob gathered, blacks armed themselves. Blacks turned the tables on the whites, firing into crowds and randomly pulling whites off streetcars. In all, ten whites and five blacks were killed or mortally wounded that night.

Finally, city leaders and members of Congress realized the situation was out of hand. President Wilson mobilized 2,000 troops to stop the rioting.[25]

There was a human toll, but a sense of pride prevailed for many in the African-American community, for having gone on the offense, for having defended themselves. A black woman who had witnessed the fighting described her feelings in a letter to a newspaper:

> *The Washington riot gave me a thrill that comes once in a life time . . . at last our men had stood up like men . . . I stood up alone in my room . . . and exclaimed aloud, 'Oh, I thank God, thank God.' The pent up horror, grief and humiliation of a life time—half a century—was being stripped from me.*
> —A Southern black woman, letter to the *CRISIS*

A few days later the summer's greatest violence erupted in the Great Emancipator's home state. Beginning on July 27, Chicago endured thirteen days of race-based rage and warfare.

Chicago had been a highly segregated city since the beginnings of the Great Migration. The African-Americans who streamed northward on the Illinois Central tracks found living space on the city's overpopulated South Side.

During the sweltering late July days, Chicagoans flocked to its greatest asset—the beautiful beaches of Lake Michigan. Blacks found areas there divided by race as well.

On the 27th a group of young black men swam near the line dividing the 29th Street beach. One unknowingly drifted into the area reserved for whites. A group of men began throwing rocks at Eugene Williams. The young man was hit and subsequently drowned. The ensuing mayhem brought a policeman who arrested one black man and none of the white men involved. Racial tensions escalated between mobs and gangs of both races. When the fighting finally stopped in the second week of August, the toll was frightening. Twenty-three blacks and fifteen whites lay dead. Five hundred thirty-seven were injured, and over one thousand black families were left homeless.[26]

At the end of 1919's Red Summer, the October 3 edition of the *Arkansas Gazette* shouted the following headline:

NEGROES PLAN TO KILL ALL WHITES

The subheads that followed were just as sensational:

SLAUGHTER WAS TO BEGIN WITH 21 PROMINENT MEN AS THE FIRST VICTIMS

"WE JUST BEGUN" PASSWORD
Blacks Had Armed Themselves and Planned
to Kill Every White Person in Sight
When Plot was Exposed[27]

What, in reality, happened in the early morning hours of October 1 was very different than the story reported. Elaine, Arkansas, was a very different setting for violence than Washington or Chicago. Located 150 miles due east of Little Rock near a bend in the Mississippi River, the sleepy hamlet lay in the middle of thousands of acres of farmland. These were the plantation cotton acres of the antebellum South. For blacks it was a land frozen in time.

The African Americans who lived outside Elaine and the much larger county seat of Helena were the people the Great Migration had left behind. Their life experience had been the reason people had dared leave family, friends, and ancestral roots. They were sharecroppers.

Between the end of the Civil War and 1919 life had changed little for blacks in the Deep South. Emancipation and Reconstruction were important and noble words that meant little to the bottom line of day-to-day survival. Freedom, citizenship, and voting rights rang hollow when it came to feeding a family. Most newly freed slaves had no money, no education, no job skills, and no hope. The Southern economy evolved from a plantation owner–slave basis to a land owner–sharecropper one. Little had changed. Many blacks remained on the same land, often living in the same squalid cabin. Now they paid rent in the form of half of what they could raise on their land. Whites substituted their method of control over blacks, handily moving from the whip and gun to the pocketbook. It was every bit as effective.

The only time the sharecropper saw money was at settlement time after harvest. That was when the landowner took the crop to market to be sold. Of course, there are always variables in the life of a farmer. Was it a good crop or a bad one? Was there enough rain? Was the price a fair one? In the case of the black sharecropper there were some implacable constants as well.

In between harvests, life depended on credit. The necessities of life—food, clothing, seed, etc.—had to be purchased at the plantation store at excessive prices, and arbitrary and usurious interest rates. Debts were to be reconciled with the crop settlement. However, whites were the only ones who witnessed the transaction and no itemized accounting or bill of sale was ever produced for confirmation. The land owners often gave their sharecroppers whatever they wished, and it was seldom fair. It was certainly never enough to pay off debts. It was an important unwritten law of the cotton country that sharecroppers could not quit and leave a plantation until their obligations had been settled. Whites devised a quasi-slavery by means of an economic stranglehold.[28]

The black population of Elaine hoped to change this system, but not in the way described in the *Gazette*. On the evening of September 30, 1919, approximately 100 African-American farmers met at a church in Hoop Spur in Phillips County, near Elaine. They were led by Robert L. Hill, the founder of the progressive Farmers and Household Union of America. Their purpose that night was to discuss methods for obtaining better payments for their cotton crops from the white plantation owners.[29] Tensions in the area had been high, and coordinators posted armed guards near the door. Whites did not want labor organizers in the area. The white control of the sharecropper system was a tenuous one. It was also a dangerous one in Phillips County, where blacks outnumbered whites approximately ten to one. When two deputized white men and a black trustee approached the building to ostensibly break up the meeting, shots rang out. To this day no one is sure who fired first. One of the white men was killed and the other wounded. The black trustee rushed back to Helena to report the incident.

The parish sheriff called for a posse, which soon grew into an armed and angry white mob of 500 to 1,000 men. Fighting erupted around Hoop Spur and lasted for three days. Gangs of whites combed the woods killing black men, women, and children. Finally, 500 federal troops were brought in and they disarmed both parties. In the end, five white men and between 100 and 200 blacks lay dead.[30]

Justice was not kind to the black community. Two hundred eighty-five blacks were arrested and placed in stockades. Seventy-three were charged with murder, conspiracy, and insurrection. Not a single white was charged. A dispatch from Helena to the *New York Times* blamed the riot on propaganda distributed among the blacks by white men—and that a plot existed for a general uprising against the whites. It was rumored a white man had been arrested, alleged to have been preaching social equality among blacks. The headline had read, "Trouble traced to Socialist Agitators."[31]

The Red Summer of 1919 had been a wake-up call for white America. In cities across the land blacks had dared resist the status quo. They had fought back. It was a time of both terror and exhilaration for black Americans.

Harlem poet Claude McKay had been a witness to the riots in New York City in the summer of 1919. He summed up the feelings of many African Americans in "If We Must Die":

> *If we must die, let it not be like hogs*
> *Hunted and penned in an inglorious spot.*
> *While round us bark the mad and hungry dogs,*
> *Making their mock at our accursed lot.*
> *If we must die, O let us nobly die,*

So that our precious blood may not be shed
In vain; then even the monsters we defy
Shall be constrained to honor us though dead!
O kinsmen we must meet the common foe!
Though far outnumbered let us show us brave,
And for their thousand blows deal one deathblow!
What though before us lies the open grave?
Like men we'll face the murderous, cowardly pack,
Pressed to the wall, dying, but fighting back!
—Claude McKay, "If We Must Die," 1919

Timing was everything. If there was ever a time and an appetite for Edward and Bessie's Klan, it was now. Yet Clarke and Tyler weren't satisfied with the profits wrought from the transitional distress felt by the Great Migration.

"Madness is badness of spirit when one seeks profit from all sources."

—Aristotle

Any good marketer works toward fully exploiting every accessible market. Bessie and Edward, therefore, sought other targets of white hatred.

They pulled memberships in from the West Coast where the black population was relatively small. Klan chapters were organized in both California and Oregon. The target there: Asians.

The Chinese had first come into San Francisco in significant numbers when gold was discovered at Sutter's Mill in 1848. They were among the throng of fortune seekers who came from all corners of the globe. The Chinese met immediate discrimination, however, and were allowed to work only those claims already mined and abandoned by whites.

Their fortune came with the construction of the monumental Transcontinental Railroad in the 1860s. Organizers of the eastbound Central Pacific Railway had a problem, a severe labor shortage. The task of punching through the rugged High Sierra Mountains was both backbreaking and dangerous. New sign-ons often rode the rails to the worksite, only to drop their sledgehammers and head for potentially bigger pay days in the goldfields. Charles Crocker, the general manager of the Central Pacific, needed a solution. Progress had slowed to a snail's pace, and his bosses were demanding action. He turned to the Chinese. White Americans had generally considered them too small for the backbreaking work. Crocker's answer was, "They built the Great Wall, didn't they?"[32] The Chinese proved highly disciplined and hardworking, organizing themselves into work gangs with self-appointed foremen. The great railway confronted some of the most difficult terrain and weather conditions ever faced by an engineering project. Thousands of Chinese died dealing with the dangerous explosives used to blast away solid rock.

In 1869 the golden spike was struck at Promontory Point, Utah, linking the Central Pacific and the Union Pacific. By then, the Chinese were firmly established on the West Coast and more came every year. So many, in fact, that Congress passed the Chinese Exclusion Act in 1882, prohibiting further immigration.[33] That act opened the door to Japanese immigration. According to the 1920 United States Census, the foreign-born Chinese and Japanese populations in America totaled approximately 125,000. Whites feared the founding of a new Japan in America. By 1920 nearly 70,000 Japanese had settled in California, comprising around two percent of the state's inhabitants.[34]

These Asian Americans were an easy target for the Klan and their promoters. Skin color and facial features made them easily identifiable. Their language, religious beliefs, and customs were odd and threatening to white Americans. They were a minority, making them easy prey.

Bessie and Edward's kleagles also found recruits in areas with Jewish populations, mostly in larger Eastern cities. Jews have long been the victims of discrimination. Always in the minority, they have historically been at the mercy of cruel and ignorant majorities. The lynching of Leo Frank, outlined earlier in this book, is a classic example of the often violent hatred experienced by many Jews.

But Edward and Bessie identified a market for their biggest new target, one that was both white and European, just like the average Klan member. These people were indistinguishable from other white Americans in almost every way. The difference was religion. They were Catholic, and the Klan had Henry the VIII to thank for their windfall.

There has been a strong element of anti-Catholicism throughout America's history. The origins of this animosity can be traced to sixteenth-century England.

The story of Henry is well documented. Born in 1491, he was the third child (and second son) of King Henry the VII and Elizabeth of York. His older brother, Prince Arthur, was destined for the throne. In order to cement an alliance with Spain, Arthur was married at age fourteen to Catherine of Aragon, the youngest daughter of King Ferdinand and Queen Isabella. Henry, on the other hand, was given numerous titles and a first-rate education, becoming fluent in Latin, French, and Spanish. It was expected he would go on to a distinguished career as a cleric.

Then, Arthur died at age fifteen and the king offered his younger son in marriage to Arthur's young widow. For the arrangement to be legal, young Catherine had to claim her union with Arthur had never been consummated and Queen Isabella induced Pope Julius II to issue a dispensation of affinity in the form of a Papal Bull. After a long on-again, off-again engagement, Henry VII's death on April 21, 1509, put the wedding on the royal schedule. The seventeen-year-old Henry married Catherine on June 11, 1509. Thirteen days later, on June 24, the two were crowned at Westminster Abbey.

As a monarch Henry had many plans for England, not the least of which was producing a male heir. Catherine had six pregnancies. Two boys were stillborn or died during childbirth. Another, named Henry, died after fifty-two days of life. A daughter was stillborn and another died within one week. The only child to survive was Mary, born on February 18, 1516. Henry became impatient with Catherine's inability to produce the male heir he desired.

He also had become enamored with a young woman in the Queen's entourage named Anne Boleyn. Anne resisted the King's advances, saying she would only succumb as Henry's legal wife. This made Henry desire the young woman more, and he appealed to Rome for an annulment. Rome did not cooperate with the headstrong king. Henry had long been unhappy with major decisions in England being settled by Italians. The marriage issue proved to be the last straw. Henry declared himself the Supreme Head of the Church of England, separating itself from the Roman Catholic Church.

This act began an ecclesiastical ping-pong match that ultimately would make Bessie and Edward very rich.

The Church of England Henry had created remained essentially Catholic, thus angering Protestant Reformers and followers of Martin Luther.

Henry did marry Anne Boleyn and on September 7, 1533, she gave birth to a daughter christened Elizabeth. Subsequent pregnancies ended badly, including the miscarriage of a son after fifteen weeks. The inability to produce a son, marital incompatibility, and rumors of plots against the King led to Anne's execution at Tower Green on May 17, 1536.

On the day following Anne's death, Henry became engaged to Jane Seymour, one of Anne's ladies in waiting. In 1537 Jane finally produced a son for Henry, and she died shortly after a difficult childbirth. The future king was named Prince Edward.

Three more wives followed: Anne of Cleves, Catherine Howard, and Catherine Parr. None of these unions produced a child. Catherine Parr's important contribution was to reconcile Henry with his two daughters, putting them back into the line of succession following Edward.

On January 28, 1547, Henry died at the age of fifty-five. Nine-year-old Edward ascended to the throne of England. Change within the Church of England followed almost immediately.

The young regent began his rule with the help of a council led by the Lord Protector, Edward Seymour. In religious matters Edward fell under the influence of Thomas Cranmer, the Archbishop of Canterbury. Cranmer, a leading reformer, found an ardent pupil in the adolescent king. Together, they introduced a series of initiatives that took the English Church from one that was essentially Catholic to one that was institutionally Protestant. Edward allowed clergy to marry, imposed compulsory services in English, ordered images and altars to be removed from churches, eliminated the Mass, and introduced *Cranmer's Book of Common Prayer*. England had done a 180-degree turn to Protestantism.

Then, in February 1553, the young monarch fell unexpectedly ill. On the sixth of July he was dead. Fifteen-year-old Edward VI had ruled England for six years and 159 days. The cause of death has been attributed to tuberculosis or acute bronchopneumonia. Rumors of a Catholic poisoning plot have been largely dismissed.

Mary, the daughter of Henry VIII and his first wife, Catherine of Aragon, ascended the throne on October 1, 1553. On his deathbed Edward had tried to block Mary's succession fearing she would lead England back to Catholicism. He failed, and she did.

Mary was raised Catholic by her mother. She had always rejected her father's break with Rome and Edward's establishment of Protestantism in the Church of England. Mary and her Spanish husband, Philip, persuaded Parliament to repeal the Protestant religious laws passed by Henry, returning the English church to Roman jurisdiction. The ruling reaffirmed clerical celibacy and married priests were removed from their church positions.

In 1554 the Heresy Acts were passed and many leading Protestants were thrown into jail. Nearly 300 of these leaders were burned at the stake, including Thomas Cranmer. This cruel policy earned the queen the title of "Bloody Mary." The victims became martyrs and anti-Catholic sentiments strengthened among the English people.

England was fully on its way to a restored Catholicism when Mary died during an influenza epidemic in 1558. She had been queen for five years and four months, and did not leave an heir. In just over eleven years England would have four Tudor monarchs. Next in line was Elizabeth, the daughter of Henry and Anne Boleyn.

Elizabeth went on to rule for more than forty-four years. Her era is well chronicled. English drama flourished thanks to William Shakespeare and Christopher Marlowe. Sir Francis Drake and other English seafarers mastered the world's oceans. And, the British Navy defeated the Spanish Armada in one of history's greatest naval encounters in 1588.

To survive for so long on the throne, Elizabeth practiced the art of compromise. Her religious policy could well be described as pragmatic. She sought a Protestant solution that would not offend Catholics too greatly. Elizabeth's newly minted Church of England was very Protestant, but included many Catholic elements. She allowed Puritans (those wanting to purify the Church of all things Catholic) to have a voice in Parliament. Elizabeth would not, however, tolerate radicals pushing for far-reaching anti-Catholic reforms.[35]

These radical Puritans also became separatists. They were persecuted in England and sought a land where they could worship their personal brand of Protestantism. Their destination became England's North American colonies. They would carry with them a virulent, at times toxic, strain of anti-Catholicism. Historian Arthur M. Schlesinger Sr. called it "the deepest bias in the history of the American people." John Higham described anti-Catholicism as "the most luxuriant, tenacious tradition of paranoiac agitation in American history."

Anti-Catholicism took root with the first English settlers. Monsignor John Tracy Ellis wrote, "A universal anti-Catholic bias was brought to Jamestown in 1607 and vigorously cultivated in all the thirteen colonies from Massachusetts to Georgia."[36] In 1642 the colony of Virginia enacted a law prohibiting Catholic settlers. Five years later Massachusetts passed similar legislation.

The only charter given a Catholic was to George Calvert, Lord Baltimore, for his colony of Maryland. Even there Protestant settlement soon dwarfed that of Catholics. In 1634 Maryland recorded only 3,000 Catholics out of a population of 34,000 (9%). Pennsylvania, a haven of religious toleration, had fewer than 1,400 Catholics out of a population of 200,000 (0.7%) in 1757. In 1785 the newly formed United States contained nearly 4 million people. Of those, only 25,000 were Catholic (1.6%).[37]

Much of the Protestant intolerance could be attributed to a fear of mysterious Catholic rituals and a perceived allegiance to a foreign power, the Pope in Rome. Founding Father John Adams once attended a Catholic Mass in 1774. He enjoyed the homily but ridiculed the rituals of the parishioners. In 1778 John Jay, the first chief justice of the Supreme Court, urged the New York legislature to require office holders to renounce foreign authorities in all matters ecclesiastical as well as civil. Thomas Jefferson wrote, "History, I believe furnishes no example of a priest-ridden people maintaining a free civil government. . . . in every country and in every age, the priest has been hostile to liberty. He is always in alliance with the despot, abetting his abuses in return for protection to his own."[38]

One of the earliest violent manifestations of anti-Catholicism was the New York Conspiracy of 1741. The incident occurred during a war between Britain and Spain as well as a time of slave revolts in South Carolina and the Caribbean.

In March and April of that year, thirteen fires erupted in lower Manhattan. At one of the fires a black slave was arrested as he fled the scene. Soon thereafter, a sixteen-year-old Irish indentured servant named Mary Burton began to implicate blacks and poor whites as part of a conspiracy to kill whites and overthrow New York government. Burton had been arrested for theft and was pressured by authorities to cooperate.

In a scenario akin to the Salem Witch Trials, a mass hysteria overtook the city. By the time the trials had finished, 160 blacks and 21 whites had been arrested. Seventeen blacks and four whites were convicted and hanged. Thirteen blacks were burned at the stake. Burton fingered a number of white Catholics as leaders of the revolt including a tavern owner and his wife, and a prostitute. They were hung in June 1741. Finally Burton accused John Ury as a principal in the uprising. Ury was a recent arrival in New York and worked as teacher and tutor. He was an expert in Latin, which convinced the court that he was a Roman Catholic priest and Spanish secret agent. Ury was hung on the last day of August. In 1742 Burton received a 100-pound reward with which she used to buy her freedom.[39]

One hundred years later another series of violent, religious riots broke out—in Pennsylvania. Known as the Philadelphia Bible Riots, they were a result of growing anti-Catholic sentiment over the increasing number of Irish immigrants flowing into the country.

The trouble began when Bishop Francis Kenrick asked that Catholic students not be required to begin each public school day with readings from the Protestant version of the Bible. He requested the students be allowed to read the Douai version used by Catholics. The Board of Controllers agreed, saying that no child should be forced to participate in religious activities, and that children should be allowed to read whichever version of the Bible their parents wished.

Anti-Catholic, Nativist groups twisted this message into a story that Catholics were insisting all Bibles be removed from the schools. A group called the American Protestant Party held a meeting on May 3, 1844, in the heavily Catholic Kensington district of Philadelphia. Violence broke out and by the time fighting had ceased four Protestants were dead. On May 7 the Nativists returned in force, calling on Americans to defend themselves from "the bloody hand of the Pope." Thirty homes were burned. On May 8 two Catholic churches and a seminary were put to the torch. Fourteen people died, fifty were injured, and over two hundred were left homeless.

On July 3 the mob returned. Cannon and musket shots filled the Philadelphia streets. Another fifteen to twenty people died and at least fifty-six were wounded. Five thousand militia troops finally quelled the riots. In the wake of the unrest, Catholics began the creation of a Catholic school system, and Philadelphia established a formal, professional police force to protect the growing city.[40]

The largest of the Nativist Protestant movements of the mid-nineteenth century was a group known as the Know Nothings. Catholic immigration to the United States had exploded during those years. Civil War historian James McPherson estimates that immigration during the first five years of the 1850s was five times greater than the decade previous. Most of the new arrivals were poor Catholic laborers from Ireland and Germany. This new reactionary Know Nothings began in 1843 in New York and was semi-secret in nature. Members asked about activities were to reply, "I know nothing," and membership was limited to Protestant males of British lineage over the age of twenty-one. By 1854 Know Nothing numbers had increased to an estimated one million and the group had become a political force. They elected several mayors and were influential in many states. In 1856 former President Millard Fillmore ran on their national ticket and received twenty-three percent of the vote.[41]

The violent disposition of the Know Nothings demonstrated itself on August 6, 1855, in Louisville, Kentucky. In an attempt to keep Catholics from the ballot box in a hotly contested race for governor, Know Nothing followers attacked Catholics throughout the city. Nearly 100 died on "Bloody Monday." People were dragged from their homes and beaten in the streets.[42]

There was one more conspicuous anti-Catholic organization in America prior to the Simmons Klan. It began in 1887 as Catholic immigration continued to swell. The Irish were now established. The newcomers came from Italy and Poland. From 1890 to 1900 over 650,000 Italians came to America. From 1900 to 1910 another two million would arrive.

Between 1870 and 1914 nearly 2.6 million Poles left Europe to make the United States their home. Few in this group spoke English, and almost all were Catholic.

The new Nativist group was the American Protective Association (APA). Their goals included restricting Catholic immigration, making the ability to speak English a prerequisite to American citizenship, removing Catholic teachers from public schools, and banning Catholics from public office. By 1896 the APA boasted a membership in the millions.[43]

Bessie and Edward knew their marketplace and fashioned a product guaranteed to sell. Historian Nancy McClean summed up the situation: "Klan leaders constructed a new kind of reactionary populist politics that yoked white supremacy to one hundred per cent Americanism, anti-Semitism, anti-Communism, hostility to immigrants, antipathy to liberals, and support for old time religion (Protestant)."

Things were changing, and white Protestant America was fearful. The status quo was in jeopardy.

Fear can be an easy sell. It was, indeed, fertile ground. Bessie and Edward had tapped into a huge and receptive marketplace of fearful white Protestants.

Business was good.

CHAPTER 7
Power Play

"Anyone who has the power to make you believe absurdities has the power to make you commit injustices."

—Voltaire

Don't kill the goose that laid the golden egg.

—Moral of Aesop's Fable No. 87

It is not known if Bessie and Edward anticipated the cascade of membership applications and fees that began streaming into their Atlanta offices. What is certain is that they were very pleased. They had tapped into a rich vein of white, Protestant, Nativist sentiment that held the potential for spectacular profit. Their object was to keep their contract with Simmons in force and to maximize every possible revenue source. They had hit the mother lode.

Clarke was quoted as saying there were only ten to fifteen klans, and approximately a membership of 3,000 when the contract with Simmons was signed. Within the first three months of the new Propagation Department's stewardship, that total had grown by 48,000, a factor of fifteen times the original membership. Clarke said, "In all my years of experience in organization work I have never seen anything equal to the clamor throughout the nation."[1]

Never once in any literature is it mentioned that Bessie and Edward had any misgivings over what they were selling. Robert Duffus wrote an article about these days in the October 1923 issue of *World's Work*.

In his piece, Duffus called Clarke and Tyler "Salesmen of Hate." They were organizing and facilitating racial and religious hatred as well as contributing to lawlessness and acts of violence. According to Duffus, "Whatever their beliefs about the Protestant religion, white supremacy, or one hundred per cent Americanism, Mr. Clarke and Mrs. Tyler both took up the Klan frankly to make money. If in order to make money it became necessary to stir up racial and religious passions, they were willing and able to do it."[2]

What followed was a year and a half of remarkable activity from Clarke and Tyler as they squeezed every dollar out of their golden goose.

The ticket to maximizing profit for the newly minted Propagation Department was William Joseph Simmons. Bessie and Edward had seen more in the Imperial Wizard than a man who needed help. They had sensed in Simmons a man they could manipulate and control. They soon discovered the Colonel had little inclination for oversight.

Although the kleagles were selling an idea, there was a very tangible, built-in follow-up sale. The ideology of the Klan had great appeal to many, but the organization's image clearly lay in the sinister-looking robe and mask. The anonymity provided by the regalia allowed for secretive and impersonal hate. Bessie and Edward saw yet another opportunity.

In the days prior to the June 1920 contract with the Southern Publicity Association, Simmons acquired robes from the W. E. Flodding Co. of Atlanta. The regalia was purchased for $3.75 and provided to members at cost. Simmons said, "We control the manufacture of our paraphernalia so that no outsiders can put up a counterfeit organization and counterfeit it." Edward immediately saw the next opportunity. He quickly terminated the agreement with Flodding and chose a new firm, Gate City Manufacturing. Edward told Simmons that Flodding was raising prices to $7.50 due to post-war cotton prices. Gate City would manufacture the robes for only $4.00. Edward also told Simmons they should sell the regalia to members at $6.50 to cover for shipping and other costs.[3]

This new arrangement was with C. B. and Lottie Davis, the owners of the Gate City Manufacturing Company. The records of Fulton County show their application for a corporation charter was filed on June 9, 1920—two days after the signing of Bessie and Edward's contract with the Klan. There is little doubt that C. B. and Lottie were actually Clarke and Tyler.[4] Their actual cost to produce a robe was only $2, netting a one hundred percent profit on every sale to the Klan.[5] Additionally, sales to new members came through Propagation Department kleagles in the field. A commission was paid to all levels of the organization. Therefore, Bessie and Edward were effectively "double dipping." There are no business records for Gate City, but it can be assumed this was a significant revenue producer.

Edward and Bessie's ability to operate within the Klan was dependent on financial records and reporting. Under Simmons there had been none—there were virtually no records kept during its first four years. So, in another deft move, Edward hired a bookkeeper, not for the Propagation Department, but for the Klan in general. His name was N. N. Furney, and it appears his loyalty was to the man who had hired him, not the Imperial Wizard.[6] Simmons had no head for numbers and was oblivious to day-to-day operations at Klan headquarters.

Bessie and Edward knew that with increased exposure would come increased scrutiny. The art of public relations has a great deal to do with image creation and maintenance. To succeed on a grand, national scale, the Klan had to become more acceptable. It had to come out of the shadows and into the daylight.

The Klan was William Joseph Simmons, and his Klan was a secret order. There was no public face to the organization. It met in secret, and its core reason for existing was mysterious and sinister. It was time to go public. The Klan needed a mailing address, and it would no longer suffice to work out of Simmons's parlor. The operation moved to the Southern Publicity Association offices in the Flatiron Building.

Soon Edward and Bessie began receiving more and more press inquiries as the movement spread across the country. Along with those queries came requests to interview the Imperial Wizard. This presented a problem. Simmons was used to running his own show and could be unpredictable. As a former Protestant minister, he was used to commanding a room from the pulpit. He was also accustomed to speaking emotionally, melodramatically, and seldom spoke from a prepared text. David Mark Chalmers, in his *Hooded Americanism: The History of the Ku Klux Klan*, recounts a time when Simmons addressed an audience of Georgia Klansmen:

Colonel Simmons silently took a Colt automatic from his pocket and placed it on the table in front of him. Then he took a revolver from another pocket and put it on the table too. Then he unbuckled his cartridge belt and draped it in a crescent shape between the two weapons. Next, still without having uttered a word, he drew out a bowie knife and plunged it in the center of the things on the table. "Now let the Niggers, Catholics, Jews, and all others who disdain my imperial wizardry, come on."[7]

In November 1920 the Klan became involved in Florida elections. Since the days of Reconstruction, whites tended to vote Democratic as a response to Radical Republican policies. Blacks, if they dared go to the polls, voted Republican. In Jacksonville that year, 1,000 men attired as Klansmen marched as a warning to African Americans not to vote. In Orlando another 500 marched. On Election Day, two prosperous blacks attempted to vote in Ocoee, a suburb of Orlando. Whites blocked their way. Fearing for their lives, the men retreated to a home in the African-American section of the town. The mob followed and shots rang out. Two whites were killed. The settlement was set afire, and blacks attempting to escape the flames were shot. Two churches, a lodge hall, a school, and twenty houses were destroyed. An Orlando newspaper reported five deaths.

Simmons reportedly later talked of the incident, congratulating Florida for "killing thirty-six niggers."[8]

This type of language and behavior was incendiary. Bessie and Edward had a problem countering acts of violence being attributed to "night riders," men disguised in sheets and masks. They did not need their leader fueling the flames.

Edward and Bessie began to actively mold the Imperial Wizard's image. Edgar Fuller, a former Clarke associate, said that Simmons, "possessed none of the qualities to lead a great movement or to effect a great organization of men."[9]

The first step was to cancel all public appearances and speeches. It is not known how Simmons reacted to the quarantine. Edward could be very persuasive. The Colonel proved easily swayed by the forceful and dynamic promoter. According to Fuller, Edward "proceeded to create then offer to the American people an extraordinary man, capable of worldwide vision, and of unifying the white peoples of the earth in one great fraternity . . . the picture of a man marvelously endowed and gifted almost beyond mortal ken."[10]

When Simmons did re-emerge, his speeches were written for him and his talking points were well established. The first test case for this new strategy came in early January 1921. Edward and Bessie invited a reporter for the *New York Herald* to Atlanta for a tour of Klan headquarters.

A basic principle of media relations is to always control the content. It was Bessie who would be the reporter's guide. She was particularly adept at disarming men. The object was to portray the Klan as a benevolent and business-like fraternal order. They succeeded on every level. For five consecutive days the Klan received what amounted to free advertising in America's largest city.

The series opened on page one of the Monday, January 10, 1921, *Herald*. The headline proclaimed:

KU KLUX KLAN
TO INVADE NORTH
IN NATIONWIDE DRIVE

> . . . As a fraternal order duly chartered under the laws of the State of Georgia, announcing that it stands for law, order, and Americanism, it has spread throughout the South and is extending its secret membership in the North. A correspondent of the New York Herald has learned firsthand from the leaders of the movement what they are doing and what they expect to do . . .

The correspondent learned exactly what Edward and Bessie wanted him to learn. He reported that Simmons would soon begin a tour of some of the large cities of the North where small beginnings had been made by organizers. He reported Simmons will "prove the new Ku Klux Klan stands for the broad principle of Americanism. That it is not narrow or impelled by race prejudice, that it seeks law and order and that it should appeal to all 100 per cent native born, white Americans of the North as well as the South."

The article reads like a press release. It listed the Klan's four fundamentals: "1) Devotion to the fundamental principles and ideals of the founders of the United States, 2) An unequivocal belief in white supremacy, 3) A belief in the separation of Church and State, and 4) The protection of women's honor and the sanctity of the home."[11]

Day two of the series extolled the crime-fighting virtues of the Klan, giving an example from Birmingham, Alabama, when 700 Klansmen turned out to aid the police.[12]

On day three, Wednesday the 12th, the article talked about 1,500 new members joining each week and about moving into a larger and more modern building. Simmons was quoted saying, "New Klansmen were selected because of merit and a reputation for integrity and high moral character. They are not herded in with beating of drums and sounding of horns."[13]

Thursday gave three examples of the Klan's good works. The first was the story of a virtuous young woman whose husband drank too much "hooch" and took to beating his wife. A number of Klansmen, including many leading citizens, took the young man out into the woods and taught him the error of his ways.

Story number two told the tale of a black organization raising money for needy children at Christmas. They had fallen short of their goal. The local Klan called the head of the group to their offices and made a significant contribution.

In the last case, the Klan intervened in a potentially violent labor strike, preventing serious difficulties.[14]

On Friday the 14th the series concluded with the Klan's campaign against Bolsheviks who were trying to organize workers against the government.[15]

After five days of free publicity, membership efforts spiked in the New York Domain.

A few weeks later, Edward and Bessie persuaded the producers of Fox News Weekly, a theater newsreel, to portray the Klan favorably.[16]

On the evening of January 27, 1921, Bessie and Edward staged a spectacular show in Birmingham, Alabama. For the first time, the press and the public would be invited to a Klan initiation ceremony. It was a serious shift in publicity strategy. This type of event had always been ultra-secretive and shielded from the public. On that night 500 new candidates marched solemnly into the Alabama State Fairgrounds. They were surrounded by hundreds of hooded Klansmen, each holding aloft a red and white cross. Two giant searchlights illuminated the scene. Mounted Klansmen patrolled the perimeter. As the 500 initiates marched to the base of the Imperial Throne, the searchlights were extinguished. There were another 1,000 Klansmen assembled behind the throne in the shape of a cross. Each lit a small cross they were holding. Simmons stood, resplendent in purple satin robes, on the throne with a tall blazing cross on either side. He administered the oath to the new Klansmen exactly fifty-five years to the day Nathan Bedford Forrest had become the original Klan's first Imperial Wizard. It was grand theater, brilliantly staged by Edward and Bessie.[17]

The image makeover would continue. In early 1921 Simmons was given a new home. Located at 1840 Peachtree Road, it was formerly owned by Atlanta capitalist John Bratton and lay in the center of a highly fashionable district of the city. When he engineered the purchase, Edward would maintain:

> *The use of the Klan funds for what would appear to be a private purpose is justified in this way. Col. Simmons was at the time living at an unpretentious part of the city and in no way, as I viewed it, in keeping with his position and it was therefore in the interest of the Klan to put him in a better home and one that would reflect credit on the organization. Moreover, Col. Simmons earned this and more too, because for four or five years he had devoted almost his entire time to the creation and preservation of this organization, at times actually going hungry in order that the bills of the Klan might be met and the work kept alive.*[18]

The price of the home was $25,500, a purchase of over $310,000 in today's dollars. The Colonel would be seen as a successful and respectable member of Atlanta society at this address, and the home would be known as KlanKrest. The details of the purchase were as follows: Ten thousand dollars was paid in cash, $7,000 coming from the Klan treasury and $3,000 in a loan from Edward and Bessie. The remaining was in the form of a note for $15,500. The transaction was facilitated by a brand new firm called Clarke Realty and the deed was made out to Edward Y. Clarke. It appears Edward made a commission from the sale, was making interest on the personal loan to the Klan, and was the legal owner of the home.[19]

A few months later in 1921 Clarke Realty was involved in another transaction. Another grand home on Peachtree Road would become the official offices of the Ku Klux Klan. It had been owned by Mr. E. M. Durant of Atlanta and would be known as the Imperial Palace. This purchase price was $35,000, or approximately $425,000 in 2014 dollars. A payment of $10,000 in cash was made from the Ku Klux Klan treasury and the remaining $25,000 was secured through notes given by Edward to be paid over a period of five years. Again, Edward was named on the title. He claimed he wrote a letter to Simmons saying the property had been purchased in Edward's name but would belong to the Klan whenever it assumed or paid the obligations then existing. Edward justified the method of the purchase by saying he hoped to keep the Klan name out of the negotiations for two reasons. First, there was an impression that the Klan had a great deal of money and that would have raised the sale price. In addition, Edward wanted to hide the fact that the building would house business offices because the area was zoned residential.[20] He most certainly awarded himself another sales commission as realtor. No records exist, but it is possible he charged the Klan rent on the building as its landlord. As bookkeeper, Mr. Furney would have been a critical component in all these Klan-related financial matters.

In less than a year of the signing of the contract with Simmons, Edward and Bessie had over 1,100 kleagles in the field. In Edward's words, they were "making things hum all over America."[21] The salesmen were instructed to use whatever pitch was most likely to work in a particular community. If a community was afraid of labor unions, the Klan was against socialist-inspired alien organizers. In large cities in the North the message was that the Klan was anti-Catholic and anti-Jewish. If immigrants were taking jobs, the Klan was one hundred percent American. If a town was "dry," the Klan knew how to deal with bootleggers. In the West the Klan was against Mormons and Asians. Of course, in the South, the Klan was expert in the art of controlling the black man. *The Birth of a Nation* continued to be shown across the country, and kleagles targeted theatergoers. Scott Cutlip in *The Unseen Power*, his history of public relations, describes those days:

> *The impact of Clarke's program was quickly and strongly felt in the Southwest—Texas, Louisiana, Oklahoma, and Arkansas. It then fluttered about the Southeast and in the Northwest, surprisingly capturing Oregon. By the summer of 1921 it had crossed the Ohio River into the Midwest, the Potomac into the Northeast, and was creeping up the Atlantic seaboard. In less than fifteen months, Klan membership mushroomed from 4,000 to nearly 100,000, and initiates had spent over $1,500,000 in "Klecktokens" (the fees donated for a membership, white robes, literature, and paraphernalia).[22]*

Edward had been a Protestant minister, and he immediately saw a connection between Christian fundamentalism and the Klan's core message. The local preacher was often the most influential citizen in each community. Win them, Clarke believed, and you win the town. Kleagles were instructed to stress a shared concern about bootlegging, crime, and vice and to give the ministers free Klan memberships. Sales materials and flyers stressed a fundamentalist Christian message. One effective flyer, called "The Klansman's Creed," stated:

> *I believe in God and in the tenets of the Christian religion and that a godless nation cannot long prosper. I believe that a church that is not grounded on the principles of morality and justice is a mockery to God and man.[23]*

One particularly effective sales strategy was known as the "church visit." *Literary Digest* wrote in 1922, "Scarcely a Sunday passes without the publication of a Klan visit to a church somewhere, either to signify approval, sit decorously through a sermon, or present a donation." Often these visits were arranged in advance with the preacher. One scenario was a silent mid-service interruption with dozens of hooded Klansmen walking down the church aisle to the pulpit and handing a donation to the minister. Their exit would often be accompanied by applause from the congregation. At times the minister arranged for the organist to play a rousing version of "Onward Christian Soldiers."[24]

Bessie and Edward soon expanded this concept with the establishment of a Klan Speaker's Bureau, probably building on the idea of George Creel's "four-minute men" idea. Professional orators dubbed Klokards were sent throughout the country to speak at civic and fraternal meetings. Many were recruited from the ranks of famous Protestant clergymen. These men did not work on a commission basis as the kleagles did, but instead received a salary. This was at the height of the popular Chautauqua Movement, when Americans flocked to meetings to hear public oratory. When they attended a Klokard lecture, they often heard such talking points as:

> *Catholics, aliens, Jews and Negroes were a threat to the American way of life. The sole weapon against them was the Klan. True Americans should join the Klan. Morals in the United States were deteriorating. The sole weapon against Sin was a Protestant alliance with the Klan. If you are on the side of God, join the Klan.[25]*

Edward cleverly rationalized that these speakers were doing the general work of the Klan and were not involved in the Propagation Department. Therefore, he had their fees and travel expenses paid out of Simmons's twenty percent.[26]

The spectacular early sales returns of the Propagation Department enabled Edward and Bessie to further cement their position within the Klan. In January 1921 Simmons was persuaded to name Edward as Imperial Klaliff of the Klan. This position was part of the Imperial Kloncillium, or national cabinet, and was the equivalent of vice president of the organization. The small-time Atlanta publicist was now number two in the fastest-growing organization in America.

In this new role, Edward immediately made two calculated moves. First, he gave the Imperial Wizard a raise. Simmons was receiving a salary of $100 a week and claimed that during the early difficult days of the organization he had not drawn any salary. In 1921 Edward increased the compensation to $1,000 a month, two and one half times his rate of pay. Clarke was obviously very powerful in the Klan structure and a favorite of Simmons, so the Imperial Kloncillium did not challenge the increase. Next, Edward proposed back pay for the Imperial Wizard to make up for all the sacrifices Simmons had endured for the first five years of the Klan's existence. The number settled on was $25,000 to be paid out in five installments of $5,000 each. Again, the proposal passed.[27]

Edward's motive had nothing to do with fairness and gratitude. He wanted to keep Simmons satisfied, prosperous, and delighted with the growth and management of his Klan. Edward and Bessie did not want Simmons questioning anything going on within the Propagation Department that would jeopardize their contract.

In fact, Simmons's control of his organization had been waning from the day he signed the agreement with the Southern Publicity Association. Charles O. Jackson, in his article "William Simmons: A Career in Ku Kluxism," said, "the monarchy of the Invisible Empire became a triumvirate in which the old Wizard played an ever-decreasing role . . . the two publicists infiltrated the organization and consolidated their control over its administration, [a] process reputedly facilitated by Simmons's excessive drinking."[28] Simmons did have a taste for alcohol. And Bessie and Edward made sure the Imperial Palace of the Klan, a champion of Prohibition, was always well stocked for the Imperial Wizard.

It was apparent to all where the power in the Klan lay. All of the growth in the organization was directly attributable to the newly formed Propagation Department and control over the new members remained with Edward and Bessie's kleagles. The contract stipulated that the salesmen would organize provisional klans within their districts. As long as the local klan remained provisional, new members could be added at the contracted rate ($8 of the $10 to the Propagation Department, $4 of that directly to the kleagle). When that klan received an official charter, the payment dropped to $2 ($1 for the kleagle) for a six-month period. After that time there were no more commissions. Obviously, there was no incentive to apply for charters and to turn a klan over to the central Klan. The kleagles remained intensely loyal to the team making them rich.

Simmons apparently realized his power within the Klan was slipping. His absences from the office grew more frequent. When he was there he had little to do. A Macon, Georgia, newspaper man who visited the Imperial headquarters commented, "Mr. Simmons hangs around the office when Mr. Clarke has need of him, possesses the biggest sounding title, and draws a regular check—as a stockholder of the ideas."[29]

Bessie had been busy during this time as well. Always the entrepreneur, she purchased a press operation and began to publish a newspaper, *The Searchlight,* that would become the semi-official organ of the Ku Klux Klan. The banner that headed the first page of each issue proclaimed "Not a Moulder but a Chronicler of Public Opinion" and the paper's motto announced, "Free Speech, Free Press, White Supremacy." To give the new publication instant credibility, and a substantial subscriber base, Bessie sought and procured a joint sponsorship with the Junior Order of United American Mechanics. The JOUAM was a popular Anglo-Saxon, anti-immigrant fraternal organization with similar philosophies to the Klan. In the early twentieth century they boasted a national membership of approximately 200,000. In fact, Bessie was a member of its auxiliary, the Daughters of America.[30]

Copies of *The Searchlight* were sent to every kleagle for distribution to his local klans. Subscriptions were strongly encouraged. Copies were also placed with local newsstands. The newspaper sold for five cents and was distributed as far west as Butte, Montana. Prestigious companies such as Coca-Cola, Studebaker, and the Elgin Watch Company advertised in the pages of *The Searchlight.* Bessie hired J. O. Wood, a member of the Atlanta City Council, to edit the publication. The associate editor was Wood's law partner, Carl F. Hutcheson, a member of the Atlanta Board of Education. The editorial stance of the paper was decidedly anti-Jew, Catholic, Communist, and black. There are no circulation numbers or revenue statements for *The Searchlight,* but the income potential was sizable.[31]

There were other synergies in owning *The Searchlight* operation. Bessie used the presses to produce the printed materials used by the Propagation Department. She printed flyers, forms, brochures, pamphlets, and handbills at a handsome profit in the absence of a competitive bidding process. Edward, in turn, probably paid the bills out of the Klan General Fund.

Bessie and Edward at this time also established a newsletter network with their kleagles in the field for circulating sales strategies and success stories within the sales force. Undoubtedly the Searchlight Printing Company was involved with this work as well.[32]

The Propagation Department also became a movie producer. In an effort to exploit the popularity of the message generated by *The Birth of a Nation*, the Klan produced its own film, *The Face at the Window*. Bessie and Edward's newsletter of April 22, 1921, urged Klansmen to see the movie because "it strikingly depicts the serious working of those forces which are antagonistic to all the principles for which the Ku Klux Klan stand and which would tear down and scatter to the four winds those principles, ideals, and institutions inseparably associated with our Government." The "face" was that of Bolshevism and an attempted violent overthrow of the United States. Just as in *The Birth of a Nation*, the Klan rode to the rescue in the dramatic final scenes.[33]

One final bit of image building occurred in 1921. The September 12 *New York Times* announced that the Klan had acquired Lanier University, a Baptist institution located in the Druid Hills section of Atlanta. Colonel Simmons would become the college's president and Lanier would be devoted to the teaching of principles of "one hundred per cent Americanism." General Nathan Bedford Forrest, grandson of the original founder of the Klan, was appointed secretary and business manager. The school had been founded four years earlier by Baptist minister C. Lewis Fowler. Fowler had hoped for a large gift from Coca-Cola founder Asa Candler, but that money had gone to Emory University. Faced with enormous financial problems, Fowler had turned to the Klan. In return for $22,000, Simmons would become president and the board of trustees would be Klan appointed.[34]

Bessie and Edward were becoming incredibly wealthy as promoters of the Ku Klux Klan, and there seemed to be no end in sight. We have no record of what Edward did with his share of the profits; we do know that Bessie decided to build her dream house.

Sometime in late 1920 Bessie purchased twenty acres of land on Howell Mill Road in fashionable northwest Atlanta. Perhaps this was a leap of faith on her part. The contract with Simmons and the Klan was only three or four months old, but Bessie was a shrewd and insightful businesswoman. She knew the new venture would be highly successful, be her ticket to riches and respectability. She could no longer be known as the Queen of Pryor Street. The spectacular home she built on the site would announce to the world that Mary Elizabeth Cornett had beaten all odds and succeeded on a grand scale.

Construction began immediately on a house designed to look like an antebellum plantation mansion. The front lawn was ringed by mature trees and a nearly 300-foot-long driveway led from Howell Mill Road to the front door. On January 30, 2006, the Mary Elizabeth Tyler home was added to the National Register of Historic Places. The registration form describes the residence:

> *Built as a Classical Revival-style house, the exterior is dominated by a two-story classical portico supported by colossal Corinthian columns and a one-story front porch that wraps around the sides of the house. The recessed classical entrance features a leaded fanlight and sidelights. A second story balcony is located above the main entrance. The Georgian plan house featured four unequal-sized rooms divided by a wide center hall. The front and rear parlors on the south side shared an interior chimney. The dining room and the smaller library on the north side each had a chimney. The stair at the rear of the hall rose half a flight to a landing where two stairs led to the second floor. The second floor accommodated three bedrooms and a sleeping porch. A bathroom was located between the front bedrooms above the center hall.[35]*

There were two out buildings, a large garage, and a caretaker's cottage.

The home is an excellent example of the Classical Revival style of architecture popular throughout Georgia from the 1890s to the 1930s. It employed Greek and Roman details drawn from grand southern homes built in the early 1800s. It is said that Classical Revival homes were associated with economic success, social acceptability, and cultural achievement. The poor, uneducated young girl who was married and a mother at sixteen had become a rich and powerful woman.[35]

Edward was a frequent guest at the Howell Mill mansion after its completion in the spring of 1921. Membership forms streamed into the Imperial headquarters. The possibilities for making money seemed endless.

CHAPTER 8
The Whistle

"The world is a dangerous place, not because of those who do evil, but because of those who look on and do nothing."
—Albert Einstein

"All tyranny needs to gain a foothold is for people of good conscience to remain silent."
—Thomas Jefferson

"A good many things go around in the dark besides Santa Claus."
—Herbert Hoover

"You shall know the truth, and the truth shall make you mad."
—Aldous Huxley

On the evening of March 16, 1921, nine men quietly walked through the dark, silent streets of Johnson City, Tennessee. They congregated in the offices of a prominent local businessman, where they were greeted by a man wearing a white robe and a cape lined in red satin. His head was covered by a peaked helmet in which two eyeholes were cut. That night the nine aliens became naturalized citizens of the Invisible Empire.[1]

If the psychologist, looking over the diversified and con-

> *flicting interests and classes of the American people, attempt-*
> *ed to find a common state of mind, he would probably dis-*
> *cover one thing that applies to all American men, without*
> *regard to "race, color, or previous condition of servitude."*
> *He would learn that there is a common American trait pos-*
> *sessed by the white man and the Negro, the Jew and the*
> *Gentile, the Catholic and the Protestant, the native and*
> *the foreign-born—in fact by every conceivable group of the*
> *males of the United States.*
> *They are all "joiners"!*
> *One has to search far and wide for an American who does*
> *not "belong" to some sort of organization, and who would*
> *not, under proper circumstance, join another.*
> *I am a joiner-by-birth.*[2]

Those were the words of one of the Johnson City nine, Henry Peck Fry. The forty-year-old from Chattanooga never became a high-ranking Klan official, nor was he an important government office holder. He was merely one of the tens of thousands who gravitated to the hooded secret order. Henry Peck Fry, however, was Edward and Bessie's worst nightmare. Fry was a whistleblower.

He was born on September 27, 1880, to George Thompson Fry and Amelia Cooley Fry in Atlanta. His father had lived in Virginia until 1868 before moving to Georgia, where he practiced law and served two terms in the state legislature. During the Civil War the elder Fry had been a colonel in the Confederate Army. The family had a strong military tradition. Henry's great-great-grandfather, Col. Joshua Fry, served with distinction in the Revolutionary War and died during an early Indian War. Another ancestor, Col. Charles Fleming, fought in the same War and was killed at the Battle of Brandywine. General Patrick Peck was killed in the Mexican War. The family believed they had been represented in every war in which the United States had been a participant.

Another Fry family legacy was public service and the law. Henry's other great-great-grandfather, Adam Peck, was once chief justice of the Tennessee Supreme Court and helped write the state constitution. Jacob Peck, a great uncle, also served as chief justice. Henry's father was a highly respected attorney.

Much was expected of young Henry Peck Fry.

In 1890 Colonel Fry moved his family to Chattanooga, Tennessee, where Henry continued his education. He left high school without graduating and entered the prestigious Virginia Military Institute (VMI). VMI was known as the "West Point of the South." Confederate legend Stonewall Jackson had once been an instructor at the school, and one of Henry's classmates, Gen. George C. Marshall, would be the architect of the Marshall Plan following WWII.

Henry was an apt student, graduating in 1901, and distinguishing himself as both a mathematician and a tactician. After graduation he was offered and accepted the position of major and commandant at the University of the South in Sewanee, Tennessee. Henry taught during the day and began reading law in the evening.

After seven months in Sewanee, Fry returned home to Chattanooga to continue his study of law while working as a reporter for the *Chattanooga Evening News*, where he earned a reputation as a clear, exact, and forceful writer.

On June 13, 1903, Henry Peck Fry gained admittance to the Tennessee bar and joined the noted firm of Frazier and Coleman. In less than seven months he argued his first case before the state supreme court.

Fry quickly gravitated to politics and was elected county revenue commissioner. His motto was "honesty is the principal requisite in the administration of public affairs." He also put his military training to good use when he was elected captain of Company M, Frazier Guards, Third Regiment, Tennessee National Guard. His company, while he was in service, was said to be the most efficient in Tennessee, so pronounced by Inspector General S. D. Tyson.

Henry was becoming a pillar of the Chattanooga community. He was a member of St. Paul's Episcopal Church as well as Temple Lodge No. 430 of the Free and Accepted Masons; of Park Lodge No. 75, Knights of Pythias; Hill City Lodge No. 245, Independent Order of Odd Fellows; and as an officer of Chattanooga Lodge No. 91, Benevolent and Protective Order of Elks.

So prominent was young Henry Peck Fry that he was included in the 1905 edition of *Notable Men of Tennessee*.[3] At the tender age of twenty-five his future seemed bright and prosperous. He was an intelligent, energetic, and eclectic Southern gentleman. His personality was dominated by rigid discipline and a strong belief system. He was honor bound by many oaths taken as a soldier, lawyer, elected official, and fraternalist. There was yet one more complex facet to his life. Henry Peck Fry was also dedicated to the cause of white supremacy.

He wasn't a radical, violent proponent of the movement, his participation more rational and intellectual. In 1906 Fry wrote and self-published his personal treatise on the race problem in America, with the rather cumbersome title, *The Voice of the Third Generation: A Discussion of the Race Question for the Benefit of Those Who Believe that the United States Is a White Man's Country and Should Be Governed by White Men.*

Fry's dedication page read:

> *To the American people hoping that, in the interest of true Americanism, the purity of the United States Government, and the perpetuation of the theory that this is a white man's government, Almighty God will send the message herein contained to every thinking man in the nation and that "The Voice of the Third Generation" will be heard and its counsels heeded.*[4]

Page one of the thirty-two stated Fry's hypothesis. There was one, and only one, solution to America's race problem. "The race problem will vanish into the gloom of an unpleasant memory of unpleasant events, if one thing is done by the American people, THE REPEAL OF THE FIFTEENTH AMENDMENT TO THE CONSTITUTION OF THE UNITED STATES."[5] The Fifteenth Amendment, ratified after the Civil War, gave black men the right to vote by specifying, "The right of citizens of the United States to vote shall not be denied or abridged by the United States or by any State on account of race, color, or previous condition of servitude."

Fry called the Fifteenth Amendment "the most glaring piece of legislative stupidity of which lawmakers have ever been guilty."[6] He claimed blacks were an inferior race of people unfit to exercise the privileges of American citizenship. Slavery should never have been introduced, but blacks had been treated kindly in the South and had committed very few crimes. The book stated that the Civil War was not about slavery, but instead states' rights. Fry praised Abraham Lincoln for never intending equality, preferring a policy of compensated emancipation and colonization. He squarely placed the blame on Andrew Johnson and the Thaddeus Stevens–led Radical Republican Congress.

The book rambles through a historical argument for his race's superiority. Fry places the evidence of great "Caucasian" accomplishments— Greek, Roman, European, even Egyptian—in comparison with black Africans living for centuries in primitive jungle savagery.

He explained the genesis of his book title. The first generation in the Southern states were the active participants in the Civil War. They were, according to Fry, brave, chivalrous men of knightly bearing who had covered themselves in honor and glory. The second generation consisted of those born during or shortly after the Civil War. The third generation was Fry's generation. These were men born since Reconstruction, then between the ages of eighteen and twenty-eight, and not directly familiar with the events following the Civil War. Fry believed they were the most patriotic of Southerners—college educated and equipped to solve the South's race problem. This generation was not violent, but instead, rational and well intentioned.[7]

As a lawyer, Fry made the argument that the Thirteenth, Fourteenth, and Fifteenth amendments to the Constitution were not worth the paper they were written on. Amendments require a certain percentage of ratification by states to become law. Because Southern states under military supervision during Reconstruction were not allowed to be a part of the process, there were not enough Northern states to reach the percentage.

Fry's philosophy regarding race can be summed up by the following: "A Negro is a Negro regardless of a smattering of education he may have, and the protection of the government makes him more vicious than in his ordinary condition."[8]

Fry's book constitutes intellectual racism. For most racists the issue is visceral, emotional, and void of logic. It is rare for someone to form an educated argument, commit it to paper, and publish it at his own expense for all to see.

Fry's military life continued through an association with Leonard Wood, one of the most famous soldiers of his generation.

Leonard Wood began his career as a doctor, graduating from Harvard

Medical School. His first military assignment was in Arizona fighting the last campaign against the Apache leader Geronimo. He was decorated for his actions in taking charge of a unit after its officer was killed, and for surviving a harrowing 100-mile journey through dangerous Indian territory. He returned to Washington to become the personal doctor to several American presidents. When the Spanish-American War broke out he received a command in Cuba. On the day of the charge at San Juan Hill, one of his junior officers was Teddy Roosevelt. In the early 1900s he would serve as military governor of Cuba and governor general of the Philippines. The high point in his career would come in 1910 when he was named Army chief of staff.

As the head of the Army, Leonard Wood began modernizing the military for a future war in Europe. He saw a need for training and preparedness and established the framework for what would become the Reserve Officers' Training Corps (ROTC).[9] In 1916 Henry Peck Fry served as Wood's personal representative, enrolling men at military training camps. Together, Fry and Wood would author a military training guide, and, later in 1916, with Wood's help, Henry established the first military correspondence school, The American Military Institute.

The school was short-lived, however, with the onset of America's involvement in WWI in 1917. Fry rejected a number of staff assignments and enlisted as a private in the Army. He did not want a desk job, instead hoping to see combat in Europe. He quickly was promoted to sergeant, then second lieutenant, and first lieutenant. A promotion to captain was pending when the war ended on November, 11, 1918. His unit remained at Camp Funston, Kansas, and never made it overseas.[10]

Fry's contact with the Ku Klux Klan came in upper East Tennessee during the early months of 1921. The account comes from *The Modern Ku Klux Klan*, a book written by Fry in 1922. He described the region as a place where one would least expect a movement like the Klan to establish a foothold, as the black population was small, orderly, well behaved, and industrious. There was a small Catholic presence, few Jews, and a "paucity of foreign population." It was overwhelmingly American and uniformly Protestant.[11]

He had been sent by a Chattanooga business house on an extended trip through East Tennessee. There is no other record of who Fry was working for or the type of business being done. He made his headquarters a boarding house in Johnson City. In early March Fry noticed a "young man of pleasing personality" staying in the same home. On the 16th they spoke for the first time at the breakfast table. Fry asked what the young man was selling as most of the residents were traveling salesmen. According to Fry the man noticed the Masonic pin on his jacket and showed Henry a local newspaper clipping announcing the arrival of a Ku Klux Klan organizer. They had a long talk. "He was an excellent salesman of his proposition, and in a few minutes he had me completely sold." Fry was aware of the organization "and was curious to see what it was all about, but principally because I thought it was a fraternal order which was actually a revival of the original Ku Klux Klan which played so important a part in the history of the South during the days of the Reconstruction."[12] This would line up with his feelings expressed in *The Voice of the Third Generation*.

That very evening Henry Peck Fry joined the Klan. He maintained he knew nothing about the structure of this new Klan, but he assumed it would function like any other standard fraternal order and that it would be a pleasure to belong to it.

Fry demonstrated immediate interest in the organization and began assisting in membership recruitment. In early April the local kleagle received a promotion and Henry was named his replacement. In the commission he signed on April 8 there was a pledge of "whole-hearted loyalty and unwavering devotion to William Joseph Simmons as Imperial Wizard and Emperor of the Invisible Empire."[13]

Fry took to the duties of kleagle with great energy. He expressed the opinion that the best way to learn about a fraternal order was as an organizer. For nearly three months Fry worked and observed. Before long he began to have doubts. According to his book, "a feeling developed within me that there was something wrong with the organization—that it was not the sort of fraternal society to which I had been accustomed for nearly twenty years."[14] He began noticing the Klan goal of infiltrating politics, the law, and the military in order to establish an Invisible Empire within the United States. He rankled at the thought of an emperor elected for life. And he saw the operation as a money-making scheme benefiting a select few. He also observed an organization, built on absolute secrecy, as potentially dangerous and radical.

The average person might not have questioned the inner workings of the Klan. Or, he might simply have resigned if he found things not to his liking. Henry Peck Fry was no ordinary man. He felt a struggle developing within himself. In *The Modern Ku Klux Klan* he reconstructed how he resolved his moral conundrum.

> *The portentous nature of my conclusions, however, weighed heavily upon me, and after the most serious consideration, I finally decided to repudiate the entire organization. I finally decided to expose the whole system, calling public attention to what seems to me to be the greatest menace that has ever been launched in this country.*[15]

This seems to be a classic example of a whistleblower—a person willing to risk everything to right a wrong. Fry was a highly principled idealist, devoted to honor and country.

> *There were, of course, dangers and potential regrets.*
>
> *My decision to take this step was a most difficult one to reach. In the first place, to give to the public the facts and inside workings of the "Invisible Empire" means to subject oneself to the penalty of death for disclosing a secret of the order.*
>
> *The most disagreeable feature of the whole procedure is the absolute necessity of going on record publicly as violating a solemn oath, a pledge of honor, and an obligation that would ordinarily be considered sacred. Is a man, having taken an oath, ever justified in breaking it?*[16]

Fry answered his own question. In his mind, if the oath is illegal and could incite a riot or lawlessness, a man is not only justified in breaking it, but is morally required to break it.

I have, therefore, deliberately and with careful thought, decided to violate and repudiate this obligation... The question as to whether I am right or wrong is one that will have to be decided by public opinion. . . . If I am wrong in my viewpoint, I do not deserve to be allowed to mingle with honorable men and women, and should be set apart from my fellows as a social outcast.

On the other hand, if I am right in the stand that I take, that the Ku Klux Klan is a secret, political, military machine, actually developing into an Invisible Empire; . . . if I am correct in my position and the whole scheme is an attempt to create class hatred and antagonism, which in the end will array race against race and religion against religion; if my contention is just that the proposition is a money making scheme; and, if the public adopts my viewpoint to the extent of demanding that the organization be legislated out of existence and made an outlaw to the world of open things, then I shall feel satisfied that the violation of this oath has been a public service.

There is no middle ground. I am either entirely right, or else I am entirely wrong.[17]

With the instincts and training of an experienced journalist, Fry gathered all the information and documents available to him. He formally resigned his commission as a kleagle on June 15, 1921. His final act was to write a long and scathing letter to the Imperial Wizard withdrawing himself as a citizen of the Invisible Empire.

Henry Peck Fry began his journey to north.

CHAPTER 9
The World

"Were it left to me to decide whether we should have a government without newspapers, or newspapers without government, I should not hesitate a moment to prefer the latter."

—Thomas Jefferson

"There can be no higher law in journalism than to tell the truth and to shame the devil."

—Walter Lippmann

"Never pick a fight with people who buy ink by the barrel."

—Bill Clinton

In the biggest city in the world, 1921 had been a very interesting year.

Warren G. Harding was president, and the events that would lead to the Teapot Dome Scandal were in their infancy. A little-known Austrian named Adolph Hitler became chairman of the fledgling German Nazi Party, and the Chinese Communist Party was formed by Mao Tse-tung. A wealthy New York politician, Franklin Delano Roosevelt, contracted polio.

Albert Einstein won the Nobel Prize in Physics and made a grand visit to America.

Fatty Arbuckle signed a million-dollar film contract and decided to throw a wild party. His trial for rape and murder would have profound impact on the movie industry. At the box office people rushed to view *The Kid* and *The Three Musketeers*.

In the world of sports, Big Bill Tilden won the Wimbledon title and Behave Yourself bested the field at the Kentucky Derby. The legendary Jack Dempsey knocked out Georges Carpentier in Jersey City in front of 80,000 adoring fans.[1] The fate of the 1919 Black Sox was finally meted out.

One of the biggest New York City stories in the summer of 1921 involved a stick-legged, pot-bellied, baby-faced kid named George Herman Ruth as he mounted an assault on the baseball record books.

The largest city in the world was also the center of the print and journalism universe. Henry Peck Fry had come to the right place.

> *Always fight for progress and reform, never tolerate injustice or corruption, always fight demagogues of all parties, never belong to any party, always oppose privileged classes and public plunderers, never lack sympathy with the poor, always remain devoted to the public welfare, never be satisfied with simply printing news, always be drastically independent, never be afraid to attack wrong, whether by predatory plutocracy or predatory poverty.*
> —Joseph Pulitzer, from the masthead
> of *The New York World*

New York City was a news town because of a frail, hard-driving Jewish Hungarian named Joseph Pulitzer. He was born on April 10, 1847, into a family of successful merchants in the town of Mako, Hungary. His father, Philip, retired and moved his family to the cosmopolitan capital city of Budapest. There Joseph was educated by private tutors and became fluent in three languages.[2]

When Philip died, the family's fortunes reversed and they became impoverished. Seeking escape and adventure, young Joseph tried to enlist in the armies of various European nations. He was continually rejected due to his tender age and generally poor health. There was, however, one nation in the mid-1860s with an insatiable appetite for soldiers and little regard for restrictions.³ On the other side of the Atlantic, the United States was locked in a brutal civil war and was experiencing horrific casualties.

Young Pulitzer disembarked in New York City on September 30, 1864. At the age of eighteen, he immediately enlisted in the Lincoln Cavalry and served for nearly eight months with Philip Sheridan's Union troops. His limited English proved not to be a problem as most of his regiment consisted of German speakers.⁴

At war's end the young immigrant found himself penniless and with few prospects. Eventually he boarded a train for St. Louis, Missouri, a city where he had heard German was as useful as it was in Munich. Once there, Joseph had difficulty holding any job for long. Either he was too frail for heavy labor, or too proud and temperamental to take orders from others. Between and around jobs, Pulitzer spent every moment studying English and reading voraciously.⁵

He began to study for a career in law, and in 1867 Joseph Pulitzer became an American citizen. By 1868 he had been admitted to the bar, but found the practice of law difficult and tedious. The turning point in his career occurred late in 1868. The German-language newspaper in St. Louis, the *Westliche Post*, needed a reporter and Pulitzer was offered the job.⁶

Joseph had found his calling. He had a flair for reporting and a work ethic that followed him the rest of his life. A sixteen-hour day was a normal day. The new American also developed a love of politics. He joined the Republican Party and quickly became a candidate for Missouri State Representative. His boundless energy earned Pulitzer a seat in Jefferson City in 1870. At the *Westliche Post*, his hard work had earned him the title of managing editor and a proprietary interest, purchased on credit, in the paper. Less than six years "off the boat," Joseph Pulitzer was living the American Dream.

He soon sold his share in the newspaper for $30,000 and made plans to travel in Europe.⁷ But before he could set sail, Pulitzer had met and fallen in love with Kate Davis, a beautiful young woman who was a member of Washington, D.C.'s, high society. His chances were slim with Kate and even slimmer with her family. He was Jewish and spoke with a guttural accent. What could he offer her? To be the wife of a newspaper reporter offered little social status. The wife of a lawyer was more acceptable, but Joseph had no interest in practice. He decided to return to St. Louis, writing to Kate that he needed to "become worthy of you, worthy of your faith and love, worthy of a better and finer future."[8]

He apparently established his worthiness. They married in 1878 and had six children together—three boys and three girls.

The turning point in Pulitzer's journalistic career came later in 1879 when he learned of the impending auction of the bankrupt *St. Louis Dispatch*. Willing to risk his entire savings of $5,000, Pulitzer entered the bidding. When the action stopped at $2,500, the boy from Hungary had become the owner of an English-language newspaper. He immediately threw considerable energy into producing a first edition. The following day the owner and editor of the rival *St. Louis Post* sensed serious competition and offered to merge the two newspapers. The *St. Louis Post-Dispatch* was born.

Pulitzer boldly announced that the paper "would serve no party but the people." His philosophy emerged in one of his first editorials when he proclaimed, "What is the great demoralizer of our public life? Of course, corruption. And what causes corruption? Of course, the greed for money." It was a dangerous path, to attack the rich and powerful. But it would prove to be a formula for success. *The Post-Dispatch* would wage numerous crusades attacking monopolies and fraud.

A second key to its success was publishing stories focusing on crime and violence. Critics attacked the *Post-Dispatch*'s overt sensationalism. Meanwhile, Joseph's work ethic and attention to detail were already becoming legendary. Readership soared. Pulitzer bought out his partner and dominated the St. Louis news scene. He also became a wealthy man.[9]

In the spring of 1883 Joseph decided to vacation again in Europe. However, he never boarded the ship in New York Harbor. Upon arriving in the Big Apple, Pulitzer learned the struggling *New York World* was for sale. The twenty-year-old *World* had started as a one-penny religious paper. After enduring a series of failures and owners, the paper had fallen into the hands of the infamous "robber baron" financier Jay Gould. The paper had a circulation of around 15,000 and was losing $40,000 a year. Gould was looking to cash in. He wanted $500,000— and for the buyer to purchase the *World* building for $200,000 and retain the newspaper's staff.

The thirty-six-year-old publisher was beset with anxiety. Could he compete in the overcrowded, highly competitive New York newspaper world? Was he physically up to the task? And, could he negotiate with the ruthless Gould? He told Kate he wanted to drop out of the talks. She persuaded him to continue.

Joseph did just fine in the negotiations, and Gould was the one who backed down. Pulitzer paid $350,000, payable in installments. He leased office space rather than buy the building, and was free to hire his own editorial staff. He had gained entry into a very select club. Pulitzer owned a newspaper in America's largest city. He had gained a platform to express his beliefs and to accomplish his personal goals.[10]

The skinny Hungarian immigrant had lofty aspirations. He had always been fascinated by American politics. He now had a vehicle to shape and influence the direction of government. He wanted to elect a president. Joseph also looked to sell millions of newspapers. The only place to do that was New York City. His third goal was to be an agent of change, to make the life of the common person better. In his quest to achieve these things, Joseph Pulitzer would invent the modern newspaper.

Instead of writing for the wealthy and literate, Pulitzer instructed his reporters to write to and for the masses. Nearly one-half million immigrants were flowing into New York City yearly. Most stayed there in overcrowded, substandard tenements. The oversaturated job market kept wages low and conditions deplorable. One in five Americans could neither read nor write. Many others were barely literate. The potential to effect change was enormous, as was the opportunity to sell newspapers. Pulitzer gave his reporters their working orders. "Heretofore you have all been living in the parlour and taking baths every day. Now I wish you to understand that, in future, you all are walking down the Bowery."[11]

He changed the way newspapers looked and felt. News writers wrote differently. Readers now saw brief, bold, large headlines. Sentences were short and simple. The vocabulary used was informal and basic. Reporters and editors were to look for stories on the exploitation of the masses and to develop crusades for their betterment. Pulitzer also wanted stories on sex, crime, gossip, and tragedy. There would be few dull front-page articles on the economy and politics in the new *World*.

One of the most revolutionary ideas Pulitzer would implement was his use of photos and illustrations. He had undoubtedly noted the role they had played in the downfall of Boss Tweed and Tammany Hall ten years earlier. William "Boss" Tweed was the infamous leader of the New York City Democratic machine in the late 1860s and early 1870s, and they met in a building called Tammany Hall. Tweed and his corrupt cronies controlled every aspect of life in the city while amassing huge personal wealth. *Harpers Weekly* magazine and its brilliant cartoonist, Thomas Nast, took on the machine. Nast's powerful cartoons played a significant role in toppling the evil empire. Tweed once lamented, "Stop them damned pictures. I don't care so much what the papers say about me. My constituents don't know how to read, but they can't help seeing them damned pictures!"

It was more expensive to print photos and illustrations, but Pulitzer sensed their impact. Technology was changing the newspaper business in large urban areas. Mass transit had dramatically altered the way people got to work. Instead of reading the newspaper at home, many people now consumed their news on the train. Home subscriptions became less important. New Yorkers bought at the subway newsstand, and the competition among the city's many dailies was fierce. Those bold, sensational headlines coupled with graphic, sometimes lurid, photos and illustrations sold newspapers.

Pulitzer also realized his readers needed to escape the rigors of their hard lives. For men he began to print a sports page with schedules and stories on baseball, horse racing, track, tennis, boxing, and football. For women, the *World* published advice columns on how to be socially proper. A fictional "Edith" would write to her country cousin "Bessie" on how to act in the big city. Another, written by "Jenny June," told women how they could claim their rightful place in society through hard work.[12]

Pulitzer and the *World* also began the time-honored tradition of the comics page.

Above all, Joseph Pulitzer was at heart, first and foremost, a journalist. There were bold and sensational headlines, but he expected them to be backed up with solid facts. The walls of the *World*'s newsroom were plastered with posters demanding "Accuracy! Accuracy! Accuracy!"

Pulitzer supplied this advice to his writers:

—Be accurate.
—Be concise.
—Never write about a trivial topic.
—Be absolutely fair.
—Write about current concrete topics, never about abstractions.
—Whenever possible, use facts, figures, and statistics.
—Rise above partisanship and popular prejudice.
—Do not talk about public people in private.
—Use word pictures to describe events so that readers feel as though they were on the scene.
—Make sure your opening sentence and paragraph are particularly striking.
—Use history when possible to make an argument stronger.
—Book reviewers should state first the most interesting points of the book, then the focus of the book, then—if there is room, the reviewer's opinion.[13]

Pulitzer hired the best people, paid them well, and demanded much of them. No one worked harder than Pulitzer himself. Never a robust man, he endured a life of failing health as a result.

The formula worked. In two years the readership of the *World* had grown from 15,000 to well over 150,000. It became the most widely read newspaper in the world.

There would be competition. In 1894 William Randolph Hearst bought the struggling *New York Journal*. He immediately increased the number of pages, cut the price, and copied the techniques Pulitzer was using at the *World*. Hearst even tried to hire the *World*'s staff.

Much to Pulitzer's angst, Hearst cared little about news gathering. His was an evening paper. The writers at the *Journal* would wait until the morning edition of the *World* arrived and simply rewrite the stories for their edition. It is reported the staff would chant, "Sound the cymbals, beat the drums; the *World* is here, the news has come."[14]

Hearst made great gains in readership. The competition became in-

tense between the two newspapers. The biggest battleground was over
Cuba and its rebellion against Spanish rule. Each paper sent reporters
to capture the drama of the situation. The reports were full of accounts
of torture, and slaughter of rebels at the hands of their colonial masters.
One *World* headline screamed, "Blood on the roadsides, blood in the
fields, blood on the doorsteps, blood, blood, blood!" Pulitzer's principles
of accuracy and truth seemed suspended over the Hearst threat. The
Journal was no better. Both newspapers agreed on a need for American
action. Their only disagreement came over the number of readers.

The climax arrived with an explosion in Havana Harbor that destroyed the American naval battleship *Maine*, killing 250 sailors. Both
newspapers lay the blame at the feet of the Spanish even though no
proof existed for the claim. Other newspapers decried the actions of
Hearst and Pulitzer. An enraged populace cried for war. Congress's declaration made it official. The "Splendid Little War" was over in less than
three months. Four hundred Americans were killed in battle, but another 5,000 died of malaria, typhoid, dysentery, and yellow fever. The
United States gained an overseas empire much to the dismay of many
Americans.[15]

Pulitzer later would regret the excesses his newspaper had committed.
He had violated his own journalistic principles in his desire to defeat
Hearst.

Meanwhile, Pulitzer's already frail health continued to worsen. His
eyesight was failing, and he was unable to tolerate even the slightest
sound. He isolated himself from his family aboard his yacht as he traveled throughout Europe seeking a cure. Wherever he was, Pulitzer kept
in touch with the news and his newspaper.

Joseph Pulitzer died aboard his yacht, *Liberty,* on October 29, 1911,
near Charleston, South Carolina. In his will he left $1.5 million for the
founding of Columbia University's Graduate School of Journalism. He
also gave $500,000 to endow the national awards for books, drama,
music, and journalism that carry his name. His old foe, William Randolph Hearst, said, "A towering figure from national and international
journalism has passed away; a mighty democratic force in the life of
the nation and in the activity of the world has ceased; a great power
uniformly exerted in behalf of human rights and human progress has

ended. Joseph Pulitzer is dead."[16]

Following Joseph Pulitzer was a very daunting task. He had hoped his three sons would carry on in his absence. In his 1904 will he left instructions for them that they accept "the duty of preserving, perfecting, and perpetuating *The World* newspaper in the same spirit in which I have striven to create and conduct it as a public institution, with motives higher than mere gain."[17] The Pulitzer family dynamic made picking up where Joseph left off not so straightforward. Pulitzer's health history and devotion to work left him little time for the children. Kate was left to raise the family alone. The boys, Ralph, Joseph Jr., and Herbert never showed the drive and dedication of their legendary father. Ralph and Joseph both attended Harvard University. Neither did well, and Joseph was expelled. When Ralph went to work for the *World* he returned late from a vacation and his father demanded his resignation. The youngest, Herbert, was clearly his father's favorite, but was only sixteen years old. Even then he showed little interest in the family business.

Joseph Jr. left for St. Louis to assume the reins of the *Post-Dispatch*. Ralph and Herbert were responsible for the *World*.

The *World* remained competitive largely through the efforts of the day-to-day editorial management. Frank Cobb had been hired by the elder Pulitzer and continued as the managing editor. One other hire during the final years of Joseph Pulitzer's life turned out to be monumental for the New York daily. He was the man pundit, and first columnist to win a Pulitzer, Westbrook Pegler would describe as "all gall, divided into three parts—Herbert, Bayard, and Swope."[18]

Herbert Bayard Swope was a superstar in the world of journalism. He was born in St. Louis, Missouri, on January 5, 1882, the son of Isaac Swope, a watchcase manufacturer, and Ida Cohn. His life parallels that of Joseph Pulitzer in a number of ways. He received a solid early education, including from the University of Berlin. When his father died, Swope also had to find a job. Attracted to journalism, he found work at Pulitzer's *St. Louis Post-Dispatch* in 1899 as a political reporter. After a brief stint in Chicago, Swope moved on to reporting for the *New York Herald*. He remained there until 1907. During this period he also experienced health problems, suffering and recovering from tuberculosis in 1905. After two years of unemployment, the reporter was hired by the

New York World in 1909.

It didn't take long for Herbert Bayard Swope to establish himself as an enterprising and tireless reporter. His first major coup exposed the Rosenthal-Rose-Becker scandal. Charles Becker was a corrupt police lieutenant who had befriended a criminal named Herman Rosenthal. When Becker began to harass him, Rosenthal threatened to expose police corruption. Becker then hired hit man Jack Rose to murder his former friend. Within hours of Rosenthal's death Swope's story of the accusations and murder hit newsstands. He quickly obtained a copy of Rose's confession. Swope followed up this feat with his stories on the Triangle Shirtwaist Company fire in 1911. One hundred and fifty women were trapped on an upper floor when the fire broke out. Employers had locked the doors to prevent workers from leaving the plant floor. Many women perished in the building, while others jumped to their deaths. The tragedy would lead to improved fire regulations in the city. In 1912 his account of the sinking of the *Titanic* appeared on the pages of the *World*.

With Swope's growing reputation came a promotion to city editor in 1915. However, the pressing news of the day was international. World War I was raging on the European continent, and America, still sitting on the sidelines, yearned for news. Swope was designated special staff and assigned to Germany. His reports appeared in fourteen nationally syndicated installments between October 10 and November 22, 1916. The prizes endowed by Joseph Pulitzer in 1911 were awarded in 1917. The Pulitzer for reporting that initial year was given to Herbert Bayard Swope for the series "Inside the German Empire."

At war's end Swope was part of a team sent to Paris to cover the peace conferences. He was named head of the U.S. press delegation and worked to improve press access to information. In a move that cemented his status as an inventive and unstoppable journalist, Swope donned the tails and top hat of a diplomat and entered the hall at Versailles. Reporters were banned from the talks. Swope enjoyed a front row seat as the Allies presented their terms to German representatives. The *World* had yet another exclusive.

In 1920 Swope was named executive editor of *The New York World*. His challenge was to keep the paper relevant and profitable amid growing competition and a shrinking budget.[19] The motive of "mere gain" Joseph Pulitzer had warned against was important in Ralph Pulitzer's administration. Seven major daily newspapers vied for readership in the city. *The American, The Telegram, The Tribune, The Times,* and *The Sun* all joined *The World* with six-figure circulations. In addition, a new threat had emerged from the west. In 1919 Joseph Medill Potter, the grandson of *Chicago Tribune* founder Joseph Medill, had begun publishing *The New York Daily News.* The slick tabloid had grown rapidly in its first years.[20]

Swope had a purpose in his new role. He once said, "What I try to do in my paper is to give the public part of what it wants to have and part of what it ought to have, whether it wants it or not."[21] One thing Swope gave his readers was the Op-Ed page. Now a staple in American newspapers, it was Swope who created it. He explained his thinking behind the idea: "Nothing is more interesting than opinion when opinion is interesting, so I devised a method of cleaning off the page opposite the editorial, which became the most important in America."[22]

The *World* became a newspaper that showcased some of the finest writers in America. During Swope's tenure at the *World*, the list of contributors included Heywood Broun, Ring Lardner, H. L. Mencken, Dorothy Parker, Will Rogers, H. G. Wells, E. B. White, and Alexander Wollcott among others.[23]

When Henry Peck Fry came to New York City with his tale of the inner workings of the Ku Klux Klan, he came to see Herbert Bayard Swope.

But why New York, and why the *New York World*? There were large newspapers in the South, but perhaps they would be hesitant to publish an exposé against the Klan. The North was a better alternative, with a more liberal journalistic tradition. In the days prior to the Civil War many Northern newspapers took up the abolitionist cause. The *World* had a solid reputation, but there were other powerful, crusading papers in New York as well as in Boston, Philadelphia, and Chicago. Still, Fry arrived, Klan documents in hand, at Swope's doorstep.

Fry's place in history has always been presented as that of a man who chose the moral high ground—as an insider so outraged by what he knew of the Klan that he felt compelled to expose its evils to the world.

He is portrayed uniformly as an honorable man.

He was, admittedly, a white supremacist and a joiner of fraternal organizations. We know from his 1906 manifesto, *The Voice of the Third Generation*, that his belief systems seemed to line up with those of the original Klan and with what he knew of Simmons's modern version.

In Fry's 1921 book, *The Modern Ku Klux Klan*, he detailed his growing moral outrage with the Klan he had come to know from the inside. The Klan, in Fry's opinion, was different from fraternal organizations he was familiar with. It was sinister and dangerous, fueled by greed and potentially threatening to the fabric of American democracy and law. He was moved to action. Henry Peck Fry was, indeed, a classic example of a whistleblower.

New information, however, suggests another possible path to Swope's door at the *World*.

On April 1, 1941, the Virginia Military Institute Archives received a document entitled "Personal Data—Lieutenant Colonel Henry Peck Fry." Fry, at age sixty-one, had submitted to his alma mater a four-page, single-spaced, typewritten account of his life.

It turns out that Henry's journalistic endeavors did not end after his 1903 acceptance into the Tennessee Bar and the esteemed firm of Frazier and Coleman. After his one year at the *Chattanooga News*, he continued to write for the *Chattanooga Times* between 1903 and 1907.

Fry apparently left Tennessee in 1907 and moved to the New York metropolitan area. In that year he became a member of the New York Bar Association, and in 1915 he joined the New Jersey Bar. His biography mentions he practiced in both states.

The story gains a level of intrigue during this time period. Ever the multitasker, Fry continued newspaper work as a freelance writer between 1907 and 1915. He contributed to the *New York Morning Sun*, the *New York American*, the *New York Globe*, the *Philadelphia Public Ledger*, the *Philadelphia Record*, and the *Philadelphia North American*.

Henry Peck Fry also claimed that between 1907 and 1915 he wrote for Joseph Pulitzer's *New York World*. It is not known if Fry and Swope were acquainted. There was overlap in their careers, however, as Swope's tenure at the paper began in 1909.

The final stunning bit of information on Henry Peck Fry comes from another document at VMI.

Fry died at the age of seventy-five on Wednesday, February 8, 1956, at his home in Alexandria, Virginia, after a long illness.[24] He had lived in the Washington, D.C., suburb for ten years. Three days later, on Saturday the 11th, the *Alexandria Gazette* published his obituary.

It was a short article. Paragraph one announced funeral services. The second paragraph identified him as a writer, a former newspaperman, a WWI veteran, a graduate of VMI, and a classmate of General George C. Marshall. The next paragraph broke new ground on the life of Henry Fry.

> *During the 1920s Col. Fry gained fame as a newspaper reporter who wrote a blistering exposé of the Ku Klux Klan. Then a member of the New York World staff, he joined the secret organization by concealing his identity as a reporter.*[25]

It is not known how the *Gazette* learned this information. Fry had never married. It is possible this was a case of a dying man embellishing his legacy at the end of his life. It is a very different account, indeed, than the one he had written in 1922. These new facts call into question Fry's motives for his actions in the early months of 1921.

It certainly is possible that Fry joined the Invisible Empire with the purest of intentions. And, certainly, other men left the organization when it did not meet their needs or expectations. Most of those men did not feel compelled to expose the Klan's deception to the world, and very few were experienced newsmen. Fry's background suggests he was highly principled and capable of taking action. As an attorney and a journalist he was aware he would need evidence to support his story. And, he would need a platform to broadcast his message to the greatest number of people. He was familiar with the *World* and Joseph Pulitzer's philosophy of exposing corruption and protecting the rights of the common man—a philosophy that had survived his death under men like Herbert Bayard Swope. This would seem to be a plausible explanation and would remain aligned with Fry's rationale in his 1922 book.

However, the *Alexandria Gazette* obituary may have been correct. Swope was a creative journalist capable of pushing the envelope on a story. Instead of being the recipient of the story, he may have instead been the creator of it.

There was precedent at his very own *New York World*. The world's most famous, and one of the first, undercover investigative journalists had been hired by Joseph Pulitzer in 1887. Her name was Nellie Bly.

Elizabeth Jane Cochran was born May 5, 1864, in Cochran's Mills, Pennsylvania, ten miles south of Pittsburgh. Her father had begun life as a mill worker, but by the time of Elizabeth's birth had purchased the mill and much of the land around it; hence the name Cochran's Mills.[26] As a teenager the young girl moved to Pittsburgh. She was a bright and strong-willed young woman. Outraged by a sexist column in the *Pittsburgh Dispatch*, Elizabeth wrote a fiery rebuttal to the editor using the pen name "Lonely Orphan Girl." The editor was so impressed with the letter that he offered the man who wrote it a job with the paper. When he learned the man was Cochran he withdrew the offer, but Elizabeth was able to persuade him differently. There were few female reporters at the time and all used pen names. The *Dispatch* editor chose "Nellie Bly" for his new hire, adopted from the title character in a popular song by Stephen Foster.[27]

Nellie was assigned to the "women's pages," covering fashion, society, and gardening—the usual assignment for a woman reporter. But she didn't stop there. Nellie produced articles on the plight of female factory workers. At twenty-one she served for six months as a foreign correspondent in Mexico. Her criticism of the dictator, Porfirio Diaz, triggered her return to the United States to avoid imprisonment.[28] When Bly was again banished to fluff assignments, she resigned in May 1887 and set out for New York.[29]

After a futile four-month job search, a penniless and desperate Bly burst into the offices of *New York World* editor-in-chief Col. John A. Cockerill armed with a fistful of story ideas and suggestions, "as desperate as they were startling to carry out." Cockerill listened to the ideas and offered no immediate response. He was probably a bit overwhelmed by the brash young woman before him, and he needed to confer with Pulitzer. He gave Nellie a $25 retainer to keep her from going to his competitors until a decision could be made.[30]

On September 22, 1887, Nellie had her answer. Her proposal to travel to Europe and return steerage class to report on the experiences of an immigrant was rejected. Instead Cockerill hired her to fake insanity and get herself committed to the Women's Lunatic Asylum on Blackwell's Island. Over the years credit for the idea was claimed by Pulitzer, Cockerill, and Nellie.[31]

Nellie checked into a boarding house for working women after having prepared for the assignment by practicing deranged expressions in front of a mirror.[32] Before long, someone there summoned the police because of her highly unusual behavior. A judge ordered the "pretty crazy girl" to be examined by several doctors. She was deemed to be demented and a hopeless case. The head of the insane ward at Bellevue Hospital pronounced her "undoubtedly insane." Nellie was committed to the asylum and found deplorable conditions: rotten food, undrinkable water, untreated waste, vermin, and an abusive medical staff. She wrote:

> *What, excepting torture, would produce insanity quicker than this treatment? Here is a class of women sent to be cured. I would like the expert physicians who are condemning me for my action, which has proven their ability, to take a perfectly sane and healthy woman, shut her up and make her sit from 6 a.m. to 8 p.m. on straight back benches, do not allow her to talk or move during those hours, give her no reading and let her know nothing of the world or its doings, give her bad food and harsh treatment, and see how long it will take to make her insane. Two months would make her a mental and physical wreck.[33]*

After ten days the *World* had Nellie removed from the asylum. Her articles, "Ten Days in a Mad-House," caused a sensation and made Bly instantly famous. Many of her recommendations for improvement of the mental health system were adopted, including increased funding and improved assessment procedures. Within months, Nellie had written two more exposés.[34] In one she pretended to be a maid in order to report on abuses by employment agencies for domestic help. In the second, she posed as an unwed mother to reveal the clandestine trafficking of newborns.[35]

Perhaps Nellie's most famous story began at 9:40 a.m. on the morning of November 14, 1889. Fifteen years earlier Jules Verne had published his wildly popular *Around the World in Eighty Days*. The account of Phileas Fogg's adventure was decidedly fictional. Nellie intended to recreate the feat and actually beat the time. Bly left from Hoboken Pier for Europe aboard the steamer *Augusta Victoria*. She traveled alone with a coat, a hat, some English gold pounds, and a simple piece of hand luggage.[36] Nellie cabled reports back from exotic locales, an eager nation breathlessly following her progress. The *World's* circulation soared. On Saturday, January 25, 1890, she alighted from an eastbound train in Jersey City, New Jersey, at 3:51 p.m. Nellie had traveled over 24,000 miles in seventy-two days, six hours, eleven minutes, and fourteen seconds. She had become an international celebrity.[37]

In 1895 Nellie retired from journalism and married a millionaire industrialist forty years her senior. After his death she ran his steel company. Business downturns saw her returning to newspaper work with the 1913 women's suffrage convention and then reporting from Europe during WWI. As Henry Peck Fry was heading to New York City in 1921, Nellie Bly was writing a regular column for the *New York Evening Journal*. She died six months later at the age of fifty-seven from the effects of pneumonia.

Bly biographer Brooke Kroeger said this about Nellie: "Nellie Bly was one of the most rousing characters of the late nineteenth and early twentieth centuries. In the 1880s she pioneered the development of "detective" or "stunt" journalism, the acknowledged forerunner of full-scale investigative reporting."[38] It was part of what historian Frank Luther Mott called Pulitzer's "New Journalism," the exploitation of scandal or shocking circumstance by a clever and talented writer who donned a disguise to get the story. He deemed it sensationalist in character and something altogether new in the field.[39]

Had Swope resurrected the "stunt" model with former *World* reporter Henry Peck Fry? The Klan was secretive and mysterious. It was also violent and growing at an incredible rate, including in the state of New York. An insider's view of the menacing Invisible Empire would certainly be a must-read for New Yorkers. Fry, a natural choice. He was a Southerner, a member of multiple fraternal organizations, and a published racist. It is possible Fry needed the money. His American Military Institute correspondence school had gone out of business, and there is no mention of his activities after leaving the Army at the conclusion of the war.

Fry's 1922 book *The Modern Ku Klux Klan* lends more to the mystery. Fry does not say for whom he was working on his assignment in Johnson City, Tennessee. He did seem to seek out the man who was the local Klan organizer, and he joined the society almost immediately. Fry threw himself at once into becoming a kleagle and learning all he could of the Klan. After only three months he resigned, taking with him all the materials and documents he could gather.

Yet, Fry's book says nothing of this type of relationship with the *New York World*. Why?

It may have had to do with Fry's unique and complicated personal identity. Everything in Fry's life revolved around honor.

Not everyone in the news business embraced stunt journalism, believing that posing as something other than a reporter was inherently unprofessional. That may have been the case with Fry. The practice also had primarily been the domain of women reporters.

As a military man, honesty and loyalty were fundamental character traits, as was his oath to defend the Constitution.

Neither would Fry want to jeopardize his standing in the fraternal world. He did not want to be known as someone who would take a solemn oath under false pretenses.

A final important consideration was Fry's standing as an attorney. Lawyers are sworn to uphold the law and adhere to ethical standards that frown on deception. Interestingly, when Fry joined the legal profession in Chattanooga in 1903, there was a law on the Tennessee books concerning the Klan. Article VI of the Annotated Code of Tennessee (1896) concerns preservation of public peace. The KuKlux Law (6668) is found on page 1,634, undoubtedly a holdover referring to the original Reconstruction-era Klan. It made it illegal to travel in disguise and to alarm the citizens of the state. The penalty for doing so was a fine and imprisonment at the discretion of the local judge.[40] A more important item to an attorney in that same code had to do with professional conduct. Entry 5781 on page 1,437 says that a lawyer could be struck from the rolls if guilty of "acts of immorality, or impropriety, as are inconsistent with the character or incompatible with the faithful discharge of the duties of his profession."[41] If considering an undercover assignment Fry would likely wrestle with issues of misrepresentation as misconduct. American Bar Association Rules of Professional Conduct address these areas. A lawyer is required to be truthful when dealing with others on a client's behalf. A case could be made for Fry being the representative of the *New York World*. The code states that it is wrong for a lawyer to engage in conduct involving dishonesty, fraud, deceit, or misrepresentation.[42]

There were a number of reasons why Henry Peck Fry would want to conceal the fact he was working for the *World*. It is possible Fry could have taken the assignment with the stipulation that his true role in the investigation be unpublished. In fact, the *World* would never admit to any affiliation or special arrangement with Fry. And, it appears Fry intended to tell his own version of the story using many of the materials he had gathered for the newspaper, securing his place in history as a man of unquestioned honor. George Orwell once said, "Autobiography is only to be trusted when it reveals something disgraceful. A man who gives a good account of himself is probably lying." Until the writing of this book, *The Modern Ku Klux Klan* has been the only source quoted on Henry Peck Fry's role in the *New York World*'s 1921 exposé of the Klan.

It appears Fry's admission to someone during his final years in Alexandria, Virginia, may very well have been the truth.

Whatever the genesis and the motive of the story, Swope now had his opportunity to expose the devil and sell a lot of papers. Because of his limited staff and funding compared to other newspapers, Swope had developed a practical philosophy on news coverage. He said he would "pick out the best story of the day and hammer the hell out of it."[43] This was one terrific story, and the *World* would use everything in its tool belt.

During July and August 1921 Swope sent out a team of reporters across the country to find reports of Klan violence. In all, some thirty writers would contribute to the story. He put one of his best men in charge.

Forty-two year old Rowland Thomas was an interesting choice. He was a hybrid—a writer who made his living both as a journalist and as a fiction writer.

Thomas was born Stanley Powers Rowland Thomas in 1879 in the small Maine town of Castine. He was the son of Lewis J. Thomas, a Congregational minister, and his wife, Annie. He apparently grew up in a family of some means, and one that valued education. Thomas attended Edward Little High School in Auburn, Maine, before moving on to Harvard University where he graduated with *summa cum laude* and Phi Beta Kappa honors in 1901. Rather than settle in to some comfortable and predictable lifestyle, young Rowland immediately set sail for the Philippines.[44] This was no youthful lark to the tropics. In 1901 the archipelago was a war zone. The "splendid little," brief war that was the Spanish-American War had spawned a bigger, nastier, longer, and more brutal conflict.

At the conclusion of the Spanish-American War, peace treaty negotiations commenced in Paris. On the table was a proposal that America pay Spain $20 million for the Spanish possessions of Puerto Rico, Guam, and the Philippines. The debate at home was intense. Should the United States follow the lead of the European powers and acquire an empire? Many leading capitalists said "yes." However, there were those who saw this course as against the principles of the Declaration of Independence and the Constitution. How could a nation that rebelled against colonialism become a colonial power? Mark Twain, for one, said "no" and was instrumental in forming the Anti-Imperialist League. He once said that if America procured itself an empire "Old Glory should have its white stripes painted black and its stars replaced with skull and crossbones."[45]

President McKinley wrestled with the question. Prior to the war he confessed he could not have come within 2,000 miles of placing the Philippines on a map. A deeply religious man, McKinley finally turned to divine help. He reported that he had knelt down in prayer. The answer came and he decided to uplift and civilize and Christianize them (the Filipino people). Of course, the Spanish had occupied the islands for 400 years and most of the native people were Catholic. The Senate ratified the treaty by a margin of only two votes. A subsequent Senate resolution promising eventual independence to the Filipino people was defeated only by the tie-breaking vote of the vice president.[46]

Later McKinley rued the decision. In referring to Admiral Dewey's victory in Manila Bay during the Spanish-American War, he said, "If old Dewey had just sailed away when he smashed the Spanish fleet, what a lot of trouble he would have saved us."[47]

The Filipinos had been fighting a war of independence against their Spanish rulers under the leadership of Emilio Aguinaldo. When the Spanish left and the Americans took their place, the Filipinos assumed the United States would grant them their freedom. When this did not happen, the war continued, but now against the United States.[48]

The Philippines War is underreported in American textbooks, lost between the Spanish-American War and World War I. It was very much like Vietnam, but sixty years earlier. More than 60,000 American troops fought for there for three years, between 1900 and 1902. Some 4,000 died. At least 20,000 Filipino rebels were killed, and civilian deaths are estimated conservatively at over 200,000.[49] It was vicious jungle warfare against an often invisible enemy. Atrocities are attributed to both sides. Twain referred to American troops as "our uniformed assassins" and the killing of Filipinos as "a long and happy picnic with nothing to do but to sit in comfort and fire the Golden Rule into those people down there and imagine letters to write home to the admiring families, and pile glory on glory."

In 1901 the preacher's son from Maine entered the fascinating and dangerous Philippines. It is very likely he was among a group of over 500 young educators (mostly men) who arrived aboard the *U.S.S. Thomas*. Called Thomasites, they were there to teach English to the Filipinos. Twenty-seven would die from jungle disease and rebel attack.

Rowland thrived in the Philippines. He is listed as an acting superintendent in the Education Department in Manila in 1902 and worked for the Supreme Court of the Philippines in 1903 at the age of twenty-four.[50]

When he returned to the United States, Thomas hoped to embark on a career as a writer. But what to write? As with many writers, Rowland wrestled with inspiration. He discussed the process in the preface to his first book of short stories, *The Little Gods*:

For the life of me, as I was sitting here this sunny late Oc-

tober morning, I could not write, a distressing condition, truly, for one who lives by writing. . . . Then all at once, it seemed, familiar voices called to me from that East we deem so old, and I was there.[51]

And from the Epilogue:

The East is for tasting of life, the West for living it.

The answer was in the Philippines. He had spent his time there well, listening, observing, and experiencing. The result was a short story "Fagan" It is the tale of an enormous, black Army infantryman in the Philippines War, a man unable to conform to military life, who deserted and met an unsettling end.

Thomas entered "Fagan," and another story, "The Valley of Sunshine and Shadow," in the 1905 *Collier's* Short Story Contest.

Collier's in 1905 was one of the most popular magazines in America. It advertised itself as a publication specializing in art, social commentary, journalism, and literature. As a progressive, "muckraking" magazine, *Colliers* had a well-earned reputation as a social reformer featuring authors such as Jack London, Ida Tarbull, and Upton Sinclair. As a literary magazine *Collier's* had few peers. With a circulation of more than a quarter million readers, the magazine was an important platform for writers both established and beginning. The annual Short Story Contest was a big deal.[52]

On page 13 of the February 11, 1905, issue, *Collier's* officially announced the winners of the competition. The first prize of $5,000 had been awarded to Rowland Thomas of Peabody, Massachusetts, for "Fagan." The twenty-five-year-old outdid some of the finest writers in the country. The money was significant, between $70,000 and $75,000 in 2014 dollars. A picture and bio accompanied the announcement. Rowland appears as a handsome young man with dark wavy hair, crisp bow tie, and a confident air. Contest Judge Walter H. Page wrote of Rowland's submission:

"Fagan" which seems to me the best, deals with fundamen-

*tal human passions. It is well and simply constructed, for
it is a straight narrative of a man's life; but it is so told
as to move naturally to a climax—an inevitable climax.
It shows, too, the self-restraint of good storytelling, only the
main facts are set down. Conventional "literary" adorn-
ment—it has none. It has directness and simplicity and
strength—nothing else.*[53]

Page's evaluation of Rowland's style was essentially correct. "Fagan" is simple and earthy. The dialogue is sparse and Thomas shows a great ear for regional dialect. His descriptions of the land and Philippine culture indicate a keen power of observation and attention to detail. These are also the traits of a good journalist. A career of another writer parallels that of Thomas. Twenty years Rowland's junior, Ernest Hemingway would follow a similar route, bridging the worlds of fiction and journalism. He, also, would look abroad for adventure and inspiration. Their styles share many similarities. *Collier's* also published Hemingway's work.

In 1909 Little, Brown and Co. of Boston published *The Little Gods,* a collection of Rowland's Philippine short stories. Rowland continued to travel. A passport application indicates he spent time in 1911 and 1912 in Egypt, India, and Java. That travel provided the stimulus for two novels. *Fatima,* a story based in Egypt, was released in 1913. The following year brought the publication of *Felicidad,* a tale with a South Sea island setting.[54]

In 1915 Rowland Thomas joined the staff of the *New York World* as a reporter. Perhaps he needed the regular paycheck that went with journalism. He grew in stature with the newspaper, and his overseas experience proved invaluable. Subsequent passport applications show travel to Japan and China in 1919 and an assignment as a correspondent to Mexico in 1920.

The summer of 1921 provided Rowland's greatest challenge. Thomas and his reporters swept through the United States looking for evidence of Klan violence. The wealth of information on the inner workings of the organization provided by Fry was invaluable.

On Tuesday, September 6, 1921, coverage began. The *World* ran with the following bold front page headline:

SECRETS OF THE KU KLUX KLAN EXPOSED BY THE WORLD; MENACE OF THIS GROWING LAW-DEFYING ORGANIZATION PROVED BY ITS RITUAL AND THE RECORD OF ITS ACTIVIES

Directly below the headline were three large photos with the caption, "The Big Three of the Ku Klux Klan." The center photograph was of a stern-faced William Joseph Simmons. On his left was a smiling Bessie Tyler, resplendent in a scarf and an aviator's helmet. On the right was a steely, firm-jawed Edward Young Clarke.

Below those pictures Swope placed a facsimile of the front and back of a crudely written postcard. It was addressed to "Mr. Editor—The Evening World—Pulitzer Bldg,—New York City." On the other side an ominous message was scrawled:

> If you all print that article Tuesday about Ku Klux Klan—Watch out. You nigger lovers—you dirty Yanks—Why don't you come down, Mr. Editor, below the Mason and Dixon Line—come down to Georgia—Georgia will show you all what we think of you, Yank. You will seal your death warrant. T.N.T. for you all.

The card was unsigned and had allegedly been received the day previous.

Rowland began the series with these words:

> What is the Ku Klux Klan? How has it grown from a nucleus of thirty-four charter members to a membership of more than 500,000 within five years? How have its "domains" and "realms" and "Klans" been extended until they embrace every state in the Union but Montana, Utah, and New Hampshire? What are the possibilities of an order that preaches racial and religious hatred of the Jew and the Roman Catholic, of the Negro and the foreign born citizen? What are the possibilities of a secret orga-

nization that practices censorship of private conduct behind the midnight anonymity of mask and robe and with the weapons of whips and tar and feathers? What ought to be done about an order whose members are not initiated, but "naturalized," whose oaths bind them to obedience to an "Emperor" chosen for life? What ought to be done about an organization, with such objects when the salesmen of memberships in it work first among the officers of the courts and police departments, following then with the officers on the reserve lists of the military and naval forces? At the end of months of inquiry throughout the United States and in the performance of what it sincerely believes to be a public service, The World this morning begins the publication of a series of articles in which answers to these questions will be offered, set out against the vivid background of as extraordinary a movement as is to be found in recent history.

It was the *World's* opening shot. For twenty-one consecutive days Swope ran front-page articles assailing the Klan and the Big Three. New Yorkers latched onto the story. *World* readership increased by more than 60,000. Much of America joined in on the daily revelations. Swope had organized a syndicate of eighteen newspapers who carried the series, including *The Boston Globe, The Cleveland Plain Dealer, The St. Louis Post Dispatch, The Milwaukee Journal, The Houston Chronicle, The Seattle Times, The Dallas News,* and the *New Orleans Times Picayune.* Later in the series, the Hearst-owned *Atlanta Georgian* would join the roster. On day one, Swope claimed a combined circulation of nearly two million readers nationally would learn of the inner workings of the Klan.

Rowland followed his opening shot in the September 6 installment with a general indictment of Col. Simmons's Klan. He sketched a brief history of the Klan, old and new. Thomas wrote, "Now the Negro has become a side issue with it. Today it is primarily anti-Jew, anti-Catholic, anti-alien, and it is spreading more than twice as fast through the North and West as it is growing in the South." Rowland spoke of local or sectional prejudices and hatreds, using the example of the Pacific Coast, where he stated the Klan had beckoned to "Japophobes" claiming that the yellow man was plotting to incite the black man in America to rise against whites. In the East, he wrote, the Klan preached that alien-born men and women, even those naturalized, had no place in America.

Rowland's second point on opening day centered on the enormous profits being realized by "the employment of a large number of professional salesmen." He asserted that since the inception of the Modern Klan membership "donations" and the sale of regalia had yielded at least $5 million and "probably a considerably greater sum." The Klan had become "a thriving business in the systematic sale of race hatred, religious bigotry, and 100 percent anti-Americanism."

Finally, Rowland accused the Klan of focusing efforts to enlist town and village authorities as well as judges and the members of police forces. The goal, according to Thomas, was the ability to work without fear of interference in "setting up an invisible, Klan-controlled super government throughout the country."

Rowland closed his salvo with the words of an unnamed man who knew the Klan intimately from the inside (presumably Fry):

> It would be impossible to imagine an attitude more essentially lawless. Ku Kluxism as conceived, incorporated, propagated, and practiced has become a menace to the peace and security of every section of the United States. Its evil and vicious possibilities are boundless. It is nothing more or less than a throwback to the centuries when terror, instead of law and justice, ruled and regulated the lives of men.

On page two readers saw a picture reported to be of Simmons in his dark wizard's mask and robe shaking the hand of a white-robed Klansman. In the background was a cross and an American flag.

A headline proclaimed "PUBLIC OFFICIAL FIRST SOUGHT BY THE ORGANIZERS OF THE KLAN." There was also a "Tabulation of Ku Klux Klanism, and official Action." Examples included:

> —Violation of legal rights of individuals by masked mobs wearing Ku Klux regalia ... 62

> —Tar and feather parties conducted by masked regulators using Klan regalia ...21

> —Individuals seized and beaten by masked mobs in Klan
> regalia ... 25

Near the end of Tuesday's edition of the *World*, in the Sports section, were two interesting items. Babe Ruth had hit his fifty-first home run for the Yankees, and a large, circular-shaped ad with an illustration of a hooded Klansman bore a bold message: "The Ku Klux Klan exposed. The whole Truth about it—Now appearing every morning in *The World*."[55]

It had been an auspicious start. Readership of the *World* took a marked upward turn. Reaction to the first installment was overwhelmingly positive for the *World*, and negative for the Klan.

Day Two, Wednesday, September 7, was all about Henry Peck Fry.

KU KLUX KLAN'S INVISIBLE EMPIRE OF HATE SCORED BY ARMY OFFICER WHO ABANDONS IT; DEPARTMENT OF JUSTICE TO MAKE INQUIRY

Below the headline was a facsimile of the official commission certificate of a kleagle in the Klan. It was Fry's, dated 7 April 1921. It was signed by Col. Simmons and placed Fry in the Realm of Tennessee.

The new kleagle was authorized to secure charter members, collect kontributions (the $10 fee), administer the Oath of Allegiance, and organize klans among other duties. He was not authorized to incur debts on behalf of the Klan without written permission.

There was a second major headline:

CAPT. HENRY P. FRY, SOUTHERNER, DISILLUSIONED AFTER SERVING AS KLEAGLE OF ORDER RESIGNS MEMBERSHIP IN LETTER DENOUNCING "UGLY STRUCTURE AND NEFARIOUS POTENTIALITIES" CONDEMNS OUTRAGES PERPETUATED BY USE OF WHIP, TAR AND FEATHERS

A major article followed.

By day 2, the government had already begun to react. A sidebar revealed, "Burns (chief of the Bureau of Investigation) to investigate the Klan. House and Senate inquiries promised. Attorney General Daugherty aroused by revelations in The World. Congressmen demand prompt action."

On page two another handwritten threat was reprinted, this time with a drawing of a skull and crossbones. On the same page the *World* announced it would decline to publish any advertisement of the Ku Klux Klan.

New Yorkers anxiously awaited the next installment.[56]

The Day 3, September 8 *World* declared that the Ku Klux Klan had used the New York Army and Navy Club mailing address to sell memberships. On page one there were copies of ads and letters using the club address of Box 36, 18 Gramercy Park, New York City. The *World* implied that this was using the mails for the purpose of inciting violence. There was also a copy of a certificate of a $10 donation (essentially a receipt), called a klecktoken. A smaller page-one article reported the "White House Gets Storm of Protest Against the Klan."

On page two the first anti-Klan cartoon appears. It was reprinted by permission from the previous day's *New York Call*. It showed gullible men labeled "coward" and "moron" intently listening to the sales pitch of a hooded Klansman. An article on that page informed that "MORE NOTED MEN VOICE DEMAND FOR KU KLUX KLAN SUPRESSION."

On page ten, the editorial page, Rollin Kirby got into the act. Kirby was the main political cartoonist for the *World* and a journalism legend. During the 1920s he would win Pulitzer Prizes for his editorial cartoons in 1921, 1924, and 1928. Kirby once said that "the idea is 75% of a cartoon. Given a good idea, one can get by with mediocre drawing, but good drawing never makes a good cartoon if the idea is weak."[57]

He found his good idea for his September 8 Klan cartoon. It showed an arm labeled "U.S." reaching down and grabbing the throat of a Klansman. The caption read "THROTTLE IT!"

Babe Ruth hit his fifty-second home run.[58]

On Friday, September 9, copies of the *World* hit newsstands with the following headline:

THE WORLD EXPOSES ROSTER OF KU KLUX FORCE PEDDLING KLAN MEMBERSHIPS ON FEE BASIS, DESPITE ORGANIZER'S BOAST THEY WORK IN DARK

There was a large photo of Klansmen in full regalia gathered around a flag and a cross. The caption read, "Administering the oath of the KKK on Stone Mountain, twenty miles out of Atlanta."

The main article explained the pyramid sales structure of the Klan Propagation Department in great detail. A smaller piece led with the headline "U.S. Government to Act Vigorously Against the Klan." A smaller headline read, "Post Office official inquiring into use of mails."

The blockbuster that Friday appeared on page two. Printed there was a copy of the Kleagle Pledge of Loyalty, followed by the name and addresses of hundreds of Bessie and Edward's kleagles. One example was the listing of the names of eighteen men in Illinois working out of the Klan office at 2742 North Clark Street in Chicago. This was a stunning piece of reporting. Only two months earlier, on July 2, 1921, Clarke had sent this memorandum to Simmons, "We are completely camouflaged in each of these places (domains) and it will be almost a miracle if we are located [i.e., discovered] in any city where headquarters have been established."

The cover was blown.

Babe Ruth launched number fifty-three.[59]

Day 5, Saturday, September 10, 1921:

THE WORLD EXPOSES KLAN'S OATH BOUND SECRET RITUAL AND KU KLUX TESTS OF RACIAL AND RELIGIOUS HATE; U.S. JUDGE ORDERS GRAND JURY TO INVESTIGATE MENACE

A very long article followed describing the initiation ritual in great detail. The front page also showed a copy of a questionnaire given prospective members. Of the approximately twenty questions were these, "Are you gentile or Jew?" "Were your parents born in the United States?" "Are you white or colored?"

At the bottom of the page was a small article in which famous American Federation of Labor leader Samuel Gompers called the Klan "a thing abhorrent to the right minded." In fact, with each edition of the *World* more and more articles were appearing from religious, political, and civic officials condemning the Klan.

Page two this day featured a photo of the front page of the Kloran, the sect's "holy book." Below that the *World* published a list of Klan officer names.

> Klaliff—Vice President
> Klockard—Lecturer
> Kludd—Chaplain
> Kligrapp—Secretary
> Klabee—Treasurer
> Kladd—Conductor
> Klarogo—Inner Guard
> Klexter—Outer Guard

America was being handed a primer on the inner workings of the Klan. The Invisible Empire was becoming far more visible.

Babe Ruth tied his 1920 record of fifty-four homers and said sixty is possible.[60]

The *World* crusade had created tremendous momentum. Public outrage was growing. And, a distraction was looming on the horizon.

Edward Young Clarke. (*Courtesy of Hargrett Rare Book and Manuscriptt Library/University of Georgia Libraries.*)

Elizabeth "Bessie" Tyler reading *The Searchlight*. (*Courtesy of Hargrett Rare Book and Manuscript Library/University of Georgia Libraries.*)

William Joseph Simmons at the October 1921 House Rules Committee hearings on the Klan. (Courtesy Library of Congress.)

Simmons's hand drawn advertisement coinciding with the 1915 Atlanta premiere of *The Birth of a Nation*.

Joseph Pulitzer. (*Courtesy Library of Congress.*)

Henry Peck Fry. (*Courtesy Virginia Military Institute Archives.*)

Herbert Bayard Swope (seated) in Germany 1916. Swope received the first Pulitzer Prize for reporting. (*Courtesy Library of Congress.*)

Rowland Thomas. (*From Harvard Yearbook, Class of 1901.*)

The New York World, front page, day one of their 21-day exposé on the Klan. (*New York World September 6, 1921.*)

SEPTEMBER 18, 1921.

PUBLICITY

ILLUMINATED!

HE EXPOSES KLAN

Klan cartoon by three-time Pulitzer winner Rollin Kirby. (*New York World, September 18, 1921.*)

C. Anderson Wright, *New York American* whistle blower.

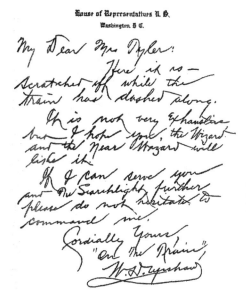

The 1921 letter to Bessie from Georgia Congressman W.D. Upshaw. (From Edgar Fuller's *The Visible of the Invisible Empire*, 1925.)

Bessie's mansion on Howell Mill Rd. in Atlanta. (*Courtesy of the Georgia Department of Natural Resources.*)

Nathan Bedford Forrest, first Imperial Wizard of the Reconstruction-era Ku Klux Klan. (*Courtesy Library of Congress.*)

Cong. Philip P. Campbell, R-Kansas, Chairman House Committee on Rules. (*Courtesy Library of Congress.*)

Hiram Wesley Evans, the KKK's Imperial Wizard following Col. Simmons. (*Courtesy Library of Congress.*)

The *World* promotes its upcoming series. (*New York World, Monday September 5, 1921.*)

CHAPTER 10
Damage Control

"It is important to preemptively strike at those who intend to do us harm."

—Matthew Levitt, anti-terrorism expert

"The only real defense is active defense—defense for the purpose of counter attacking and taking the offensive."

—Mao Tse-tung

Joshua Chamberlain was in a tight spot. He was far from his cozy academic cocoon. Bowdoin College seemed a distant and serene memory. Chamberlain was a brilliant professor of rhetoric and modern languages, fluent in Greek, Latin, Spanish, German, French, Italian, Arabic, Hebrew, and Syriac. He was loved by his students, respected by his colleagues, and held in high esteem by the administration.[1]

Now he was facing sure, nighttime death on an insignificant hilltop in Pennsylvania. It was day two of the Battle of Gettysburg and Chamberlain was at the center of the pivotal moment of the fight. Chamberlain and his 20th Maine troops had been quickly ordered to the crest of Little Round Top, a sixty-foot hill outside Gettysburg. Union generals had suddenly realized the strategic importance of this tiny bump in the land. Confederate troops were amassing to capture the hill and thus flank the Union Army. Gettysburg would be lost. History would need rewriting. The 20th Maine held the left end of the Union line. Chamberlain and his 385 men were told to hold the position at all costs.[2]

Chamberlain could have stayed out of the fight. He could have easily remained in the comfort of the classroom, but he had a strong sense of duty. His great-grandfather had fought at Yorktown in the American Revolution. His grandfather had served in the War of 1812, and his father had fought in an Indian War. Chamberlain told his employer he wanted a sabbatical to study abroad. Instead he enlisted. Because of his education, he was made an officer. Chamberlain would lead men in combat having had no military training himself.[3]

The situation on Little Round Top was desperate. Two Alabama regiments under the command of John Bell Hood mounted attack after attack. Chamberlain had sustained heavy casualties. His men were running out of ammunition. All was lost.

What would any right-thinking man do in this situation?

Chamberlain ordered a bayonet charge. His men overwhelmed the startled Confederates and saved the day for General Meade's Union Army.[4]

On Day 4 of the *World*'s investigative series Edward and Bessie ordered a bayonet charge.

Crisis management is an important part of the public relations arsenal. While you cannot predict a crisis and you cannot completely control a crisis, you can respond to a crisis in a way that regains as much control as possible for your client.

Bessie and Edward had learned early on that hiding in the shadows was the worst strategy an organization could adopt. In the beginning days of their Klan management they went public, positioning the Klan as a legitimate society. They had retooled Simmons's image to that of an upright, leading citizen living in a fine house in an upscale neighborhood. Klan headquarters acquired a public address and the press was invited in. They crafted the message and the access to it. Edward and Bessie were very good at their jobs. They administered every aspect of a money-making empire. As the stories from the *World* began to hit newsstands, a quick and well-planned response was necessary.

Years of dealing with newspapers had given Edward and Bessie significant insight into the psyche of the reporter. They knew the press needed a story. They also knew that the more facts and details they could provide, the less the reporters would rely on speculation and rumor.

The Klan needed a single spokesperson to manage and manipulate this crisis. The Klan needed a secret weapon.

Readers across America were being educated by the press about a secretive, violent, evil, male-dominated organization. Edward and Bessie needed to soften that image. They needed to deflect the stories of lynchings and tar-and-feather parties. The course they chose was fraught with risk, but also filled with potential. We don't know if Colonel Simmons agreed with the decision, but he had little voice in the matter. Edward and Bessie were clearly running the show. The official announcement would come by proclamation from the hand of the Imperial Wizard. The outside world would assume that Simmons was a strong and confident leader with a vision for the future.

Simmons's proclamation, dated September 9, 1921, and following three days of the *World*'s investigative crusade, began full of bombast:

> *To all Genii, Grand Dragons and Hydras of Realms, Grand Goblins and Kleagles of Domains, Grand Titans and Furies of Provinces, Giants, Exalted Cyclops and Terrors of Cantons, and to all citizens of the Invisible Empire, Knights of the Ku Klux Klan, in the name of our valiant dead, I affectionately greet you.*
>
> *In view of our Nation's need and as an additional force in helping on the great work of conserving, protecting and making effective the great principles of our Anglo-Saxon civilization and American ideals and institutions, the Imperial Kloncillium, in regular session assembled, after deliberate care and earnest prayer, decided that there shall be established within the bounds and under the supreme authority and government of the Invisible Empire an organization that will admit the splendid women of our great national commonwealth who are now citizens with us in directing the affairs of the Nation. Which decision of the Imperial Kloncillium I have officially ratified after serious, careful, and devoted consideration of all matters and things involved by this move.[5]*

With one bold action, the exclusive club now permitted women to be members. Bessie and Edward could not predict the fall-out of the announcement. Klan members had always pledged the protection of American womanhood, but would they embrace them on an equal basis? Women had finally secured the right to vote in 1920. Would the Klan be seen as inclusive and progressive? Or, would male members rail at the thought of allowing women into their ranks? Important for the moment was how American newspaper readers would perceive this kinder, gentler Klan. On a personal, practical level, this move could open up a major, new revenue stream of membership dues and regalia sales for the Propagation Department.

The second part of the announcement raised more than a few eyebrows:

> *I do further proclaim that in order to have the proper assistance in the formation and perfecting of this organization, I have this day September 9, 1921, selected and officially appointed Mary Elizabeth Tyler of Atlanta, Fulton County, Ga. to be my Grand Chief of Staff, to have immediate charge of work pertaining to said women's organization under my authority and direction.*

Bessie had stepped out of the shadows. She had become the first female member of the Klan and had joined Edward as one of the top officers of the society.

Simmons ended the proclamation with the full power of his office:

> *Done in the Aulic of His Majesty, Imperial Wizard, Emperor of the Invisible Empire, Knights of the Ku Klux Klan, in the Imperial City of Atlanta, Commonwealth of Georgia, United States of America, on the ninth day of the ninth month of the year of our Lord, 1921.*

> Duly signed and sealed by His Majesty
> WILLIAM JOSEPH SIMMONS,
> Imperial Wizard[6]

On the fifth day of the *World*'s Klan series, Saturday, September 10, the train from Atlanta steamed into the station in New York City. Bessie, the newly minted Grand Chief of Staff of the Ku Klux Klan, disembarked and took a suite of rooms at the swank Hotel Pennsylvania. Word of the visit was leaked to the press, and although Bessie claimed the trip was pleasure instead of business, she agreed to speak to reporters.

Clearly, this was a new experience for the hardened male members of the New York press. They were accustomed to interviewing spokesmen who would dourly read a press release and then answer questions in a careful, hesitant manner. They were not used to carrying out this interchange with a powerful woman. She had been labeled by the *World* as one of "The Big Three" of the Klan.

Bessie began by reiterating that she was not in New York on official business. She was there to shop. This was not what the press corps expected to hear from an organization in the crosshairs of a national investigation. Bessie claimed she had been "working seventy hours a week for the last three years perfecting the Klan." She was merely seeking a little rest and relaxation. This feigned indifference and nonchalance showed the Klan was not cowering from the *World* coverage.[7]

Bessie immediately had the press corps in the palm of her hand. Edgar Fuller had said of Bessie, "Her experience in catering to men's appetites and vices had given her insight into their frailties."[8] She used all her seductive and alluring powers that day at the Hotel Pennsylvania. The *New York Times* reporter clearly noticed when he wrote: "Rather tall and decidedly buxom, Mrs. Tyler is a blue-eyed, auburn-haired matron with a rosy complexion and a positive way of talking—particularly on the Klan." Later in the article the same man turned fashion reporter. "Smoothing down a few wrinkles in her black satin dress—black's her favorite color, as exemplified in black patent pumps and black beaver hat and black broadcloth cape—she asserted that one of the most prominent men in New York was the Klan's official representative here."[9] Even the reporter for the *World* got into the act, writing, "Mrs. Tyler is apparently middle aged, buxom, and of the blond type known as Titian."[10]

Edward and Bessie knew they had to change the momentum of the national Klan story. They did this by creating their own news. Present in the room was another Klan representative, Imperial attorney Paul

Ethelridge. According to Bessie, the two were unaware of each other's presence in the city and were coincidently staying in the same hotel. (It is safe to assume the two had arrived together from Atlanta.) That gave Bessie the opportunity to announce that Ethelridge was in New York "for the purpose of instituting a suit for $1,000,000 against the *World.*"

Ethelridge would say to reporters:

> *I want to say here and now that the World's position with respect to the Klan is all wrong. If you grant for a moment that there is a nationwide, law abiding, self-respecting organization embracing in its membership the highest type of citizenship in America you must necessarily admit that such an organization cannot and will not permit to go unchallenged the charges, statements, and inferences made against it by the World. The only remedy open to the organization is to bring action for libel and force the World and other newspapers to prove the truth of their assertions and insinuations.*[11]

Bessie answered more questions after Ethelridge's statement, but one final comment summed up the aura of confidence the Klan exuded. Bessie thanked the *World* for their coverage:

> *In conclusion I would like to say that the publicity given us has caused thousands of inquiries from every section of the Nation to flood our office and I now have under my personal supervision in Atlanta three secretaries constantly employed answering these inquiries. Everyone seems to want to get in, and the newspapers did us quite a favor in publishing the names of our members as well as greatly facilitating the work.*[12]

The *Times* filed the story in their Sunday, September 11, edition under the headline "Ku Klux Empress Comes Here to Shop" while the *World* countered with "Mrs. Tyler, Klan's Woman Chief of Staff, In New York." The smiling aviator cap photo from day one accompanied the article. Bessie had disarmed the New York press. She had bearded the lion in his den. She wasn't finished.

That same day the *World* published the sixth installment of the series. The headline read, "Klan's Imperial Wizard Dictates Chants of Self Adulation." Reproduced on page one was a page of the official initiation ritual. The page was filled with reaction articles damning the Klan and praising the *World*. On the editorial page Rollin Kirby weighed in with his second cartoon. In this one Uncle Sam, holding a club, was seen chasing a hooded Klansman. The caption was "Reversing It!"[13]

Bessie again appeared in the *Times* on Monday the 12th. The headline was "Woman Organizer Defends Ku Klux." As she had the day previous, Bessie talked about her reason for coming to New York, relating the details of her shopping on Saturday morning.

> *First of all, Mrs. Tyler likes New York shops although she admitted she hadn't as yet listed those maintained by Klansmen. It is a rule of the organization that Klansmen buy from Klansmen. But, somewhere Mrs. Tyler located a Klansman salesman in the chinaware department of some store. And he got her order for some china vases—"Lovely ones" as Mrs. Tyler said.*

Bessie also told the reporter that New York was a "nice town, but nowhere to rest." She was thinking of leaving the city in a day or two and looking for a quiet place. The reporter wrote: "Overwork, she said, had taxed her nerves severely and she feared a breakdown. But she wasn't too tired to defend the Ku Klux Klan."

She maintained, "The order does not foster race prejudice; but believes there is room in this country for every race. We do believe, however, that this is a white man's country as ordained by the will of God."

Bessie took exception to claims that certain Klan officials, including the Imperial Wizard, were profiting from the Klan. "I can and do truthfully state that Colonel Simmons is a poor man . . . he was receiving only $100 a week salary, and previous to that, for five years, he received practically nothing from the organization."

Finally, Bessie took on charges of the organization being anti-Jewish and anti-Catholic. "On the contrary, it (the Klan) is a Christian, Protestant organization that believes in and teaches absolute separation of church and state. . . . Any fraternal organization has the unquestioned right to select its membership, and this organization is no more anti-Catholic than the Knights of Columbus are anti-Protestant and no more anti-Jewish than the Sons of Israel are anti-Gentile."[14]

The *World*'s Day 7 headline on Monday the 12th was:

IMPERIAL WIZARD SIMMONS PARODIES CEREMONY OF CHRISTIAN BAPTISM IN HIS KU KLUX RITUAL. DEATH THREAT MADE FOR VIOLATION OF OATH[15]

On Tuesday, September 13, the *New York Times* gave Bessie a forum for the third consecutive day. The headline read, "SAYS WOMEN HERE FLOCK TO JOIN THE KLAN." A subhead continued, "First Lady of Ku Klux So Busy Answering Inquiries She Has to Employ Aid." Yet again, Bessie's social calendar led the story.

> *Just before she left the Hotel Pennsylvania last night to try to find a movie to her liking along Broadway, Mrs. Elizabeth Tyler, the "first lady" of the Ku Klux Klan, talked about how New York women were taking to the Klan.*

The article continued:

> *"The first day I arrived here," she said, "I received 300 letters from women throughout this state seeking information about the Klan. You can say quite correctly that New York women are flocking to join us."*

Bessie went on to claim that, according to the latest figures, men and women were joining the Klan "at a rate of 1,000 a day." Her last statement may have caused some unhappiness with Klansmen who hoped that the women's organization would be a separate auxiliary.

At my suggestion the women's organization will be on a par with that of the men. We plan that all women who join us shall have equal rights with the men. . . . Yes, the women's organization will have the same ritual and the same costumes. I wish that I had brought up my silk costume from Atlanta. There have been so many wild yarns circulated about the costume of the Knights of the Ku Klux Klan that I'd like to show just what the costume consists of. It isn't half as dreadful as it has been pictured."[16]

With that, Bessie left for the movies.

Ironically, on the day Bessie talked of the movies and silk costumes the *World* reprinted an inflammatory article from Bessie's *The Searchlight* newspaper. Day 8 of the series began with this headline:

KLAN PREDICTS ENEMIES OF LAW AND ORDER WILL SHRIEK WHEN KU KLUX TIGHTENS GRIP AND OPPOSITION REALIZE THEY ARE WHIPPED

Reproduced on page one was the first page of the July 2, 1921, *Searchlight*. Across the top was the paper's motto: "Not a moulder but a chronicler of public opinion." The article contained an ominous warning from an interview with Imperial Wizard Simmons. "The KKK has not yet started to work . . . . We are merely organizing at the present time . . . we are keeping records and making plans . . . The day of our activity has not yet arrived." The message was clearly a warning to the enemies of the Invisible Empire.

A front-page sidebar contained an assertion from writer and journalist H. L. Mencken that the "Klan dupes Boobs."[17]

Bessie returned to Atlanta after her whirlwind stay in the Big Apple, satisfied that she had done well. She and Edward immediately converted *The Searchlight* from a weekly into a daily for the remainder of the *World* coverage to galvanize the Klan faithful.[18]

Day 10, Thursday, September 15, presented a shocking headline to readers:

KU KLUX KLAN AS VIRULENT AS THE A.P.A. AGENTS USE PROPAGANDA CHARGING CATHOLICS ASSASSINATED LINCOLN, GARFIELD, AND MCKINLEY

The A.P.A. referred to the American Protective Association, the anti-Catholic, anti-immigrant organization that had thrived in the years at the end of the nineteenth century.

The front-page illustration was a reproduction of a flyer used by kleagles. It was titled "Do You Know?" Among the fifteen anti-Catholic accusations were these:

—*"The Pope is a political autocrat."*
—*"A secret treaty made by him started the War."*
—*"He controls the daily and magazine press."*
—*"Our war industries were placed exclusively in Roman Catholic hands."*
—*"Roman Catholics compose one sixth of our population and hold three fourths of public offices, being entrenched in national, state and city governments throughout the country."*
—*"The Knights of Columbus declare they will make Popery dominant in the United States."*

The federal government appeared again this day with an article headlined: "BURNS [director of the Bureau of Investigation] FINDINGS ON KLAN AWAITIED BY CONGRESSMEN. PLAN HEARINGS AND NEW LEGISLATION IF PRESENT LAWS DO NOT COVER OFFENSES CHARGED."[19]

Thursday the 15th was also memorable for the entry of a new competitor for the hearts and minds of New York readers. The Hearst-owned *New York American* had felt the sting of the *World*'s crusade. Most estimates peg the increased daily readership gain for the Pulitzer paper at between 65,000 and 100,000. The *American* was apparently caught off guard. They had not done the investigative months of spadework nor had they applied the manpower Rowland had had at his disposal. They needed their own Klan insider, and they needed to find him fast. On the fifteenth, nine days into Swope's series, the *American* ran the following headline on the front page of their late edition:

EX GRAND GOBLIN BARES SECRETS OF KU KLUX

Beneath the headline was the photo of a young, serious-looking man in an army uniform. The photo announced, "He Exposes Klan." The copy that followed said, "This is C. Anderson Wright, American aviator and a Grand Goblin of the Ku Klux Klan until 48 hours ago. He received a death threat which the Ku Klux Klan denies sending him. He has just resigned and beginning today tells exclusively through the *New York American* the real inside story of the Ku Klux Klan. His story is not hearsay. He sat in the Imperial Council and tells the astounding stories of the conferences he actually participated in."[20]

Unlike Henry Peck Fry, Wright was hired as a columnist and did his own writing. During the remainder of September Wright would pen seventeen articles, many of which were highly sensational and journalistically questionable.

Wright began on that Thursday with an entry about the Invisible Empire's plan to drive Jews out of New York. From Day One he labeled the efforts of Clarke and Tyler as a "mere money making scheme."

The *American* published on page two a copy of Wright's letter of resignation to Simmons written only two days prior. He made three points in that letter, labeled A, B, and C.

He said, "First and of most importance by and with Imperial authority, every oath of a Klansman was broken by yourself [Simmons] and staff which, without question of doubt, relieved me of any binding oath upon the order."

The second item had to do with Wright's role in the order. Wright was an aviator in World War I. He claimed to want to organize a national organization of fliers, hoping to attach the group to the Klan. He came with the names and addresses of aviators through his defunct magazine, *Tail Spin*. In item two Wright accused the Klan of taking that data to further general Klan membership, and not the "Knights of the Air." Finally, Wright claimed the Klan was in default regarding payments promised him.

The "C" item in the letter is of particular interest. For Wright this was a moral issue, claiming continuous drinking by staff. "I intend to expose the real internal conditions of the Imperial Empire which have only reached the selected few, even though my life has been threatened as a penalty for doing this. I do not intend longer to let decent men and women be dragged into the mire of your corrupt and disreputable so-called Imperial blessed few." Wright made the claim that, "Georgia corn whiskey was kept in quantities in the Imperial safe and under the Imperial bed of the Imperial Wizard."

The *American* concluded with a reprint of a Klan article from the previous day's *Chicago Herald Examiner*. The newspaper would continue the following day with an Anderson essay, and would for the remainder of the month. Each day's headlines were often shared with details of the sensational Fatty Arbuckle case.[21]

Friday, September 16, day 11, *The World*:

THE WORLD BARES KLUX PROPAGANDA BRANDING JEWS, NEGROES, AND FOREIGN-BORN AS DISLOYAL; CONGRESSMEN DEMAND FAR REACHING INQUIRY

There was also on page one a *Searchlight* cover claiming a "Clean Bill of Health Given the Klan," as well as a photo of a Klan parade in Houston.

On page two the *World* published a "Statement from Mrs. Tyler." Before she left for Atlanta on the 14th, Bessie penned a letter that the newspaper published in full. It was a long statement, dominating the page. It included many of the facts that had appeared in the *Times*. Bessie's New York trip had garnered considerable press coverage. As a public relations campaign, it was a smashing success.

Babe Ruth hit number fifty-five, setting a new home run record.[22]

The *American* ran Wright's claims of hearty growth in the New York Klan. In the previous year membership had surged from 250 to 15,000, reaping tremendous monetary rewards for Bessie, Edward, and the Klan treasury. There was an excerpt from a Klan newsletter announcing that the police chief of Norfolk, Virginia, was a Klan member. There was also a striking picture of Simmons in full regalia presiding over the initiation of new members in Chicago.[23]

On Day 12, Saturday, September 17, the *World* published two photos demonstrating the KKK secret handshake. On page two readers found the entire Klan oath, which included sections on "Obedience," "Secrecy," "Fidelity," and "Ishness."

Ruth added number fifty-six.[24]

The *American* countered with a blockbuster headline announcing that the Klan had brought in a single year total of $26,650,000! Wright certainly did not have access to Klan or Southern Publicity Association books, but the claim made a great headline. In 2014 dollars adjusted for inflation, that number would be in excess of a quarter of a billion dollars. Wright based his information on a national membership for the Klan of 700,000 and supposedly included the sale of regalia.[25]

On Sunday the 18th, the *World* described violent Klan acts in Beaumont, Texas, and featured another Kirby cartoon. This one showed a Klansman cowering in a spotlight. The light was labeled "Publicity." The caption was "Illuminated!"[26]

Wright and the *American* claimed plots to wreck the Knights of Columbus and the Sons of Israel. There was a picture of a fully robed Simmons kissing an American flag. There were more alleged death threats aimed at Wright, that his "head was in a noose."[27]

Even with the daily barrage of bad press, the Klan seemed to be surviving. Membership applications were, indeed, up because of the nationwide publicity. However, Day 14, September 19, 1921, could mark the beginning of the end for E. Y. Clarke and Elizabeth Tyler.

The headline was a continuation of the tone set previously, with one notable exception:

KU KLUX'S RECORD OF ATROCITIES GROWS. RECENT BEATING AND TARRING OF MEN AND WOMEN

Then came the blockbuster.

E. Y. CLARKE AND MRS. TYLER ONCE ARRESTED

The main article covered the particulars of 152 reported violent acts attributed to the Klan, including killings, floggings, tar-and-feather parties, branding with acid, and irreparable mutilations. The content was strong and damning, but it took a back seat position to a smaller headline at the bottom of page one. Rowland Thomas's investigators had unearthed the seamy details of Bessie and Edward's 1919 arrest. That headline announced:

CLARKE AND MRS. TYLER ARRESTED WHILE IN HOUSE OF ILL REPUTE

Judge in 1919 Fined Ku Klux Leaders Police Testified They Found in Resort Woman Conducted
Copyright 1921 by the Press Publishing Co. (The New York World)
ATLANTA September 19—The World's exposure of the Ku Klux took an astounding turn here yesterday when a staff correspondent obtained evidence of details which have been ongoing matters of gossip in Atlanta. This evidence shows that a few days prior to November 1, 1919, Edward Young Clarke of Atlanta who is at present, by appointment of Imperial Wizard Simmons, Imperial Kleagle or head organizer of the Ku Klux Klan, and Mrs. Elizabeth Tyler of Atlanta who recently, also by appointment and proclamation of Imperial Wizard Simmons, was made Grand Chief of the newly formed women's division of Klucksters, were arrested at midnight and in their sleeping garments in a notorious underworld resort at 185 South Pryor Street Atlanta, run by Mrs. Tyler, and taken to the City Prison.[28]

Two years earlier this had been a non-story. Bessie and Edward had spent a night in jail, brother Francis made bail for them, J. Q. took the fall for liquor possession, and they had paid their fines. Edward's wife,

May, had gone away after receiving a new house and a monthly payment. The incident had gone unreported in the Atlanta press.

On page two the *World* published copies of court dockets 17005 and 17006 dated October 31, 1919, with guilty judgments against E. Y. Clarke and Mrs. E. Tyler for disorderly conduct.

The story went into great detail. Rowland's reporter had done his homework, including interviewing the police officers involved in the arrest. He obtained the divorce papers filed by May previous to the arrest and revealed the specifics of Edward's settlement.

In 1919 this was but one of hundreds of domestic issues that passed through the Georgia court system. To a majority of Atlantans in 1919, Bessie, Edward, and May were relative unknowns. In October 1921 millions of Americans knew that Clarke and Tyler were two of the notorious "Big Three" of the Ku Klux Klan. Instead of reacting to the story, the public relations experts had become the story.

Simmons's Klan had always positioned itself as "a high class order for men of intelligence and character," one that "supported the soul of chivalry and virtue's impenetrable shield." A key point in the Klan promise was to protect "the sanctity of the home and the chastity of womanhood." Now, the organization's number two in command had been exposed. He had been arrested in his pajamas, sleeping with a woman who was not his wife; the location of the arrest—a "house of ill repute." Furthermore, Edward had not denied that he had abandoned his wife and young son for over three years.

The other woman in the triangle was no ordinary woman. Only ten days before the *World* article told of the 1919 arrest, Imperial Wizard Simmons had elevated Bessie to Grand Chief of Staff in charge of the Klan's new Women's Division. She was now stained as a home wrecker, carrying on with a married man.

The address of the tryst was another suggestive tidbit. As well as "house of ill repute," the correspondent had referred to it as a "notorious underworld resort." Most readers understood that these were euphemisms for a brothel. To make matters worse, Elizabeth Tyler was identified as the owner of the property. That alcohol had been involved worsened it still. The Klan had made a strong stand in support of Prohibition.

Edward and Bessie's initial reaction to the story in the Tuesday, September 20, *World* was to label it a lie. Bessie was quoted saying, "The attack on my personal character published in this morning's *New York World* is a malicious lie. . . . I do not believe that there was ever an American woman so persecuted and forced to make such a personal sacrifice as I am making for our cause." Edward called the *New York World,* "the biggest liar in America."[29]

A headline declared "Atlanta Police and Officialdom Seem to Aid Klan." The subhead read, "Certified copies of court records vanish from custody of Lieutenant in Department." Fortunately for the *World,* their reporter had acquired copies earlier. This account only fueled the suspicion that many high-ranking Atlanta officials were members of the Klan. Georgia Solicitor General John A. Boykin, a known Klansman, promised a "vigorous investigation."

On the 21st the *World*'s story on the arrest appeared in the *Atlanta Georgian.* Because of delivery logistics the series lagged the New York publication by two days. Edward made a desperate attempt to quash the story by sending men throughout the city to buy up copies for three cents more than the seven-cent selling price. When that failed he admitted to a *Georgian* reporter that he and Bessie had been living together in 1919 because he was "ill" and his partner had taken him in.

The two were clearly not working together at this point. Bessie made her own statement to the press, saying "Trying to injure an organization which stands primarily for the protection of womanhood by stooping so low as to attack the character of an innocent woman will not help their side. Shame on them, is all I have to say." Later, Edward stormed in the *Georgian*'s newsroom demanding a retraction, railing that he had been misquoted.[30]

The first evidence of Klan unrest over the story appeared in the *World*'s September 21 issue. On page two a headline read, "Oust Clarke and Woman, Klan Plea." In the article, New Jersey kleagle A. Donald Bate called for the dismissal of both Edward and Bessie. Upon hearing of this demand, Bessie fired Bate without consulting with either Clarke or Simmons.[31]

Looking for a vote of confidence, Bessie appeared before a closed meeting of the Klan hierarchy. She claimed the press was an enemy that would stop at nothing in their attacks on her and other Klan officials. She offered her resignation with the usual staging. As she had calculated, her offer was refused.

On Friday the 23rd this headline was published, "Clarke Out, Not I Asserts Bate." The subhead said, "Mrs. Tyler has also resigned says Kleagle active in Elizabeth, N.J." Bate protested that Bessie had no authority to dismiss him. Apparently Bate's information was true. Edward had sent Simmons a letter of resignation for him and Bessie, maintaining he was doing it to protect her from "attacks from the enemy." The letter was submitted without Bessie's knowledge and then leaked to the press.

Bessie was furious. She released her own statement calling her partner and lover "weak kneed," and attacking him for not first consulting with her. She had no intentions of leaving the Klan even if it meant working for nothing. The *World* took note of these developments:

> Atlanta, Sept. 25—Developments arising here within the last twenty-four hours give the clearest indications yet observed that "Imperial" leadership of the Ku Klux Klan has begun to wobble under the incessant fire of publicity focused on it by the outside press of the country. A slip up somewhere has resulted in a spectacular collision of conflicting statements made by Edward Young Clarke and Mrs. Elizabeth Tyler. A family "dogfight" has apparently broken up their long-established combination, and it will be difficult for Imperial Wizard Simmons himself to escape becoming involved in their quarrel.[32]

There would be yet another ill-advised reaction to the Clarke-Tyler arrest story. Bessie's *Searchlight* newspaper got into the act. A front-page editorial penned by Associate Editor Carl F. Hutcheson took a very aggressive stance. It is not known if Hutcheson acted on his own or at the behest of Bessie. It was headed, "American Patriots, Hark!" The following are excerpts from that editorial:

> *American patriots! The womanhood of this country has been criminally assaulted in the most diabolical and satanic manner known to the human race—an attempt has been made*

to ruin the character of a good woman by the most dastardly method of current times. That dastardly, cowardly, and infamous instrument of murder comprises certain daily and powerful newspapers in this country. Murder! Yes murder of the worst type! . . . Every word written in opposition to a great patriotic woman of Atlanta reeks with the blood of a grand innocent lady of southern birth and standing. . . . We issue the bugle call to all of you to buckle on your armor and defend this good lady, even with your lives. To you American patriots, we address ourselves! Unleash your dogs of war and make these hounds of convict stripe pay penalty for the great injury done. . . . If there must be war with the Roman Catholics, the Knights of Columbus, and the hireling newspapers, editors and reporters—let it come! We are ready![33]

Federal postal inspectors took note of the message and threatened action. *The Searchlight* was distributed using the mail. Section 480 of the postal regulations outlined penalties for inciting murder, arson, or assassination through the mail.

Action was required from Simmons. First he refused the resignations of his principal organizers, acknowledging he had heard rumors of the story, but attached no credence to it. The Imperial Wizard also barred Mrs. Tyler from making any further statements and publicly renounced *The Searchlight* editorial. Hutcheson wrote a retraction.

A week later Bessie sold her interest in *The Searchlight* for $1,000.[34]

The quarrel had played out on the front pages of newspapers throughout America. According to public relations professor and author Scott Cutlip, "In this comedy of errors, publicists Clarke and Tyler violated the public relations fundamental that one does nothing to keep a bad story alive."[35]

All during this story the *World* had continued its relentless front-page crusade. There was an article on how the Klan enrolled public officials, controlled grand juries, and organized and drilled Riflemen. There were continuing stories about Attorney General Daugherty and his inquiry into the Klan. On Day 19 the paper talked about plans to build a

$1,500,000 palace and a $3,500,000 regalia factory.[36]

On Monday, September 29, 1921, the *World* ended twenty-one consecutive days of front-page Klan coverage with the headline:

KU KLUX INIQUITIES FULLY PROVED, THE WORLD CONCLUDES ARTICLES

Below the main headline that last day were:

> Pretentious Absurdity, Cruel Intolerance, Ugly Terrorism and Cynical Eagerness for Money and Power, Inseparably Interwoven in Sinister Movement, Bared to the Astounded Public, Which Has Commended Exposure.

DOCUMENTARY EVIDENCE BACKED UP ALL ALLEGATIONS THAT WERE PRINTED

> This Service Rendered by the World Has Been Free of Malice, but Has Not Glossed Over Any Facts Discovered, However Damaging to Individuals or Groups—Storm of Indignation Sweeps the Country and Arouses the Government.

A humorous cartoon from the pen of Al Frueh helped cap off the series. Frueh was a regular contributor to the *World* and would later be the first cartoonist published in the *New Yorker*. His cartoon consisted of five panels showing Klansmen in various situations—playing baseball, eating at a restaurant, and so on. All of their dialogue begins with "K" or "KL." Frueh titled it, "The Koo Klanguage of the invisible Klempire."

On the editorial page Rollin Kirby contributed his final cartoon—a large, hooded, armed, angry group of Klansmen hold a sign aloft saying, "If there must be war . . . . Let it come, We are ready." Kirby's caption was "A CHALLENGE TO LAW."[37]

The next day Babe Ruth hit home runs fifty-seven and fifty-eight.

The *New York American* continued to run daily Klan articles from the pen of C. Anderson Wright.

On September the 19th, the same day the *World* broke the 1919 Bessie–Edward arrest story, the *American* and Wright declared that Edward aimed to become the world's richest man. According to Wright, Clarke uttered that statement and promised to make Wright a wealthy man if he stayed with him. On the same day Wright added another $3,500,000 to his audacious tally of Klan revenues informing that it came from selling "holy water" from the Chattahoochee River at $10 a quart (this would represent nearly 90,000 gallons!).[38]

On Tuesday the 20th the *American*'s headline stated that the Klan intended to make $7,000,000 from Anderson's Knights of the Air. On page two was the story of the 1919 arrest. It is likely this story was written from the previous day's *World* article.[39]

The *American* articles each day honed in on spectacular dollar amounts. On the 21st the headline proclaimed the Klan would get $50,000,000 in U.S. planes and airstrips for its Knights of the Air. On the 23rd Wright reported that Bessie's take with the Klan amounted to $5,000,000 a year derived from membership donations, robe and helmet sales, "canned spirits" (holy water), and *Searchlight* subscriptions. On Monday the 25th Wright announced yet another revenue stream, adding another $1,000,000: the sale of lodge furniture to local klans. On the 28th the *American* reported the existence of an enormous Klan printing plant near Stone Mountain. September the 29th told of a new degree in the order, the Knights of Mirth, which would bring in another $5,000,000 to the Klan's treasury. The last day of the month, Friday, September 30, reported yet another $2,250,000 from the new Women's Division of the Invisible Empire.[40]

Wright's information had now brought Bessie and Edward's yearly take to $14.5 million, or $7,250,000 each! There obviously was little journalism involved in the Wright columns, and the *American* could not have done much fact checking. Holy water and lodge furniture sales were wildly inflated. The Knights of the Air had never taken flight; they hadn't signed up even one member. Bessie's Women's Division was still in the planning stages. Nearly everything was speculative, creative math.

Wright had been a Klan member for only a few months in 1921. He did spend some time in Atlanta in the Imperial Palace and did associate to some extent with Edward and Bessie. However, it is doubtful that the two publicists would have confided in Wright the insider information he claimed to be privy to. He did seem to focus on Bessie and her role with the organization. On the 25th the *American* had run a boast from Bessie that she *was* the Klan, calling her the "Queen of the Klan." The headline that day stated "Even Imperial Wizard of Hooded Band Bows to Rule of Mrs. Tyler."[41] Fry's material for the *World* was more objective. He had never been to Atlanta. He contributed organizational details and Klan documents.

No longer did the *World* run daily front-page headlines and articles, but it didn't let the story die. Reporters continued to dig. Sources rose to the surface. Leads were followed.

Attorney General Daugherty continued his investigation of the Klan. Postal authorities questioned the Invisible Empire's use of the mails. Congress prepared its own hearings. Public opinion called for action.

The September 27 *World* reported, "Immediately upon the announcement by the *World* that its special series of articles exposing the Ku Klux Klan had been concluded, Invisible Empire lobbyists began to work on members of Congress to prevent a Congressional investigation." A strategy was in place to demand an inquiry instead into the dealings of the Catholic Knights of Columbus.[42]

When it became apparent the momentum leading to Congressional hearings could not be stemmed, Klan strategy changed. Instead of fighting the investigation, the Klan openly embraced the opportunity to testify. It is always best to show that one has nothing to hide. Bessie and Edward were obviously behind the Klan action described in an October 1 *World* article.

Colonel Simmons took the offensive. In an unprecedented move, Simmons sent a telegram to every member of Congress demanding an official probe. With typical Simmons bombast, the message contained 267 words. The nighttime rate for a telegram of this length sent from Atlanta to Washington, D.C., in 1921 was $3.34. The cost of sending this message to each of the 531 members of Congress was nearly $1,750. In 2014 numbers adjusted for inflation this would be the equivalent of some $22,000. The message was obvious. The Klan wanted to clear its name and did not fear the bright lights of inquiry.[43]

Simmons got his wish. The House Committee on Rules would meet on October 11. The Colonel would represent the Klan. Edward and Bessie were not called.

Another *World* article that same day, Saturday, October 1, would shock the Klan and, especially, Edward.

An eleven-year-old story had surfaced accusing Edward of financial misdeeds during his time with the Methodist Church.

CLARKE EXPELLED FROM CHURCH, ACCUSED IN U.S. COURT IN 1910 KLEAGLE AND FINANCIAL ADVISOR OF KLAN OUSTED BY METHODISTS ELEVEN YEARS AGO ON EIGHT COUNTS

A reporter from the *Atlanta Georgian* had begun digging into Edward's past, into the days before his Chamber of Commerce work. It appears Clarke had been involved in a number of stock misrepresentation schemes between 1907 and 1910. As a member of the Atlanta's First Congregational Methodist Church, he had convinced elders to invest $151,986 in the stock of the Congregational Methodist Publishing House. Edward had sold them stock based on a statement of assets prepared by himself as treasurer and business manager of the corporation, although, according to the *World*, "he knew it was not worth the paper it was printed on."

Investors began to suspect problems. On January 24, 1910, involuntary bankruptcy hearings were instituted against the Congregational Methodist Publishing House in the Federal District Court of Atlanta. The referee in the hearing, Harry Dodd, oversaw the liquidation of corporate assets. He found only $1,783 and paid the creditors at the rate of two and a half cents per dollar invested. Edward escaped criminal charges, probably because the activity was considered of the *caveat emptor*, buyer beware, variety. Few regulations existed in the securities arena at that time.

However, Clarke had faced a trial—an ecclesiastical trial. On Wednesday, February 2, 1910, Edward was brought before the members of the

First Congregational Methodist Church. In a scene reminiscent of the Salem Witch Trials or the Spanish Inquisition, Young stood accused of lying, extortion, fraudulent and unjust dealings, improper handling of funds, false and malicious slander, inordinate ambition, insubordination, and hypocrisy and treachery. Edward was present with legal counsel and flatly denied all charges. He threatened to hold criminally liable every person who voted in the meeting or was instrumental in the publication of charges.

In the Middle Ages Edward would probably have been burned at the stake. In this case the congregation voted to expel him from the Methodist Church. The story did appear in the press, but Edward never filed civil or criminal proceedings.[44]

It is probable that Bessie and Simmons were caught off guard by this new revelation. Simmons would now undergo more incriminating questions about his Imperial Kleagle at a time when he was preparing to withstand Congressional scrutiny. As for Bessie, the wedge between her and Edward was widening.

On October 11 Bessie wrote a letter that provides significant insight into the atmosphere within the Imperial Palace during these tense days. It would be the first of many pieces of correspondence between Bessie and Edward and J. Q. Jett. The "J. Q. Jett Papers" are housed deep within the Hargrett Rare Book and Manuscript Library at the University of Georgia.

The first significant information from this initial letter is that J. Q. was no longer married to Minnie Doris, and that he was no longer in the employ of the Southern Publicity Association. It appears that sometime in 1920 J. Q. and Minnie divorced. In a later 1922 letter Bessie would refer to the marriage as merely a "childish affair." Jett had left Atlanta and returned to his boyhood home of Ellijay in northern Georgia. Yet, both Edward and Bessie maintained contact with their former employee. Edward referred to him as "Quincy" and Bessie usually called him "Son." Jett was already remarried to a woman named Leastie and they had a child. The letters continued for nearly three years.

The letter of the 11th, typewritten on Klan stationery, opened:

My Dear Quincy,

I have been trying to get an opportunity to write you for some time, but have been undergoing a Government probe and quiz ever since you were here and, believe me young man, it was some trying time. But, much to my benefaction and belief, the Government officials evidently found everything clean as a pen and the business run right and in a straight-forward businesslike manner.

I believe they will have no complaints to make along these lines.

A U.S. postal inspector had been in Atlanta examining the Klan's books.

Of course you know from the papers that a Government investigation is on in full swing in Washington as well. We are waiting until this is over to comeback at our enemies in the Press.

Bessie was happy J. Q. had escaped incrimination in the *World* series. Apparently a reporter named Charles P. Sweeney had thought he found a good source in J. Q., but according to Bessie, "went to pieces and lost his head when he found that you were in the confidence of the Klan." The letter then turned personal:

I hope your little kiddie and madam are well. I greatly appreciated the fruit. It was the finest I have ever seen. My daughter has been quite ill and confined to her bed and cannot say just when she will be out again. Thanking you for your kindness in this and many other matters, I beg to remain

Mother[45]

The House Committee on Rules began hearings that day. Bessie may have sounded confident, but the situation was desperate.

CHAPTER 11
Shock Waves

"We know no masters, we acknowledge no dictators. This is a hall for mutual consultation and discussion; not an arena for the exhibition of champions."

—Daniel Webster

"The debates of the great assembly are frequently vague and perplexed, seeming to be dragged rather than to march to the intended goal."

—Alexis De Tocqueville

"Reader, suppose you were an idiot. And, suppose you were a member of Congress. But, I repeat myself."

—Mark Twain

A number of resolutions have been introduced in the House of Representatives having for their purpose an investigation of an order known as the Knights of the Ku Klux Klan. The resolutions have the usual whereases and invite to a very wide field of discovery. The resolving clauses themselves, however, direct attention to two specific matters. First of all, has the organization used the mails in such a way as to, or for the purpose of, defrauding, in violation of Federal statutes. That question no doubt will have attention, if evidence of it is developed, from the proper authorities of the Government. Another question that is presented in there

solutions is that of overt acts alleged to have been committed
by men wearing masks, which overt acts would probably
not be committed by men who did not wear such masks. If
overt acts have been committed amounting to assault, dis-
turbances of the peace of citizens and of communities, these
are matters cognizable by State authorities and should have
the attention of such authorities. The invitation to go into a
wide field of discovery should be resisted as far as possible if
that range of discovery does not lead to a corrective, either
under the laws as they now exist or the necessity for legisla-
tion to meet such conditions as may be disclosed.[1]

With those words the Honorable Philip P. Campbell of Kansas opened the Hearings of the House Committee on Rules at 10:30 a.m. on Tuesday, October 11, 1921.

This is a very powerful committee on the Hill. It is sometimes called the "arm of the leadership" or the "traffic cop of Congress." The United States Constitution states in Article 1, section 5, clause 7, that each house may determine the rules of its proceedings. The Rules Committee is in charge of determining under what rule bills come to the floor. "A rule is a simple resolution of the House to permit the immediate consideration of a legislative measure, notwithstanding the usual order of business, and to prescribe conditions for its debate and amendment."[2]

The Klan issue was a topic in the fall of 1921 that required immediate consideration. Only weeks earlier millions of Americans had waited breathlessly for each new edition of the *World*. Every politician in America had publicly decried Klan practices and had demanded swift action against the Evil Empire.

The committee had a decidedly Republican flavor. After eight years of Wilsonian Democratic governance, the 1920 election had chosen Republican Warren G. Harding to be America's next president. The Rules Committee reflected America's political bent—eight Republicans and four Democrats.

Royal C. Johnson was a Republican from South Dakota. He was a lawyer who had served as state's attorney and as attorney general of South Dakota. He was elected to the House of Representatives in 1915 and would serve there until 1932, with one notable exception. In 1918 he absented himself from the House and enlisted in the U.S. Army. There he rose swiftly from private to first lieutenant. While in France, Johnson was severely wounded by an exploding shell. He refused care and took two of his comrades to safety, earning him the Distinguished Service Cross and the Croix de Guerre with a gold star from the Republic of France.

Thomas David Schall represented Minnesota's 10th District as a Republican. He was legally blind due to an electrical shock from a cigar lighter, and was granted a full-time page to assist him in his work. After five terms in the House, Schall won election to the Senate where he served ten more years. In December 1935 he was struck and killed by a hit-and-run driver in Maryland, making him one of the few U.S. senators to die in office in a road accident.

Born in Alabama at the height of the Civil War in 1863, Edward W. Pou would relocate to North Carolina and serve that state as a Democratic representative in Congress for thirty-three years (1901–1934). When asked how to pronounce his name he said to say it as if it were spelled *pew.*

William A. Rodenberg (R–Illinois) was a school teacher turned lawyer from the Land of Lincoln who was first elected to the House in the 56th Congress (1899–1901). Over a twenty-four-year period, Rodenberg was twice defeated for re-election and twice re-elected in his ten-term political career. In 1915 he rode a train with the Liberty Bell through southern Illinois on its nationwide tour following the Panama-Pacific International Exposition in San Francisco.

Daniel Joseph Riordan (D–New York) was a New York City politician who served nineteen years in the House. He was notable for being a member of the famous Tammany Hall organization.

James Campbell Cantrill (D–Kentucky) was a University of Virginia graduate who worked his way through the Kentucky House and Senate. In 1908 Cantrill was elected president of the American Society of Equity for Kentucky, a farmer's organization. He represented Kentucky in Congress from 1909 until his death in 1923 while he was campaigning to become governor of Kentucky.

Simeon Davison Fess (R–Ohio) came from an academic background. Born on a farm near Harrod, Ohio, he graduated from Ohio Northern University in 1889, where he then taught history and law. In 1902 he lectured at the University of Chicago and then returned to Ohio to serve as president of Antioch College in Yellow Springs from 1907 through 1917. While still at Antioch, Fess was elected to Congress in 1913 where he served for five terms. In 1923, he began a two-term run as the senator from Ohio.

Porter Hinman Dale (R–Vermont) was another lawmaker who served in both the House and the Senate. Dale hailed from the bucolic-sounding town of Island Pond, Vermont. Before his political career he studied for two years with a Shakespearean scholar and actor, and served as a colonel in the state militia. Dale became a four-term member of the House of Representatives, then was twice elected a member of the Senate. He died during his second term, in 1933.

After graduating from Amherst College in 1894, Bertrand Snell (R–New York) worked as a bookkeeper and a lumberjack, eventually becoming successful in the paper mill business. In 1915 he was elected to Congress and served as a twelve-term representative until 1939. As minority leader during the '30s, Snell often fought the liberal programs of Democratic president Franklin Roosevelt.

Finis J. Garrett (D–Tennessee) was a Bethel College graduate who worked as a newspaper editor and lawyer. Between 1905 and 1929 he was a ten-term congressman (out of office from 1919–1923), including time as House minority leader. In 1927 Garrett wrote *How Andrew Jackson Applied Democratic Principles*.

Aaron S. Kreider (R–Pennsylvania) owned a shoe factory. In fact, he was once president of the United States Shoe Manufacturing Association. Kreider would serve as a representative from Pennsylvania for five terms from 1913 to 1923.

The Committee Chairman Philip Pitt Campbell (R–Kansas) was one of those people the Klan fought against—not 100% American. He was born in Cape Breton, Nova Scotia, Canada, and moved with his parents to Neosho County, Kansas, at age five. A lawyer, he was elected to Congress in 1903 and would serve ten terms until 1923.[3]

The first order of business had to do with resolutions presented to the committee. There were three. Peter Tague, representative from Massachusetts, was the first to make a statement. After a long dissertation, Tague called for the formation of a Special Committee of Congress to fully investigate the Klan (H. Res. 188), saying "If one third of all that has been said of this organization (the Klan) is true . . . there should be an investigation and the law should be made so strong . . . to inflict punishment of the law upon any man or men who would go around in the dark like cowards." Tague also asked that Congress pass an act giving the attorney general the power to investigate every organization in the country.

>CONG. POU: The courts have that authority anyway, have they not, Mr. Tague?

>CONG. TAGUE: Well, it is very evident that the courts have not used that authority where these gentlemen have been working.

The second speaker, Rep. Leonidas C. Dyer of Missouri, presented H. Res 192, which called for investigation to be done by the Committee on the Judiciary.

>CONG. DYER: Of course all of you gentlemen, who are really great Congressmen, know there is only one committee in the House that is competent to investigate a great matter such as this, and that is the Judiciary Committee.

>CONG. RODENBERG: You are a member of that committee?

>DYER: Yes.

The third and final resolution (H. Res. 191) was presented by Representative Thomas J. Ryan of New York. His concern was information received from the Internal Revenue Department "that would show certain violations of the law by the Ku Klux Klan that would deserve and merit the attention of Congress."

With the procedural formalities out of the way, Chairman Campbell turned to the first witness.

CONG. CAMPBELL: Mr. Thomas, do you desire to make a statement or submit to questions?

MR. THOMAS: Whichever way the committee thinks will best bring out points it wishes to reach.

CAMPBELL: I suggest you make a statement in your own way of what you know about the matter to which attention is directed by these resolutions. . . . State your name, whom you represent, and what your activities have been in connection with this matter.

THOMAS: My name is Rowland Thomas. I am a member of the editorial staff of the *New York World*. At the beginning of July I was assigned to the duty of investigating the Ku Klux Klan. That investigation occupied the months of July, August, and September. It was made as thoroughly as a newspaper investigation, without the right of subpoena or any other access to papers, can be made.

Rowland went on to summarize the findings of his investigative series. He talked of having staff in Atlanta and local representatives in thirty or more American cities.

MR. THOMAS: We attempted always, without bias, to get an accurate statement of the facts as known . . . . Perhaps the outstanding fact in our investigation is that during the last year a great number of acts of violence against individuals have been reported in the press throughout the United States.

Thomas said that the acts could be characterized in two ways. The Klan punished individuals either for objectionable moral conduct or for violation of statute law. The Klan was acting as a Protestant moral police force, and that "these punishments were administered in the hours of darkness by men whose identity was completely concealed by masks and whose responsibility for the acts therefore could not easily be established."

Thomas stated that the press had reported these incidents as Klan activities and that the public opinion in the communities assumed the violence was at the hand of the Klan. He went on to use the example of Beaumont, Texas, where the local klan took credit for a whipping and tar-and-feathering by publishing in the local newspaper a 4,000-word document bearing the seal of the Klan.

Rowland then told of anti-Catholic initiatives used by local kleagles, particularly in the Northeast. The target was often the Knights of Columbus. In the middle of this information, Rowland made a personal disclosure for the public record:

> *Let me state here that my mother's family has been a New England Congregationalist family ever since there was a New England, and that my father's people are Welsh dissenters even from the established Church of England for some 600 years. So that any sympathy I might have for the Church of Rome is only the sympathy of fair play in this particular case.*

Ever the journalist, Rowland wanted the world to know his work was impartial and free of prejudice.

The problem with Catholics for the Klan, according to Rowland, was that they were not "100 percent Americans." A potential Klan candidate had to be "native born, white, a gentile, and owe no allegiance of any sort to any foreign body, organization, potentate, or ruler." The reference, of course, was Catholic reverence and obedience to the pope in Rome.

Rowland recounted the case of Miss Julia Riordan, an Atlanta public school teacher, who was discharged from her position because she was Catholic. The man on the school board who pushed for the firing was an associate editor of *The Searchlight*, "which is by rumor owned largely by Mrs. Elizabeth Tyler, who manages the business affairs of the Ku Klux Klan."

CONG. RODENBERG: Is that the official organ of the Ku Klux Klan?

MR. THOMAS: They have never admitted that it was the official organ. I have to come constantly to the process of calling attention to the significance of certain things that have happened . . . About the middle of September—let me see; I can give you the date—on the eighteenth of September, which was a Monday morning, the *World* had reason to publish an article calling attention to a criminal record which existed in the cases of Edward Young Clarke and Mrs. Elizabeth Tyler—

CONG. CAMPBELL: (interposing) I suggest that matter might be omitted.

Chairman Campbell clearly did not want to get into the salacious details of Edward and Bessie's boozy, partially clad, bawdy house arrest. Rowland was able to make his point by avoiding the lurid facts. That point was that after the *World* article was published, *The Searchlight* evolved from a weekly to a daily with the express purpose of defending the Klan and Bessie. *The Searchlight* may not have been official, but it was certainly semi-official.

Rowland followed with testimony that placed Klan membership at between 650,000 and 700,000, generating nearly $7 million in "donations." He also outlined other revenue streams—robe and hood regalia, lodge furniture, and so on, which accumulated another $3 million to $4 million.

MR. THOMAS: It was obvious that *The Searchlight* was bringing a considerable income, and there were other sources of income which other people can point out more accurately than I can. So that all together they had had access to a very large amount of money, this income being the fruit of the spread of that spirit of violence and that propaganda of group dislike, suspicion, and hatred.

Thomas then stated that the Klan intended to establish an invisible empire with "a chief man who had taken the title of emperor," and that "every man who joined this order pledged himself to obey without question all the instructions of the emperor, who had been elected for life." It can be assumed the irony of this information was not lost on the committee. Catholics were un-American for their devotion to the pope. Were Klansmen equally un-American for their obedience to the Imperial Wizard?

Then came a revelation that certainly piqued the interest of the panel:

> **MR. THOMAS: Emperor Simmons more than once made statements that members of the Congress of the United States—both representatives and senators—belonged to his invisible empire, and therefore were under his imperial orders. He boasted that governors, mayors, and other administrative officers, members of city councils were members of this invisible government, and that sheriffs, policemen, police chiefs were members, and that judges on the bench were members of it.**

Rowland ended with, "This, in brief, is my statement of the basic findings of our investigation."

Under direct examination, Thomas then answered a number of questions.

Chairman Campbell inquired into specific acts of violence to citizens. Rowland recounted the tale of J. C. Thomas of Atlanta, a hot dog vendor who was abducted by three men in March of 1921. Mr. Thomas had been receiving threatening notes regarding his alleged improper moral behavior with a woman and his selling of food to Negroes. The men took him at night to an abandoned park with the intent of administering a flogging. Thomas, instead, produced a knife, killing one man and slashing the others. He was subsequently acquitted of manslaughter charges in the name of self-defense. The two surviving attackers, a Mr. Pitts and a Mr. Shite, were charged with abduction. They were defended in court by W. S. Coburn, a supreme attorney of the Klan. Their charges were dropped.

Congressman Fess asked if the threats came through the mail. Rowland said he had no information on that matter.

Congressman Kreider inquired about the duties of a grand goblin. Thomas outlined the organization of Edward and Bessie's Propagation Department, saying it covered from "Connecticut to Portland, Oregon" and from "Chicago to the extreme South." He knew of activity in the Dakotas, Arizona, and California.

> CONG. FESS: Is there any organization in the District of Columbia?

> MR. THOMAS: There is, yes, Dr. Fess.

Finally,

> CHAIRMAN CAMBELL: I think that is all, Mr. Thomas.

The next witness called was C. Anderson Wright, the *New York American* Klan contributor and former head of the Knights of the Air.

> CHAIRMAN CAMPBELL: State your name for the stenographer.

> MR. WRIGHT: C. Anderson Wright.

> CAMPBELL: State where you reside.

> WRIGHT: New York City. I was formerly a member of the New York Klan, King Kleagle, assigned as chief of staff of the Invisible Planet, Knights of the Air.

Wright clearly had an agenda in mind as he began his statement:

> MR. WRIGHT: I wish to say, gentlemen, that the investigation should be made on account of race and religious hatred above all, and especially that the real power behind the Klan is a woman, Mrs. Elizabeth Tyler, co-partner of Edward Young Clarke, owners of the Southern Publicity Association; that Mrs. Tyler absolutely dominates and runs the Klan through Imperial Kleagle Clarke and everything is done at her direction.

CONG. CAMPBELL: Is she over the Imperial Wizard?

WRIGHT: Not officially, no, sir, but unofficially, yes. It is an absolute fact—there is no question about it—that Mrs. Tyler and Mr. Clarke own the Klan and control the Klan in every way.

Where Rowland had been professional and factual in his testimony, Wright was accusatory and sensational. The scope of the investigation had to do with violence, depriving citizens of their civil rights, using the mails for the purpose of inciting hatred and violence, and potential tax evasion. Wright's focus on Bessie had nothing to do with facts. It was personal. He went immediately into Edward and Bessie's personal relationship.

MR. WRIGHT: Mrs. Tyler and Mr. Clarke, at the time I was in Atlanta, were living together on an estate. I visited their home many times. I can—

Campbell again took the high road.

CONG. CAMPBELL: We do not care to go into that phase of it at this time.

MR. WRIGHT: I can back all this up by documentary evidence I have published in the *New York American* and affiliated papers throughout the country in my articles. . . . I claim that they have evaded the war tax or income tax, that they call their initiation a donation to get from it . . . that they make an enormous profit on their regalia; that their *Searchlight*, the semi-official organ, which is owned by Mrs. Tyler, prints treason and goes through the mails. . . . I will be very willing to answer any questions, as I was in the Imperial Palace for quite a time and knew everything that went on there.

Under questioning from Rodenberg and Pou, Wright explained his aviation background, his joining the Klan, and his assignment as chief of staff of the proposed Knights of the Air. He went on to describe the Imperial Palace and the offices of the Southern Publicity Association. He talked of Edward and Bessie's contract with Simmons.

CONG. CAMPBELL: How long ago was this?

MR. WRIGHT: This was just a little over a year ago. At that time, as I am told by Mr. Edward Young Clarke, the Klan had about 1,000 or 2,000 members; today they boast of 700,000 members. Whether this is true I cannot say, because I did not have access to their records.

This lack of factual evidence had certainly not impeded Wright's sensational financial assertions in his *American* articles.

Wright outlined the Klan sales organization and how any eligible man was granted entry no matter their character or anything else.

CONG. RODENBERG: In other words, the man who solicited them passed on their qualifications?

MR. WRIGHT: He wanted to earn his $4, so it would not be very hard to pass him on.

CONG. POU: You think Colonel Simmons was not after the money?

WRIGHT: I think Colonel Simmons was absolutely sincere. I think he has simply been led astray. . . . and was made just a figurehead by this Mrs. Tyler.

Wright was asked about his proposed aerial department. "We felt that we should get a fraternal order together of flyers to promote commercial aviation and give the boys a chance to fly. We are all reserve officers . . . and since we have been out of the Army we have never seen an airplane. . . . We all got together and tried to do something for the flyers. Then along came the Ku Klux Klan and I looked at it very favorably; it looked like a most wonderful organization, and it looked like this man who was behind it, Colonel Simmons, as I then thought was the man to get behind the flyers and organize them into units. . . . I had no money absolutely, and the idea was to get the colonel to finance it." The theme of having no money would resurface later.

Wright said he contacted Clarke who brought him to Atlanta for discussions. Almost immediately, Wright realized he would have little contact with Simmons. Initially Wright saw Clarke as a visionary partner in his new venture. Soon he realized Edward saw the unit as yet another personal revenue stream. He saw Bessie as just plain ominous.

Clarke signed a lease for office space for the Knights of the Air in Atlanta under the name of the Southern Publicity Association. Edward installed a man named Paydon as secretary and named Wright chief assistant. His reasoning was that Wright was a northerner and, as such, people in Atlanta would not trust him. He recounted what happened when Bessie heard of the office: "all of a sudden into the office burst Mrs. Elizabeth Tyler: she looked around and said the office was fine and all that, and who was to pay for this? I said, 'Why, Mr. Clarke signed the lease and told me to furnish it; I suppose the Klan is.' She said, 'Well, Mr. Clarke did this without my authority, and I won't have it.'" This seems an early indication of tension between Edward and Bessie.

Wright told of meetings held at Bessie's home on Howell Mill Road. "Clarke had taken Mr. Paydon and I out to this place of Mrs. Tyler's, or his place; I do not know whose place it is, but it is a very elaborate place out in the country, with even a lake in it, boats and everything, and he has every animal on it from a bear to a peacock, and I was taken out there for two days."

Wright had still not been paid even $1 and his situation was becoming dire. He contended he started getting suspicious when Clarke decided only Klan members could be officers in the Knights of the Air, and that all equipment the Klan got (planes) should be in his name, and not the Klan's. "Then Mrs. Tyler said, 'The papers are attacking us too fiercely; we will have to lay off for the time being.'"

MR. WRIGHT: I was dumbfounded. She had called me in, and I said, "Mrs. Tyler, my dealings have been with Mr. Clarke and

Col. Simmons. What right have you to give directions as to what I should do?" She said, "Well, Mr. Wright, Colonel Simmons is sick and compelled to be away part of the time, and you know that Mr. Clarke has been sick at home now for several days, so therefore I am in charge and am really the Ku Klux Klan."

Wright then disclosed another item illustrating a possible rift between Edward and Bessie:

MR. WRIGHT: I will cite one instance which I think caused Mrs. Tyler to be bitter against me. Mr. Paydon and I decided we would get an apartment to live in instead of living at the hotels. So Clarke said, "Be sure to get an apartment big enough for me to have a room at." That was the start, I think, of Mrs. Tyler getting suspicious of Clarke, and then she started to call a halt on both Mr. Paydon and me.

It was not long after this that Wright resigned from the Klan. "I was absolutely broke. They had not lived up to their obligation, or I should say Clarke had not. . . . I was pretty much up against it." Congressman Rodenberg asked if the Klan had threatened him for his articles in the press on the organization. Wright said not officially, but on the previous Friday he had been fired from his position as a sales manager for his exposure of the Klan. Rodenberg then asked if Wright had received any threatening letters.

MR. WRIGHT: I have received hundreds of them. My articles have appeared in twenty-six newspapers and everyday they send me a pack of them.

After a few more questions, Wright was excused. His testimony had shed light on his motivations for writing the *American* columns. He was broke, and there was no love lost between him and Bessie.

Next came the statement of O. B. Williamson.

CONG. CAMBELL: Mr. Williamson, state your name and your

business.

MR. WILLIAMSON: O. B. Williamson. I am a post office inspector.

CAMPBELL: As a post office inspector, have you made any investigation of the order of the Knights of the Ku Klux Klan?

WILLIAMSON: Yes, sir. I have made an investigation of the order. I spent some seven days in Atlanta, and have made a preliminary investigation of the business of that concern.

Inspector Williamson began by stating that he had gone to Atlanta and interviewed Clarke, Tyler, and Colonel Simmons, and that he was freely given all he asked for. Among those requests was all the Klan's printed materials and advertising pamphlets.

MR. WILLIAMSON: I have looked over the constitution and the laws of the Klan and I do not see anything in these that would have a tendency to incite murder.

Williamson then focused his efforts on a phrase from the Imperial Proclamation that stated the Klan was formed, "not for selfish profit, but for the mutual betterment of our oath bound associates."

He questioned Clarke about the purchases of the Imperial Palace and KlanKrest (Simmons's residence), and the association with Lanier University. The Imperial Palace on Peachtree Road had been purchased in June 1921 at a cost of $35,000. The $10,000 down payment came from the Klan treasury, but the property was deeded to Edward. According to Clarke this was done to avoid adverse publicity and to keep the price low. Additionally, the area of the home was residential and business usage was not allowed. Clarke claimed to have notified Simmons of the purchase arrangement. On October 4 (the day Williamson began his investigation) Clarke, through a Klan attorney, formally transferred the deed to the Klan.

The house at 1840 Peachtree Simmons called home was next in the discussion. It was purchased for $25,500. That $10,000 down payment was made up from donations from Klan members, money from the treasury, and a small loan from Bessie and Edward. The deed was still in Edward's name. Clarke justified the purchase because Simmons had been living in "an unpretentious part of the city" and he needed a home that would reflect credit on the organization.

The deal with Lanier University was explained by Clarke in the following manner. The University had approached the Klan with an offer for the Invisible Empire to buy the college. There was a large debt assumption deemed to be too high. The Klan countered with a "donation" of $22,474.32. With that donation came Simmons's appointment as president and the naming of a new Klan-appointed board of trustees. Williamson apparently had no problem with any of these financial dealings.

A discussion ensued on the manufacture and sale of robes and the deal struck with Gate City Manufacturing and Mr. C. B. Davis in 1920.

Williamson's statement continued with an attempt to sort out the revenue streams of the Klan operation. Clarke had made the distinction that the Klan was indeed a not-for-profit. However, as a result of the contract signed between Clarke and Colonel Simmons, the Propagation Department run by Edward and Bessie was organized for profits. Williamson submitted a copy of that contract to the panel.

The next submission was a financial statement of the Propagation Department provided by Edward covering the period of time from June 1, 1920, to September 24, 1921. Income from klecktokens ($10 initiation fees) was $860,000, representing 86,000 new members. After all disbursements (commissions to kleagles, the Klan's $2, salaries, rent, telephones, postage, etc.) a total profit of $32,000 was listed. The Klan received $170,000 and Edward and Bessie were paid $15,000 in executive salaries. This was a significant discrepancy from Wright's claim of nearly $15,000,000 for the Southern Publicity Association principals.

A balance sheet of the Klan dated October 1, 1921, was submitted. It showed, in neat columns, total receipts of $308,661.43 and disbursements of $308,661.43. Attached were figures showing Klan assets of $104,932.15 and liabilities of $104,932.15—a perfectly balanced balance sheet. The numbers provided by Edward and the Klan bookkeeper showed a modestly profitable Southern Publicity Association and a perfectly not-for-profit Ku Klux Klan.

It appears O. B. Williamson, postal inspector, accepted the numbers and explanations without question.

It must be noted here that there were no records prior to June 1920. Simmons was notoriously unorganized. The record keeping materialized at the time of Bessie and Edward's contract with the Klan. In his new role as a member of the Imperial Council, Edward had hired N. N. Furney to handle the books.

Congressman Snell questioned Williamson on the 86,000-member number. Both Thomas and Wright had estimated the total to be between 500,000 and 700,000.

> CONG. SNELL: That is quite different from what was testified to here this morning.

> MR. WILLIAMSON: Yes, sir, it is.

> SNELL: These are the actual numbers that you have?

> WILLIAMSON: They are.

> CONG. RODENBERG: Mr. Williamson, during your investigation did you visit that magnificent
> estate that is supposed to be occupied by Mr. Clarke and Mrs. Tyler?

> WILLIAMSON: I did not.

> RODENBERG: Had you not heard of this estate, this magnificent palace?

> WILLIAMSON: I never did before.

> CONG. POU: You did not hear of it in your investigation while you were in Atlanta?

> WILLIAMSON: I did not.

POU: Then you believe it to be mythical?

WILLIAMSON: It must be.

Congressman Rodenberg seemed to have some doubts about the Williamson investigation.

CONG. RODENBERG: Did you make an inquiry?

MR. WILLIAMSON: I made an inquiry of people who know the local situation and got no information of such a place.

CONG. SNELL: Then you had heard about it?

WILLIAMSON: I heard the scandal hinted at by the *World*, and that was why I made such an inquiry.

RODENBERG: If such a place is in existence it would surely be a matter easily ascertained.

CONG. POU: Surely.

RODENBERG: I would rather believe your statement that it does not exist because I would not think much of your inspection if you had not found it and it existed.

WILLIAMSON: I talked to Mrs. Tyler about it, of course, I got her story that there was no such place.

Later, Royal Johnson asked about the "holy water" sales reported by Wright in the *American*.

CONG. JOHNSON: The *New York American* published an article recently to the effect that these people sold a quart of Chattahoochee River water for $10 a quart, for anointing purposes in some of their ceremonies. Did you find any record of that?

(Laughter)

MR. WILLIAMSON: I did not. I do not believe it. I did talk to Mrs. Tyler about that; she told me it was not true.

JOHNSON: She said it was not true?

WILLIAMSON: Yes, sir.

Under questioning Williamson admitted he had spoken only once to Colonel Simmons because he was not in the office and trying to rid himself of a severe cold. All of his exposure was with Edward and Bessie, and they were in complete control of operations.

CONG. CAMPBELL: Then, in your investigation, did you discover whether Colonel Simmons knew very much about what was going on in the local klan, or in the imperial Klan at Atlanta?

MR. WILLIAMSON: Well, if I am permitted to venture an opinion, I should say that he did not know a great deal about the business operations of the Klan.

Finis Garrett weighed in with a question.

CONG. GARRETT: Mr. Williamson, what was the attitude of this man Clarke and this lady about exposing their records to your investigation?

MR. WILLIAMSON: They made no objection, but gave me everything I called for.

Some members of the panel seemed skeptical as to the depth of Williamson's work. He had not gone beyond the data presented to him—data given him by Edward and Bessie. The two publicists knew that if they feigned compliance and transparency, and did it with a smile on their faces, a lower-level inspector like O. B. Williamson would accept their books as honest and accurate.

The next witness was William J. Burns.

CONG. CAMPBELL: Mr. Burns, will you state your full name to the stenographer?

MR. BURNS: William J. Burns.

CAMPBELL: You are connected with the Department of Justice?

BURNS: Director of the Bureau of Investigation.

CAMPBELL: Are you making an investigation into this (the Klan) matter?

BURNS: We are.

CAMBELL: Have you concluded your investigation?

BURNS: No.

CAMPBELL: Are you ready to make a report?

BURNS: Not yet.

CONG. GARRETT: Is it moving right along?

BURNS: Yes, sir.

Finis Garrett had left the hearings earlier in the day when C. Anderson Wright had testified. Garrett asked that Wright be recalled. After a few preliminary questions, Garrett probed the relationship between Edward and Bessie, and the Imperial Wizard.

CONG. GARRETT: Now, how long have you known Mr. Simmons?

MR. WRIGHT: I have never met Mr. Simmons, but I have been told a lot about him by Mr. Clarke when I joined the Klan in New York City.

GARRETT: I got the impression from your testimony this morning—and I want to see if I am right about it. This committee is making these inquiries, of course, with a view of determining whether it is proper to authorize a congressional investigation of this matter, and you are the only person who has been a member of the Klan who has been before the committee and presumably you know more about it than anybody else here testifying. I got the impression that the principal reason why you thought there ought to be an investigation was on account of the financial end of it, as handled by Mr. Clarke and Mrs. Tyler?

WRIGHT: Not only the financial end, but the whole thing—the moral end of it. They are teaching one thing and practicing themselves an entirely different thing; they are preaching one doctrine and living another.

GARRETT: Now, do you mean that Clarke and Mrs. Tyler are doing that, or do you mean that the organization as an organization is doing that?

WRIGHT: The only people I ever dealt with, or have received a commission from, or had any dealings with, financial or in any other way, were Mrs. Tyler and Edward Young Clarke . . . and I was a Klansman.

Garrett and Rodenberg continued to question Wright until 4:55 p.m., whereupon the committee adjourned. It had been an eventful day. They would reconvene on Wednesday at 10:30 a.m.[4]

On the evening of the first day of hearings, Tuesday, October 11, dramatic news made its way north out of Atlanta. The October 12 *New York Times* told the story:

FIRE AT MRS. TYLER, THREATEN SIMMONS

Attempt is Made to Kill Woman Official
Of Ku Klux Klan in her Home outside Atlanta
Special to the New York Times

Atlanta, Ga. Oct. 11—With most of the leaders of the Ku Klux Klan in Washington attending the Congressional Hearing on the proposal to investigate the organization, an effort was made tonight to kill Mrs. Elizabeth Tyler, assistant in the Propagation Department and recently appointed head of the Women's Department. Five shots were fired into her residence on the Howell Mill Road in the outskirts of Atlanta, but Mrs. Tyler was not hit. Mrs. Tyler earlier in the evening had been entertaining some woman friends and after their departure, she went to her bedroom and began reading. The window shade was up and a bright light was on. At 9:45 o'clock five shots were fired at the window, all the bullets burying themselves in the walls. Mrs. Tyler at once notified the county police. They responded quickly, but no traces of the assailant could be found. It is stated that bloodhounds will be used in an effort to track him. A large number of Klansmen also arrived within a few minutes and joined in the investigation. Within half an hour after the shooting there came a telephone call to the office of the Atlanta Constitution.

The night editor answered the telephone and a voice said: "I want to talk to a reporter."

"All right" was the answer.

"I just wanted to tell you that we got Mrs. Tyler tonight," came over the wire. "We'll get Simmons tomorrow."

"Who's that talking?" the newspaperman asked.

The answer was indistinct except for the words, "Good night."[5]

The next day Edward blamed the assault on gunmen from New York. According to Clarke, the information came from S. L. Savage, a former New York detective and now chief investigator of the Klan.[6]

It was almost too perfect, and most likely was. Many observers were skeptical of the facts and the timing of the event. Bessie and Edward had manipulated the press to their personal advantage before.

For one, Bessie was not the type to entertain women friends at her home. The call to the newspaper sounded like dialogue from a common dime novel. Pinning the deed on New York City was a calculated strategic move.

Appealing to gender-specific sympathies has always been an effective PR tactic. A woman had been assailed by gunfire in her home in the middle of the night! And her attackers were from New York City! The Klan's power base was Protestant rural America, and these details strengthened the Klan's position by rousing their base. The big-city East represented Catholic, immigrant, socialist evil.

Klansman and former executive secretary to Edward Young Clarke, Edgar I. Fuller claimed proof that the incident was indeed a staged hoax. In his 1925 book, *The Visible of the Invisible Empire, The Maelstrom,* Fuller asserts, "A notable instance is that of the firing upon Mrs. Tyler's mansion by the paid representative of E. Y. Clarke and Mrs. Tyler. In that case, a Greek by the name of Poulos was engaged to fire a fusillade of bullets in the home of Mrs. Tyler, that the representation might be made of an attempt to assassinate her in her home. It was a bungling job, and deceived no one. Later the pistol that was used in the firing was found in a shallow lake on Mrs. Tyler's premises, where Poulos had flung it, and was easily identified as the property of a local politician (Billy Brandt), closely identified with Clarke and Tyler."

Fuller attached a copy of a memorandum from Bessie to Klan Kashier N. N. Furney dated October 11, 1921:

> *Kindly make a check to Mr. J. O. Wood for $190.00 to cover items below:*
>
> *Paid Mr. W. H. Haemes $45.00*
> *Paid Mr. G. A. Poulos $145.00*
>
> *The above was for work in the department of investigation and has already been paid by Mr. Wood personally and a check to him for above amount would be appreciated.*[7]

Bessie and Edward were desperate to counter the news coming out of Washington, D.C.

Indeed, Bessie was very much on the minds of the committee as day two began in Washington. O. B. Williamson was recalled to the stand.

> CONG. CAMPBELL: Mr. Williamson, on yesterday you were asked about the home or the premises occupied by Mrs. Tyler. At that time you said that you did not know where she lived in Atlanta. Have you any statement now with respect to her residence?

Williamson produced a statement from Clarke saying Bessie had purchased land on Howell Mill Road eight months previous, paying $1,500 down with installments of $75 a month. Clarke had stated the home to be worth approximately $10,000 and that no Klan funds were used in the purchase.

> CONG. CAMPBELL: You never saw the home?

> MR. WILLIAMSON: No, sir, I never did.

> CAMPBELL: Did you talk to Mrs. Tyler about the home?

> WILLIAMSON: Yes. I showed Mrs. Tyler this statement and she said it was correct.

On day one, C. Anderson Wright had described a home that was quite magnificent. Anderson was recalled.

> CONG. CAMPBELL: I think you said the home in which she lived was a much more pretentious home than this is purported to be. (Referencing the Clarke statement) Is this the correct description of the house?

> MR. WRIGHT: Not by any means, sir.

He proceeded to give a detailed description of Bessie's estate. He told of a large frame house with more than ten rooms and a porch all around. It was modern in every way, with everything run by electricity or machinery. There were numerous out buildings, including servants' quarters and stables. In the back were garages for a fleet of cars. Wright could not estimate the number of acres included with the house, only that you could not see the end of it when standing on the property.

Congressman Garrett, who had been absent for a period of time the day before, then asked Wright about his deal with the *New York American*. Wright explained he had begun his series on September 15 and wrote an article a day for the next twenty days. Garrett asked about compensation and Wright admitted to receiving $2,000 with more to come. He said the final total was unresolved because the series was sold to many newspapers.

CONG. POU: Do you expect to receive as much as $5,000 all told?

MR. WRIGHT: Yes, sir.

Campbell was then prepared to call Simmons for his testimony. However, Paul Etheridge, the Klan supreme attorney, asked for a short recess because the Imperial Wizard, "is seized with a kind of nausea and thinks he would be feeling better at the afternoon session." Simmons would continually nudge his health issues into the spotlight in the days to come. Campbell was willing to resume later. Etheridge then asked the committee's indulgence to make a short statement. He was there to do a bit of damage control.

He had two points to make.

MR. ETHERIDGE: It was asserted here on yesterday by the witness, Mr. Wright, that Mrs. Tyler is in truth and in fact the official head of this organization and the power behind the throne, so to speak. Gentlemen, I have been a member of the imperial body, which is equivalent to the board of directors, of this organization for something over four years, and almost during its entire existence. I think I have attended every meeting of that body and have been called into consultation by the officials and the body itself many times . . . I wish to state that I never met Mrs. Tyler until July 4, 1921, at which time I was casually introduced to her at a Fourth of July celebration . . . . Never at any time have I ever had any consultation with her or have I known of her being called into consultation or her opinions asked for or offered regarding the workings of this organization.

Etheridge's second point had to do with Bessie's mansion. It would not do to have a mere employee of the Propagation Department living in luxury and splendor. He explained that he was the chairman of the commission of roads and revenues in Fulton County, and that as such he was very familiar with the property Bessie owned on Howell Mill Road. In fact, Etheridge knew the former owner.

"Gentlemen, that property consists of something like ten acres of as poor land as we have in Fulton County." He described a place with a modest cottage on the side of a wooded hill. The only features were a vegetable patch and a rustic foot bridge. This was hardly the estate described by Wright and seen in photos held by the National Registry of Historic Places. "I own property in more than one location in Fulton County, in the city and in the suburbs and in the country. That property, gentlemen, is not worth over $10,000."

With that, Campbell called a recess until 2:30 p.m.

The afternoon session was highly anticipated. Throughout the first day and a half of the hearings, Imperial Wizard Simmons had calmly and confidently listened to the testimony. There is a photo in the Library of Congress archives showing him leaning back in his chair, legs casually crossed, during a recess. David Mark Chalmers, in *Hooded Americanism: The First Century of the Ku Klux Klan*, gave this description based on news reports:

> *The Imperial Wizard of the Invisible Empire made a pleasing impression on the stand. His appearance was that of a politician of the old school and the Old South, a colonel of the fraternal volunteers. He moved his tall frame with*

dignity. He wore a Prince Albert coat and a stiff-necked collar, the kind where the whole of the necktie is looped with stately dignity around it. His vest was crossed by a gold chain weighted down by dangling fraternal keys. His vest pockets bulged with fountain pens and a large case for the spectacles which perched on his long, thin prominent nose. His complexion was sandy, his lips thin but firmly composed, and his red hair was beginning to recede noticeably.[8]

As Chairman Campbell began to recognize Simmons, a dramatic figure demanded to be heard. His name was William David Upshaw, a second-term representative from the state of Georgia. Known as the "Billy Sunday of Congress," he was one of the strongest proponents of the temperance movement and would in 1932 run against Franklin Roosevelt for president on the Prohibition Party ticket. Called "the driest of the drys,"[9] he took to walking on ledges to prove his sobriety and would sign letters "Yours, very dry." He had once been vice president of the Georgia Anti-Saloon League and had certainly had contact with Edward and Bessie and the Southern Publicity Association.[10] Edgar Fuller talked of the relationship in *The Visible of the Invisible Empire*: "In Georgia the Klan had a friend and champion in the person of Congressman W. D. Upshaw. Mr. Upshaw's interest in the Klan dates back to the early days of the organization. All through the movements and growth of the organization he has been closely identified with both E. Y. Clarke and Mrs. Tyler." In Fuller's book there is a copy of an undated handwritten note, on House of Representatives stationery, from Upshaw to Bessie:

My Dear Mrs. Tyler:

Here it is—scratched off while the train has dashed along.

It is not very exhaustive but I hope you, the Wizard, and the Near Wizard will like it.

If I can serve you and The Searchlight further, please do not hesitate to command me.

Cordially yours,
"On the Train"
W. D. Upshaw[11]

CONG. CAMBELL: Congressman Upshaw.

CONG. UPSHAW: Mr. Chairman, ever since I have been in Congress I have made it a rule to show every possible courtesy to my constituents when they come to Washington. . . . It is my official duty as well as my personal pleasure to present to this committee one of my prominent constituents.

CONG. RODENBERG: (Interposing) Mr. Chairman, that is not necessary. He does not need a formal introduction to the committee.

Campbell allowed Upshaw to continue. The Georgia congressman made a cryptic reference to a resolution he had penned and would address at a later date. Then he continued his introduction, "Knowing his sterling character, as I do, I am prepared to underwrite his every utterance as the truth of an honest, patriotic man." After several additional flowery statements, Upshaw concluded with: "I have the privilege, gentlemen of the committee, of presenting to you my long-time, personal friend and constituent, Col. William Joseph Simmons."

What followed would be two and a half days of grand theater. Simmons took center stage, and it would be his greatest performance. He had been a spellbinding orator in his tent meeting days in the ministry. Bessie and Edward had certainly prepared him for his appearance, but they were not in the room now.

The colonel's opening statement was calculated to arouse sympathy and to serve as an excuse for lapses in memory and preparation. It also showed his ample Southern charm and sense of humor.

COL. SIMMONS: If you will allow me just a few remarks before going into the matter, in justice to your committee, I want to state that I have been a sick man; have been confined to my bed for two weeks and left my bed to come up here. I have been out of bed only three days and in that time have undergone the hardest travel and have been in bed most of the time since I got here.

Simmons's appearance that day as described in the David Mark Chalmers book was hardly that of a man on his deathbed.

COL. SIMMONS: (cont.) I may not look sick. My sickness is not expressed in looks. I belong to the Irish race, and I believe if I was dead, I would be a handsome corpse. I have suffered with an attack of tonsillitis, combined with laryngitis, which developed into bronchitis with threatened pneumonia. So it looks like I have had all the "chitises."

Simmons launched into a personal résumé as a lawyer, Spanish-American War veteran, churchman, and member of numerous fraternal groups. Then he thanked the committee for its fairness and the press photographers for the pictures they had taken of him in the room and on the street. Then there was one more mention of his health.

COL. SIMMONS: Owing to my physical condition, I want to crave, sir, the patience of your committee in going through this statement. I will state to you frankly that at any time, under the strain of talking, I am liable to have a coughing spell that may result in a vomiting spell which has been with me now for over ten days.

Simmons would not relinquish the stand until the end of the hearings. His statement began on Wednesday afternoon and finished at the end of the Thursday session. During his testimony, Simmons would reference his illness twenty-nine times.

The colonel requested that he be able to make his statement, which had been prepared seriously and carefully, without interruption. Then he asked Campbell to swear him in so that "this statement and my entire testimony be under oath."

CONG. CAMPBELL: Neither the chairman nor any other member of this committee is authorized to administer oaths.

COL. SIMMONS: Very well; I would request it if it was within your power to do so.

CAMPBELL: It is not.

SIMMONS: Then I will proceed, Mr. Chairman, with the same consciousness of truth in making my statement as if I was under oath.

The stage belonged to Simmons and he embraced it with the zeal of his former days in the Methodist pulpit. It would be a long and winding, open-ended defense of his beloved Klan.

COL. SIMMONS: Twenty years ago I received the inspiration to establish a fraternal, patriotic secret order for the purpose of memorializing the great heroes of our national history, inculcating and teaching practical fraternity among men, to teach and encourage a fervent practical patriotism toward our country. . . . At that time I was a mere young man and knew that my youth and immature thought would not permit me to successfully launch the movement, so I kept my own counsel all through fifteen subsequent years, working, thinking and preparing my head and heart for the task of creating this institution.

Simmons recounted the October 1915 meeting during which thirty-four men signed the application for a charter. He described the betrayal by J. B. Frost and the subsequent tough times.

COL. SIMMONS: During all this time of dread and darkness I virtually stood alone, but remaining true to the dictates of unsullied honor, I steered the infant organization through dangerous channels. . . . Through the dark hours of struggle . . . for over nine months I had an average of one meal a day. I have fought a good fight. I have truly kept the faith, and God permitting me, Mr.

Chairman, I shall finish my course, with love toward all, with malice toward none. I shall pursue the right as God shall give me a vision of the right.

Simmons addressed claims of lawlessness in the Klan, "in each community where there is a Klan will be found members from the leading citizens, men who stand at the forefront in their cities. These men would not stand for lawlessness."

To the charge that the Klan was a gigantic swindle, the Imperial Wizard made it known that over a six-year period he had received only $12,000—an average of $2,000 per year.

On another matter:

> COL. SIMMONS: The charge has been made that Mr. Edward Young Clarke and Mrs. Elizabeth Tyler, who have charge of the propagation work for the Klan, have received for this work from five to twenty-five millions of dollars.

The Colonel produced a copy of the contract he signed with Clarke and a financial statement of the Propagation Department. This was the same document examined by Williamson, showing very modest numbers.

> COL. SIMMONS: The Klan contract is with Mr. Clarke, Mrs. Tyler being his first assistant and having no official connection with the Klan. . . . She is a splendid businesswoman and is employed there to look after the work of that office. During my association, and the association of other officials of the Klan, with Mr. Clarke and Mrs. Tyler their conduct and character have been of the highest.

Simmons answered claims that the Klan took the law into its own hands to terrorize citizens. "Before God and this honorable committee, I have never authorized nor signed any kind of instructions that could in any way be construed as a violation of the law. . . . No man who would break his solemn oath by taking the law into his own hands is worthy of membership in any organization or worthy to be a citizen of our glorious country."

One by one, the colonel addressed charges that the Klan incited riots . . . that the Klan assisted in the enforcement of the law . . . that it preached and taught religious intolerance . . . that they were a hideous oath bound organization of dark practices . . . that they intimidated blacks in the South.

Then Simmons turned his attention to the press.

> COL. SIMMONS: The attacks against the Klan were originated and started by the *New York World*, which is owned or controlled by a Jew, Mr. Pulitzer, whose main purpose is circulation and revenue . . . (the *World*) added 100,000 circulation and additional advertising.

On the topic of Hearst's *New York American*:

> COL. SIMMONS: Hearst's New York papers have also attacked the Klan . . . Just as Judas Iscariot betrayed Jesus Christ for thirty pieces of silver, so there was found by the Hearst papers a man, C. Anderson Wright, a former Klansman, who for money betrayed his oath. . . . When *The World* and Hearst attacked the Klan we voluntarily went to the Department of Justice and offered them all our books, records, files and every bit of information they might desire. . . . If we had been a lawless organization would we have done that? No sir. We would have tucked our great long-forked tails, folded our horns and gone to the high timber. We would never have thought of it. "He that hath light within his own clear breast may sit in the midst of night and enjoy bright day." And, Mr. Chairman, in our breasts we have that holy light that will illuminate our pathway.

As the afternoon session drew to a close, Simmons made a calculated, self-serving, and righteous offer:

> COL. SIMMONS: Standing here in the presence of God, before this committee of one of the greatest law making and deliberative

bodies in the world, and standing in the shadow of the Capitol of our great Nation, I say to you gentlemen, that if the Ku Klux Klan was guilty of a hundredth part of the charges that have been made against us, I would from this room send a telegram calling together the grand concillum for the purpose of forever disbanding the Klan in every section of the United States.

With that, the committee adjourned until 10:30 Thursday morning. Simmons had done his job well, defending the Klan against every charge, portraying the organization as innocent, noble, and unjustly persecuted.[12]

The House Committee on Rules reconvened on the morning of the third day of hearings. Simmons had not completed his statement and was allowed to continue.

COL. SIMMONS: I am here, as I stated yesterday, to present to your honorable committee facts as I honestly and conscientiously know them.

The Colonel continued to portray himself as a sympathetic martyr.

COL. SIMMONS: Sometimes, Mr. Chairman, if you please, a man who is endeavoring hard to play an honest game feels the lash and sting of unjust and unwarranted ridicule, especially when that comes from a source that he is powerless to answer back. Let that be as it may. I have drunk deep of the bitter cup of Gethsemane. In my strenuous effort to stand true to the standard of what is regarded by all men with proper perceptions the standard of unsullied honor I have been made to suffer unjustly for those things I have conscientiously endeavored to do which I knew were for the best interests of my fellows . . .

Mr. Chairman, I would not stand before you and pose as an angel, nor before the world, because I am conscious of the fact that I am not growing any wings. Sir, I have nothing back there but a pair of shoulder blades, and they are under the skin, but I can be and am sincere and honest.

The plan for the day was to enter into the record nearly every piece of printed material that pertained to the secret order. What could possibly be wrong with an organization unafraid to bare its soul to public inspection? Rather than simply submit the material, Simmons often read long passages, word for tedious word.

Exhibit A was a copy of the charter granted the Klan in 1915 from Fulton County, Georgia. A-2 was a sample of the form used to organize a local klan or subordinate lodge. Simmons began reading that entire document. When he reached a passage stating, "The Imperial Wizard has and holds the full and unchallengeable authority, right, and power to suspend or revoke this charter," Simmons interrupted himself to answer his critics.

COL. SIMMONS: It has been charged in certain newspapers that I hold an iron rod over the members of this organization and can do with them and by them as I please; that I hold imperial powers. That, like the other accusations, is also untrue.

CONG. RODENBERG: You are elected for life, are you not?

SIMMONS: Here is a peculiar feature about the Ku Klux Klan, gentlemen. It is an infant organization, and if any person on earth should have the control of the conduct and the nourishing of the baby, the mother of the baby should have that right. Are the parents imperialistic in their control of the children of their own creation?

The authority I hold in this organization may possibly be compared with the authority of a general in an army . . . He can issue his orders down the line and those orders must be obeyed, but that general cannot issue an order in violation of the regulations and rules of war.

My position in this order is a position of necessity. If I be the founder of it—I repeat the illustration, if I be the mother, so to speak, of this institution—where can there be any extreme or unreasonable imperialistic powers in the authority of the mother over her own child?

As the Imperial Wizard prepared to submit Exhibit B he felt the need to explain an unfamiliarity with all the financial figures supplied by the Klan office. He had been sick in bed or out on trips a great deal of the time. Exhibit B was a list of the monthly salaries of key Klan personnel. Simmons explained his salary of $1,000 had been set by the supreme executive committee as of August the first. He had been receiving $100 dollars a week and the committee felt an adjustment was needed. Congressman Fess then asked about a provision for back pay. Simmons thanked Fess for reminding him of that. The Imperial Concillum had decided to reward Simmons for past service in the years when he had gotten no compensation. It was decided he would get $5,000 a year for five years.

CONG. FESS: $25,000 in all?

COL. SIMMONS: Yes, sir; for five years. Of that I have received one payment, and that was just a few weeks ago. I have received only one payment.

Exhibit C was a financial balance sheet of the Klan General Fund. Exhibit D listed everything you would ever want to know about Lanier University—the board of trustees (Klan appointed), its faculty, and the courses of study. Exhibit E was the contract signed with Edward to run the Propagation Department. Fess again had a question.

CONG. FESS: Do you not think that a commission of 80 percent is inordinate?

COL. SIMMONS: If you are familiar with the organization and development of fraternal orders and have made a study of that subject, you will see that this is not inordinate. I was with a fraternal order or a fraternal insurance order with an initiation fee of $5 and I got all of that as my commission, together with a bonus of $3 from headquarters.

In a further defense of the contract:

> COL. SIMMONS: When Mr. Clarke signed this contract, he made the statement just prior to signing it, "Mr. Simmons, it is going to cost a large sum of money to organize or create an organization force." . . . The truth of that statement is borne out by the fact, according to my information, that he put $7,000 of his own money into it and borrowed $5,000 more before he got the machinery constructed to begin the work.

Exhibit G consisted of all the pamphlets and documents of the Klan. Much of this was the material Simmons had had the foresight to copyright back in 1915. There was a format for a Klan meeting, including dialogue, an opening devotional song, dedications, prayers, proclamations, and the closing ceremony. The ceremonies contained a heavily religious context. One song was sung to the tune of "America."

> *God of Eternity*
> *Guard, guide our great country,*
> *Our homes and store*
> *Keep our great state to Thee.*
> *Its people right and free.*
> *In us Thy glory be,*
> *Forevermore.*

The material drips with love, brotherhood, devotion, and patriotism. Simmons painted the Klan as an organization bathed in honor and purity for the remainder of the morning session, and then into the afternoon. The committee listened to major portions of the works verbatim.

Exhibit H was a copy of the telegram Simmons had sent to all members of Congress, and Exhibit I was a copy of a telegram sent to President Harding.

At the conclusion of the exhibits, Simmons felt compelled to once again address the issue of Bessie's influence within the Klan.

COL. SIMMONS: Going back now—and I am going to be brief—it has been conspicuously presented to your honorable body that one Mrs. Elizabeth Tyler is the supreme boss of the whole business. I want to state to you, Mr. Chairman and gentlemen of the committee, that that is an absurd untruth. . . . Mrs. Elizabeth Tyler is not my boss, and I am not a figurehead. The only head I have is a red head, and I have never been bossed by but two women, my mother and my wife.

In the remainder of the session Simmons discussed the moving of the robe manufacture contract from W. E. Flooding to Gate City.

An inquiry into the Klan's not-for-profit status ensued. The topic of calling the initiation fee a donation in order to evade the paying of taxes came up.

CONG. RODENBERG: The income tax law was not in operation long before this order started.

COL. SIMMONS: When this law first took effect I went to the income tax office in the Federal Building in Atlanta and made inquiry as to whether this organization would come under that law. . . . That gentleman informed me "You do not come under this law," and that was the end of that conversation . . . Now if it does, then we are ready to meet our obligations to the Government because we seek to meet them in all other things and we will not dodge them there.

The colonel had completed his statement after a day and a half of arduous and often compelling testimony. He now rose to his full height for a rousing and over-the-top closing statement.

COL. SIMMONS: Now, then one more point, Mr. Chairman, and I will have to close. I am sorry I am suffering as I am, but I cannot help it. Julius Caesar had his Brutus, Jesus Christ had his Judas, and our great and illustrious Washington had his Benedict Arnold. Sir, I can state to you that I can enter the fellowship of all three of those because I have suffered in my soul as a result of the treasonous and treacherous conduct of traitors . . .

Again I want to express to you, Mr. Chairman, my deep gratitude and thanks for the courtesies you have extended to me. . . .

I want to say to my persecutors and the persecutors of this organization in all honesty and sincerity, no matter to what creed or
race you may belong in your persecutions, through the medium
of the press or otherwise, that you do not know what you are
doing. You are ignorant of the principles as were those who were
ignorant of the character and work of the Christ . . .

I cannot better express myself than by saying to you who are persecutors of the Klan and myself . . . "Father, forgive them for they
know not what they do! . . . Mr. Chairman, I am done!"

The gallery burst into applause as Simmons collapsed onto the table in
front of him. Campbell asked for order. Etheridge rushed to his ailing
leader's side.

Campbell decided to adjourn the hearings until the next morning at
10:30, hoping Simmons would be recovered and ready to answer questions.[13]

CHAPTER 12
Flight

"The best-laid plans of mice and men often go astray."
—Robert Burns, "To a Mouse"

"We are not retreating—we are advancing in another direction."
—Douglas McArthur

Much had transpired since the close of the Thursday session of the House Committee on Rules. First, there had been no Friday hearings. The Simmons camp had produced a letter from a Dr. William J. Manning who was, according to Simmons, "one of the most reputable and prominent physicians in Washington." The letter stated that Manning's patient was suffering from the various "chitises" Simmons mentioned at the opening of the hearings on the afternoon of the 12th. He was running a temperature and was "much exhausted." It became necessary for his doctor to absolutely prohibit any physical or mental action the next day, and the chairman of the Rules Committee before whom Simmons was to appear was so informed. Two cultures had been taken, showing "a most virulent germ, a streptococcus." Dr. Manning concluded his letter with, "He is still suffering to a considerable degree as a result of the poison given off in his system by the organism mentioned, and is far from being a well man. So strong was his mental make-up and determination to appear before the committee again, however, that the writer (Dr. Manning) has reluctantly given his consent for Col. Simmons to appear before the committee today, October 17, 1921."

Simmons appeared to be well and confident on Monday the 17th when the hearings resumed. He was probably pleased with his performance the prior week. With very few questions from the committee, he had been allowed free rein to defend his besieged fraternal order. He had painted it as a noble, Christian-based, legal organization with nothing to hide. He had exuded Southern charm and gentility while claiming sinister motives on his attackers from the liberal Northern press.

Even though he had commanded the stage for nearly one and a half days the previous week, Simmons asked for another ten minutes to make an additional statement. Chairman Campbell permitted the request.

The colonel launched into one more attack on the *New York World*. He made claims that a *World* reporter named Robert H. Murray had meddled in Mexican politics in the years before World War I, writing propaganda-laced articles in support of the U.S.-supported president, Venustiano Carranza. Simmons called Carranza a "known enemy of the United States, who has been proven to be guilty and fully responsible for the death of over 587 American citizens in Mexico and along the border." Surely this could not be a reputable newspaper.

> COL. SIMMONS: I particularly desire to impress on your committee this fact, that in the testimony of the representative of the *New York World*, false statements and charges were made against the Klan and its officials. If the *New York World*, in the opinion of many thousands of Americans in Mexico and the United States, deliberately garbled and published false information, as some of these Americans swore was done, and if the *New York World* was a continuous distributor for several years of propaganda through its columns in the interests of the proven enemies of the United States, as sworn testimony before a Senate committee states they did, then what could our organization expect from this newspaper?

Next came a sensational allegation against the *World*.

> COL. SIMMONS: I wish to notify the chairman of this committee that there are plans on foot at the present time whereby one

of the representatives of the *New York World* is to be tarred and feathered in the name of the Klan, and that this plan has been originated and its details worked out by representatives of the *New York World* so that it will appear that the Klan did this in a spirit of revenge.

What occurred next may have been a tactical error. The colonel chose to revisit the closing moments of the Thursday session when he had collapsed upon declaring, "Father forgive them, for they know not what they do! Mr. Chairman, I am done!" First, Simmons again repeated that he had been testifying despite having come there from his sickbed. Then, he decided to relate a story he had been told about the events immediately following his dramatic collapse. According to Simmons, a gentleman, identified as Assistant Attorney General John W. H. Crim, sitting at a table a few feet away, had bounced to his feet and said "For cheap theatrical effect, damn such a fakir. I have been expecting this for many minutes!" According to sources, Crim had then gone to Chairman Campbell, and that Campbell and Crim had said the collapse was a "cheap theatrical attempt to gain sympathy."

The source of this information was the correspondent of a prominent Southern newspaper who had passed the account to Georgia congressman W. D. Upshaw.

Chairman Campbell was clearly not amused.

CONG. CAMPBELL: Mr. Simmons, let me say right here that if all the rest that you have detailed up to this time since you began this morning is as false and utterly without foundation as the statement that Mr. Crim and I had that conversation, you have given us something this morning that is absolutely of no use to the committee.

COL. SIMMONS: Mr. Chairman, I will state to you, sir—

CAMPBELL: The conversation you relate did not occur between a representative of the attorney general's office and myself.

SIMMONS: Now, then, Mr. Chairman—

CAMPBELL: (interposing) I made no such statement to any-body.

Sensing the chairman's rising anger, Simmons quickly began to back-track.

COL. SIMMONS: I am glad you make that statement. I am stat-ing that that has been reported, and I do not believe it.

Campbell had reached the end of his patience.

CONG. CAMPBELL: I think, Colonel Simmons, you have gone far enough with this kind of thing.

However, Simmons did not heed the warning. He further incurred the wrath of the chairman by demanding that C. Anderson Wright be recalled, and even suggested the appropriate line of questioning. In fact, he provided forty-five questions, reading each aloud for the record. At one point Campbell interposed:

CONG. CAMPBELL: Would you just as soon submit the ques-tions in writing? It would save us a great deal of time.

COL. SIMMONS: There is just another page of them, sir, if you would allow me to read them.

Simmons rattled off another eighteen. At the conclusion he stated, "I am ready now, sir, to subject myself to any questions."

CONG. CAMPBELL: Do you desire to stand or have a seat?

COL. SIMMONS: I will sit over here, sir.

It would be a good choice. Campbell had endured long hours of Sim-mons's self-serving and self-righteous testimony. He had been fair to the Imperial Wizard, but his level of tolerance was quickly diminishing. The histrionic conclusion to day three may have provided the breaking point.

CONG. CAMPBELL: I am desirous of securing some concrete information with respect to this organization. I think if we can have some short answers and short questions detailing matters that are of public interest it will be of service to the committee.

There would, indeed, be a series of sharp, pointed questions. By the time he was done, Campbell had asked over 330, covering twenty-seven pages of the published transcript of the hearings. It makes for fascinating reading. One can feel the tension in the room as Campbell's staccato pacing placed Simmons in an increasingly uncomfortable and defensive position. The Imperial Wizard struggled with specific information and frequently blamed his medical condition for his lack of command and preparation.

Campbell began quizzing the Imperial Wizard about the early days of the Klan.

CONG. CAMPBELL: And from 1915 down to June 7, 1920, you raised and disbursed how much money in connection with the organization?

COL. SIMMONS: I could not answer you definitely on that point because I have not had an opportunity to go back over the records, as most of them were lost in moving the office about three years ago, and I have never had occasion to reconstruct them, but it is my purpose to do so.

CAMPBELL: Well, approximately how much money?

SIMMONS: We had a membership in the spring of 1920 of about four or five thousand members.

CAMPBELL: You received for each member the sum of $10?

SIMMONS: No, sir. For the first three years the fee was placed at $5.

Campbell then referred to Simmons's own exhibit that showed a total of over $150,000. Simmons disputed that number. Campbell insisted it came from Simmons. The colonel said they came from his office and that he had not had time to review them due to illness.

CONG. CAMPBELL: Have you a roster of your members?

COL. SIMMONS: Yes, sir, not complete, however, but we have a roster going back to certain dates.

CAMPBELL: Why not all?

SIMMONS: Well, it would be too voluminous to have all that, and it is not necessary.

The questioning proceeded to a discussion of the Klan's propagation contract with E. Y. Clarke.

CONG. CAMPBELL: On the 15th of June you entered into a contract with Mr. Clarke?

COL. SIMMONS: The 15th of June of what year?

CAMPBELL: Of 1920.

SIMMONS: Yes, sir, I believe that was the year.

CAMPBELL: Under the contract with Mr. Clarke it was his duty to do the advertising, secure the members, take his $8, and give you $2?

SIMMONS: That is the substance of the contract. In other words, he was to direct the promoting of the organization and pay all the expenses of that promoting, his field men, and his clerk hire, and things of that sort; the expenses in general of the work of his department.

CAMPBELL: You had nothing to do with the field work after that?

SIMMONS: No, sir. Mr. Clarke was employed to look after that. That was his business like you would employ a man to build a home for you.

Campbell noted a disbursement for field work of $19,356 from the Klan General Fund after the commencement of Clarke's contract. Simmons explained that was for lecturers sent out to speak in behalf of the Klan.

CONG. CAMPBELL: That is an aid to or supplementary to Mr. Clarke's work?

COL. SIMMONS: It is an aid in a way, and in a measure it is supplementary, too, but this is the work of the organization itself or of the Klan itself. It is for the purpose of seeing that these local organizations are properly put in and instructed.

The financial report also noted $24,600 in traveling expenses and over $5,000 in telephone and telegraph costs. Simmons said these were incidental to the field work being done.

CONG. CAMPBELL: Your salary is now $1,000 per month?

COL. SIMMONS: Yes, sir.

CAMPBELL: Prior to that it was how much?

SIMMONS: A year ago it was not in excess of $100 a week with expenses included.

CAMPBELL: Something has been said here about some back salary being paid?

SIMMONS: The governing body, the Imperial Concillum, passed a resolution to pay me a sum that would be equal to $5,000 a year for the past five years.

CAMPBELL: How much of that $25,000 has been paid?

SIMMONS: Only one $5,000, or one payment.

This was a significant sum of money. In 2014 dollars, adjusted for inflation, the $25,000 would represent nearly $285,000.

CONG. CAMPBELL: Upon the suggestion of what particular Klansman or officer was that payment made?

COL. SIMMONS: I was present and courteously asked to step out of the room for awhile.

CAMPBELL: Who asked you to step out?

SIMMONS: I do not remember who did it.

CAMPBELL: Was it Mr. Clarke?

SIMMONS: No more than any other officer.

CAMPBELL: Were any of these men holding positions that are of pecuniary advantage to them?

SIMMONS: I think only in the way of their compensation for their services to the organization.

CAMPBELL: Mr. Clarke has a contract?

SIMMONS: Yes, sir, on a commission basis.

CAMPBELL: Could you discharge Clarke at any moment?

SIMMONS: For cause; yes, sir.

The Chairman was ready to go on the offensive.

CONG. CAMPBELL: I have a memorandum here somewhere, or a record, that shows that out of the accumulated funds of Clarke there was $111,000 that he divided fifty-fifty between himself and Mrs. Tyler. Did that come to your attention?

COL. SIMMONS: No, sir; I am not familiar with what agreement Mr. Clarke has made with those who work under him in his department.

CAMPBELL: Has it occurred to you at any time since the running of the contract that you were paying out of the $2 fund money for advertising and for promoting membership, or for securing membership, practically 70 cents out of every dollar that you get out of the $2 in the interest of Mr. Clarke's contract?

SIMMONS: No, sir.

CAMPBELL: That has not occurred to you?

SIMMONS: No, sir, it has not. It has not been done in the interest of Mr. Clarke's contract.

CLAMPBELL: Has it ever occurred to you at any time that Mr. Clarke thought he had a very good thing that might at any time be terminated by you, and that it would not be a bad thing for him and those associated with him to increase your salary, pay you in back pay the sum of $25,000, and have the deed to the home in which you lived in his name? Has it ever occurred to you that it might have occurred to Clarke that it would be a good thing for him to do that?

SIMMONS: No, sir. Mr. Chairman, every year the—

CAMPBELL: Has the suggestion ever entered your mind that perhaps Mr. Clarke and Mrs. Tyler did not have the high ideals with respect to this organization that you had?

SIMMONS: No, sir, I have no evidence of that at all.

CAMPBELL: Has it ever occurred to you at any time that they were using it as a money-making scheme?

SIMMONS: No, sir; it has not. I have no evidence that would justify any opinion on part of that nature.

CAMPBELL: The fact that they have collected $225,568.84 in one year and divided it among themselves does not suggest to you that is a pretty good thing for two persons, or a good deal of money for two persons to make in one year out of a benevolent organization?

SIMMONS: Well, sir, that might on its face appear to be a splendid sum of money, but out of that they have had to pay considerable expenses.

CAMPBELL: But you have been paying out of the $2 that came to you money for expenses incurred in increasing the membership of the order?

SIMMONS: Yes, sir, that is true.

CAMPBELL: Have they been putting anything over on you, do you think?

SIMMONS: No, sir; I have not had any occasion to be suspicious of anything of that sort up to date. They have done a splendid piece of work.

CAMPBELL: Has it not occurred to you that this idealistic organization that you have given birth to and have fostered so long is now being used for mercenary purposes by very clever people or propagandists who know how to appeal to the people of this community or in that for membership?

SIMMONS: So far, I have not. Nothing has come to my view that would prompt me to have such an opinion.

As questioning continued it became more and more apparent that Simmons had very little grasp of the day-to-day operations of the Klan. Campbell brought up the case of the Atlanta hot dog vendor, J. C. Thomas, who had been abducted and threatened.

CONG. CAMPBELL: Did you make any effort to ascertain whether or not Klansmen were responsible for that?

COL. SIMMONS: I made no effort at the time for the reason that I was in Florida sick, down sick.

CAMPBELL: Who was in charge of the Klan in Atlanta? What was the name of the man in charge?

SIMMONS: You mean, who was in charge in my absence?

CAMPBELL: Yes.

SIMMONS: The Imperial Klaliff, looking after business affairs.

CAMPBELL: Who was that?

SIMMONS: Mr. Clarke.

CAMPBELL: We have heard frequent references of your being away on account of sickness. How much time during the last year have you been away from your duties on account of sickness?

SIMMONS: In the last year, I would estimate possibly as much as four months.

CAMPBELL: And recently you have not been in the office or engaged in the work of the organization?

SIMMONS: Not in any detailed work on account of my sickness and sicknesses in my home, except to answer correspondence addressed to me personally and to have general supervision of the work.

Campbell was an experienced attorney, and he relentlessly pursued Simmons down various paths. He questioned the newsletters sent out by Clarke and Tyler to their kleagles. Many of these communications were inflammatory and contained blatant inaccuracies. Simmons admitted he had never seen any of them.

The colonel denied the Klan was recruiting police chiefs, judges, and members of Congress with the goal of building an Invisible Empire. He emphatically stated that the Klan was not assisting the police by taking the law into their own hands.

Campbell brought up the violent crimes reported by the *World* committed by men wearing masks.

CONG. CAMPBELL: And your high purpose in creating this organization at this time was for the purpose of establishing a memorial to the Klansmen of that period (the Reconstruction Klan)?

COL. SIMMONS: It was memorializing their spiritual purpose, Mr. Chairman, and the work they did to serve the civilization of our country.

CAMPBELL: Has it occurred to you that the crimes, some sixty odd in number, that have been recently charged against the Knights of the Ku Klux Klan have been made possible by the very masks, or the type of masks, that were worn in the Reconstruction period by the Klansmen of that day?

SIMMONS: You say has it occurred to me?

CAMPBELL: Yes.

SIMMONS: No, sir; it has not occurred to me. There are no grounds for that.

Simmons had steadfastly held that those crimes were committed by copycat organizations; that if his members broke the law they would be immediately expelled from the Klan.

> CONG. CAMPBELL: They are concealed from the public, their identity not to be known.

> COL. SIMMONS: The same thing might apply, sir, to the Mardi Gras.

> CAMPBELL: That is a frolic.

> SIMMONS: That is true. The Klan is just the same.

> CAMPBELL: It is an innocent frolic.

Near the end of his questioning, Campbell again returned to financial matters.

> CONG. CAMPBELL: $171,000 has been received by the Klan since June 1, 1920. You now have $12,000 in the bank and about $2,000 worth of furniture, as well as an equity in your home. What was done with the rest of the money?

> COL. SIMMONS: The statement you are quoting from—

> CAMPBELL: (interposing) I am quoting from the statement you have submitted as a part of your testimony.

> SIMMONS: You have given me an insight into a statement made prior to this year, and I did not have an opportunity to go over that.

> CAMPBELL: No, that is this year.

> SIMMONS: I know . . . this year.

CAMPBELL: The money, at least, is not now in the treasury, and the only things you have listed here show, as I have indicated, that you have assets in the neighborhood of $40,000 as the result of an income of $171,000. They are round numbers.

SIMMONS: Now, with an opportunity I can be in possession of those facts that seem to be inconsistent. On my return to the office I can get you a correction or rectify the statement there.

CAMPBELL: Does the fact that there appears to be such a discrepancy between the assets and the liabilities lead you to believe that maybe you have been used, as has been suggested here, as a man of high ideals who may not know very much about what is going on in the organization? That has been the charge.

SIMMONS: Well, that is an opinion expressed.

CAMPBELL: Does it appear to you now that there is any justification for arriving at that conclusion, in view of your statement here now that you do not know what has been done with the funds of the organization?

SIMMONS: My answer to that question, sir, would simply be it is impossible for any man heading a movement to be acquainted with and thoroughly understand all the details that are going on, no more than the president of a bank could understand all the detailed transactions of his bank. They have been entrusted to those who are employed by the bank.

CAMPBELL: Then it may be that persons in whom you have reposed the greatest confidence have taken advantage of your credulity and of your ideals and have used the organization and its funds in a way that would not meet with your approval if you knew the details of their activities and expenditures?

SIMMONS: If that were true, I certainly would like to know it.

CAMPBELL: Do you not think it worthwhile to ascertain and find out whether or not it is true?

SIMMONS: Well, that question, Mr. Chairman—pardon me— is rather irrelevant, because I am going to—

CAMPBELL: You are going to find out?

SIMMONS: I told you at the very outset that if there is any wrong it shall be righted.

Edward Pou continued the examination. The North Carolina congressman had served as a Klan apologist throughout the hearings. In the wake of Campbell's aggressive interrogation, he asked the Imperial Wizard a series of soft questions. But the damage was done. Simmons had shown that he had been an absentee leader with almost no grasp of the day-to-day operations of his organization.

CONG. CAMPBELL: I believe that is all, Mr. Simmons.

COL. SIMMONS: All right, Mr. Chairman, I wish again to thank you all for your courtesy, and I ask that Mr. Wright be put back on the stand at your discretion.

Congressman Garrett moved to have an executive session. The Committee retired to an adjoining room. After a short time they returned.

CONG. CAMPBELL: The committee is of the unanimous conclusion that no witnesses will be recalled at this time, and that no other witnesses will be called at this time. At a subsequent time, the committee will meet and decide on its further action in the matter. At present the committee is adjourned.[1]

Nothing would come of the hearings. There would be no special committee formed to investigate the Klan. There were no laws passed based on the information gleaned during the four days in October. The inaction could very well be attributed to the following:

H. J. RES. 201
JOINT RESOLUTION

Instructing the Clerk of the House to secure from the secretary of state in each State in the Union certain information about secret organizations.

Whereas there are in the United States of America many secret organizations operating in this country ostensibly for patriotic, fraternal, and benevolent purposes; and

Whereas the uninitiated regard with suspicion some of these organizations that meet behind closed doors and give cumulative evidences of surreptitious designs and questionable practices; and

Whereas many of said societies collect large sums of money from their members, and often from the public, investing these funds in the purchase of great properties and the widespread propagation of their doctrines; and

Whereas the continuation and multiplication of such secret societies with their mystic passwords, their weird rituals, their fantastic regalia, and their high-sounding titles, are regarded by many patriotic American freemen as inimical to the spirit and genius of our institutions and subversive of the broadest fellowship in our blood-bought democracy; and

Whereas only one of these secret organizations has been called by congressional resolution to appear before the Rules Committee of this House on Tuesday October 11, to give account of its principles and its proceedings:

Therefore be it resolved by the Senate and House of Representatives of the United States of America in Congress assembled,

That the Clerk of this House be, and is hereby, instructed to secure from the secretary of state in each State of the Union the name of every secret organization chartered or operating in the State without charter, and furnish the same to both Houses of Congress.

SEC.2. That the chief official of each and every secret organization in the United States of America be summoned to appear before a special committee of this House to be appointed at the discretion of the Speaker, to give account of their aims and purposes, the funds collected and expended, and also to disclose the oaths and the rituals of said secret organizations to the eyes of this Congress and before the liberty-loving people of this Republic.[2]

The author of H. J. Res. 201 was Congressman W. D. Upshaw of Georgia. This was the document he had alluded to in his introduction of Colonel Simmons to the House Committee on Rules. It is also very possible that this was what Upshaw had referred to in his note to Bessie. In that undated, handwritten correspondence, Upshaw had said, "Here it is—scratched off while the train has dashed along. It is not very exhaustive, but I hope you, the Wizard, and the Near Wizard will like it. If I can serve you and *The Searchlight* further, please do not hesitate to command me."[3]

Bessie and Edward needed a friend in Congress to defuse the growing momentum building against the Klan in Washington, D.C. The thought of further investigation and the passage of legislation that would harm the Klan greatly worried the duo.

Their solution to the problem amounted to political dynamite. They exploited America's sense of fair play to their advantage. According to Upshaw's resolution, if one secret organization was investigated by Congress, so should all similar societies. Each state was to provide the names of secret organizations operating within their borders, and the heads of those organizations were to be summoned before a House committee to answer questions on funding, oaths, rituals, and activities. H. J. Res. 201 quickly ended the official congressional scrutiny of the Ku Klux Klan.

Politicians are pragmatic individuals. For most, the greatest priority during their term is not lawmaking, but getting re-elected. Historian Charles Metz estimated that in 1920 there were between 30,000,000 and 60,000,000 fraternal memberships in the United States.[4] Most definitely a number of the congressmen on the Rules Committee were fraternalists. To pursue and persecute secret fraternal societies was tantamount to committing political suicide.

It had been a remarkable forty-two days. From the *World*'s first published story on September 6 to the sound of the closing gavel of the Rules Committee Hearings on October 17, the Klan had been dissected before the eyes of a curious nation. The dirty laundry of the Invisible Empire had been hung out for all to see.

For the moment, the Big Three had survived.

> *"I don't care what they say about me as long as they spell my name right."*
> —attributed to P. T. Barnum

> *"There is only one thing worse than being talked about, and that is not being talked about."*
> —Oscar Wilde

> *"There's no such thing as bad publicity except your own obituary."*
> —Brendan Behan, Irish writer

If it had been the *New York World*'s goal to expose and destroy the Klan, only half was true. Klan applications began arriving at an unprecedented rate. Certainly there were Americans who were outraged by what they had read, and who demanded the eradication of the Invisible Empire. However, there were untold thousands who embraced the Klan's core values. The *World* had also served to publicize the organization to those prone to joining. In one of the early installments of the series, Swope and Thomas had printed a blank facsimile of the Klan membership application. Readers had simply clipped the form from the paper, filled it in, and mailed it to Atlanta with their payment of $10.[5] There is a report that Edward and Bessie personally made $40,000 (nearly $500,000 in 2014 dollars) during the first two months following the *World's* series.[6]

Yet there was trouble in paradise. The power base Edward and Bessie had built was beginning to crumble at its foundation. One thing all the publicity had established was that the two were making extraordinary profits. During the House hearings, testimony stated that the Propagation Department had received $225,568 in payments since the signing of the contract with Simmons. Edward quickly countered that the true profit was only $16,000, with the remainder going toward expenses. Few insiders believed that number. Stories of Edward and Bessie's affair were also damaging. Along with the Klan's espousal of racial and religious hatred and the condoning of violence, there existed a self-righteous belief in Christian fundamentalism. Claims of Bessie's powerful role in the organization were also disquieting to the male membership. Even Simmons was feeling the unrest. His lack of strong leadership profiled in newspaper accounts, and his performance during the Congressional hearings, had begun to erode support among the rank and file.

The first cracks began to show only six weeks after the Congressional hearings ended. The December 3, 1921, edition of the *New York Times* detailed the story.

DEPOSED GOBLINS SAY
KLAN IS BROKEN

One of Four Domain Chiefs who tried to oust Mrs. Tyler and Clarke tells of "Smash." Say 18,000 quit in Chicago and 3,000 resigned in Philadelphia.

Four of the most powerful grand goblins in the Invisible Empire had staged a rebellion. Grand goblins were the men directly below Bessie and Edward in the Propagation Department hierarchy, and headed multistate domains. The four were: Harry B. Terrell of the Capitol Domain in Washington D.C., A. J. Pardon Jr. of the New England Domain in Boston, Lloyd P. Hooper of the Domain of the East in New York City, and F. W. Atkins of the Atlantic Domain in Philadelphia. Atkins was the spokesmen for the *Times* story.

Atkins informed that rank-and-file members had complained to their leadership about Clarke and Tyler, and their mismanagement, illegal practices, and immorality. Many in Chicago and Philadelphia had already resigned as a result. The grand goblins had investigated the matter and found conditions worse than even those that had been charged. Atkins stated, "The Ku Klux Klan is broken. 'Smashed' would be a better word. Charges against Mr. Clarke and Mrs. Tyler are said to be responsible for the disintegration."

The four domain chiefs went to Atlanta for a face-to-face meeting with the Imperial Wizard. After presenting their case they demanded Simmons get rid of Clarke and Tyler or they would resign. Again, according to Atkins:

> We talked with him (Simmons) Friday and again Saturday. Sunday we met with him at the Ansly Hotel and he said, "Boys, I love you, and I know everything you are saying is true. I have made similar investigations of this man. If Edward Young Clarke has not resigned from the Knights of the Ku Klux Klan within seventy-two hours, William Joseph Simmons will."

Atkins said this statement from Simmons had been made in front of at least twenty people. The four were sent home. The seventy-two hours came and went without action. Instead of ridding the Klan of Edward and Bessie, the grand goblins were fired. Atkins responded to the dismissal, "I say we are proud of it. We presented our ultimatum and the power that Clarke and Mrs. Tyler hold over them is such that we really stood no chance of winning."

Klan headquarters issued a press release, simply stating that the four had been banished from the Klan and that Mr. Clarke and Mrs. Tyler would remain with the organization. Simmons was quoted, "I am so little concerned over the present agitation that I am taking this opportunity, on advice of my physician, to go away for a short spell of rest and recuperation." According to the transmission, he was headed to the North Carolina shore. Simmons added, "I shall keep in constant touch with the Imperial Kleagle of the organization, Edward Young Clarke, and in my absence he is in supreme charge of the work of the organization."[7]

Edward and Bessie had won round one. A week later Simmons released a statement that a committee of thirteen had looked into the charges against Clarke and Tyler and had fully exonerated them. It is doubtful the colonel had anything to do with any of the information emanating from the Imperial Palace. He had been removed from the action.[8]

The four goblins were not finished. Their next step was legal, submitting affidavits to a court in Atlanta. They would seek an accounting of all Klan funds. "The whole crowd is rotten and we plan to prove it. We have affidavits that will support every contention we make and which will break up the Klan forever if they do not strengthen it so that it will never die."[9]

Two of those affidavits came from a disgruntled Southern Publicity Association and Propagation Department employee. His name was Z. R. Upchurch.

In the first affidavit, included in the December 3 *New York Times* story, Upchurch certified that "during a campaign for the Anti-Saloon League there were deadheads, or people who did not exist on the payroll in the hands of Clarke and the receipts were signed in the handwriting of Elizabeth Tyler, his friend and associate." The implication—ghost payrolling. Edward and Bessie had billed their client for hours not earned.[10]

The second allegation was aired in a *New York Times* story dated December 15, 1921.

CALLS KU KLUX KLAN PRACTICALLY BANKRUPT

Atlanta Leader Makes the Statement in an Affidavit Attacking Kleagle Clarke.

Special to the New York Times
ATLANTA, Dec. 14—The Ku Klux Klan is practically bankrupt, according to an affidavit made public today by Z.R. Upchurch one of the leaders of the Atlanta Klan. ... The affidavit says that the Klan now faces payments of large obligations with a depleted treasury: that it does not hold clear title to any of the real estate it has purchased, and that it has been trying to sell certificates of indebtedness to individual Klansmen in the hope of obtaining necessary funds to tide it over the emergency.[11]

Upchurch also made assertions the newspaper could not print. They were about immoral conduct between Edward and Bessie and personal observations of conditions at 185 South Pryor Street. He also charged that Edward had defrauded charitable and religious organizations of thousands of dollars while conducting money-raising campaigns, and that he was continuing such practices with the Klan.

The four grand goblins, Upchurch, and 169 other Klansmen filed a petition on December 21, 1921, for receivership of all property, funds, documents, and records of the Klan. In March 1922 the petition was denied by the Fulton County Superior Court. A subsequent appeal to the state supreme court was also unsuccessful. Bessie and Edward had dodged another bullet, but their situation required new strategies.[12]

Bessie's role in the all-male Klan had become a growing problem. By all accounts she wielded tremendous power within the organization, and she had become very wealthy.

In early 1922 an announcement notified the public that Bessie was resigning her post with the Propagation Department because of the illness of her daughter, Mrs. J. Q. Jett. This was apparently a diversionary tactic as Bessie continued to work in the Imperial Palace and collect her commissions.[13] We also know because of the J. Q. Jett letters that Minnie was no longer Mrs. Jett but that she was indeed sick. The illness turned out to be tuberculosis. The ploy seemed to work as criticism regarding Bessie's presence subsided greatly.

Then there was the matter of the Imperial Wizard. There was an impression throughout the Klan membership that the old colonel had lost control of the Invisible Empire. Should there be a grass-roots movement to replace Simmons, the results could be disastrous for the fortunes of Edward and Bessie. It was decided the Imperial Wizard should take an extended leave of absence. On June 10, 1922, the *New York Times* published the story.

LEAVE FOR SIMMONS; CLARKE TO RUN KLAN

Imperial Kleagle Will Act as
Imperial Wizard Pro Tem—
Simmons May Go Abroad

Colonel William J. Simmons, Imperial Wizard and founder of the Ku Klux Klan, at his own request has been allowed a six months' leave of absence by ranking officials
of the order. He will devote this time it is stated, to preparing the ritual and initiation rules governing the second and third degrees of Ku Kluxism.

The article went on to say there was talk of Simmons going to Europe to study conditions there. Officials at the Imperial Palace, however,
denied he was being sent overseas, and as far as they knew, he had no
intentions of going.

> *In the meantime, acting under authority of the Klan, E.Y.*
> *Clarke, Imperial Kleagle, is acting as Imperial Wizard pro*
> *tem and is signing official communications in that manner.*

Even in this release Edward ensured there were no lingering questions
about Bessie.

> *It was stated emphatically here tonight that Mrs. Elizabeth*
> *Tyler has no official connection with the Klan.*[14]

With Simmons temporarily out of the picture and Bessie hidden in
the shadows, Edward made another move to solidify his position in the
Klan. He needed to bring someone into his organization who would be
acceptable to the general membership. He found that person in a Texan
named Hiram Wesley Evans.[15]

Evans was born on September 26, 1881, in Ashland, Alabama, to Hiram Martin and Georgia Ann Evans. We know little of his early life,
except that he eventually studied dentistry at Vanderbilt University in
Nashville. He never received his degree but did set up a practice in Dallas. Like nearly every other player in this story, Evans was a fraternalist.
His claim to fame came as a Masonic leader in Texas.[16] In 1920 Evans
was drawn to the Klan and eventually became a highly successful organizer in the Propagation Department. He also became influential in the
organization as the Exalted Cyclops (chapter president) of the powerful
Dallas Klan No. 66, and the Great Titan (district commander) of Texas

Province No. 2.[17] His record was noticed in Atlanta, and Edward and Bessie developed a friendship with him.

In the late spring of 1922 Hiram Wesley Evans was brought to Atlanta to serve as Edward's assistant with the hope that his solid Klan credentials would placate dissidents within the organization. Money was flowing in at an astounding rate. By the end of the summer of 1922 the membership rolls would grow to one million.

Almost immediately Edward, Bessie, and Evans began conspiring a palace coup that would remove Simmons from the leadership of the Klan. The plan was to "kick the colonel upstairs" giving him the lifetime title of Imperial Emperor. They set November as their target date, when Simmons would return for the first Imperial Klonvocation to be held in Atlanta.[18]

One of the first moves was to give Evans a title. Edward fired the Klan Imperial Kligrapp (secretary) Louis David Wade and handed the position to Evans. This proved a mistake. Wade fought back, filed a suit, and went to the press. On July 17, 1922, the *New York Times* told the former kligrapp's story:

CHARGES KLAN HEAD
IS TAKING TRIBUTE
Wade Declares Clarke and Mrs. Tyler have Become Rich on "Ill-Gotten Gains"
SAYS THEY CONTROL FUNDS
Former Kligrapp Asserts Clarke Takes Advantage of Imperial Wizard's "Drunken Condition"

ATLANTA, Ga. July 16—Charges That Edward Young Clarke, Imperial Wizard Pro Tem and Mrs. Elizabeth Tyler, his former associate in the propagation department, are feathering their own nests to the extent of a great fortune; that the Knights of the Ku Klux Klan have become mere tribute payers, and that Clarke has either kept Colonel W.J. Simmons, Imperial Wizard, drunk or taken advantage of "his drunken condition" are set

forth by Louis D. Wade, discharged Kligrapp, in answer
to a suit for injunction filed by the Klan officers to prevent him from spreading propaganda among members
of the order detrimental to the officers.

Wade expressed outrage that persons so notorious as Clarke and Mrs. Tyler should be in absolute charge "of the destinies of an order in whose ranks there are so many upright and noble men whose characters are above reproach." He maintained Clarke was now Imperial Wizard Pro Tem, Imperial Kleagle, and Imperial Klaliff, and therefore controlled the selection of all officers of the Klan: "Any member of the Supreme Council who opposes Clarke's will is immediately dismissed."

Wade offered four very damning pieces of evidence. The first was an accusation that Edward required each officer and agent of the Klan who handled money to be bonded. Clarke obtained a blanket policy from a surety company and then charged his members premiums and pocketed a profit. The second stated "The regalia which each Klansman is required to own is manufactured at a cost of $1.90 and sold by the manufacturer at $4, and that Clarke and Mrs. Tyler own a large, if not controlling, interest in the firm manufacturing such regalia."

Wade then described a Clarke Realty deal in which Clarke had engineered a Klan purchase of 250 acres of land in Fulton County for $150,000. According to the deposed Klan officer, Edward then sold the most valuable part of the parcel to an organization in which Clarke was the dominant stockholder for $33,000. The Klan was left with the burden of $115,000 for the less valuable portion. The initial purchase may have been land for a meeting ground for the upcoming Imperial Klonvocation.

Wade's final assertion was that, contrary to public statements, "Mrs. Tyler remains at the head of the Propagation Department."[19]

Two weeks later, on August 3, Bessie typed another letter on Klan stationery to J. Q., "My Dear Son," in Ellijay. It began with talk of Minnie's continuing health problems and of the necessity of finding a specialist who understood tubercular cases. Then she made reference to J. Q. running for the Georgia state legislature: "I read your announcement for legislature with much pleasure. I am very proud of you and hope to see you win out. Your statement was good and just exactly like you." She ended with, "Give Leastie and the baby my love and keep a big share for yourself.—Mother."

A cryptic post script followed.

> *P.S. Now listen, boy, here's just a bit of motherly advice. I do believe you know that there is nothing I desire more than your happiness. I do want you and wife to get along nicely. While you, Doris, and I readily understand that your former marriage was just a childish affair, you might bear in mind that Leastie is a woman and your wife and it might not be so easy for her to understand. I do not want you to do anything that would put a single doubt in her mind as to your loyalty to her because she is nice and sweet and you have the cutest, sweetest baby in the world.*
>
> *—Mother*[20]

We don't have the opportunity to read J. Q.'s letters to Bessie, but it appears he may have been pining for his ex-wife. Bessie may have been thinking about such things because she was about to marry again, for the fourth time. Her relationship with Edward had been purely professional for some time. The tumultuous days at the end of the *World* exposé had taken their toll. On August 20, 1922, the *New York Times* announced the wedding.

MRS. ELIZABETH TYLER WEDS
Married to S.W. Grow by Imperial Chaplain of Ku Klux Klan

ATLANTA, Ga.—Mrs. Elizabeth Tyler, until recently head of the propagation department of the Ku Klux Klan, was married this morning to Stephen W. Grow, Atlanta moving picture man. The ceremony took place at Mrs. Tyler's home in Howell Mill Road. The ceremony was performed by the Rev. Caleb A. Ridley, imperial chaplain of the Ku Klux Klan. Mr. Grow is well known in the motion picture business in Atlanta. Besides his connection with W.M. Hodkinson Corporation he is associated with the

Southern Publicity Association, in which Mrs. Tyler has been interested.[21]

Very little is known about Stephen Grow. He had some connection with Bessie through the Southern Publicity Association, although his role with the firm cannot be established. His work with the Hodkinson Corporation would have been in the distribution arm of the movie industry. William Wadsworth Hodkinson has been called by some "The Man Who Invented Hollywood." Hodkinson became one of history's first movie theater owners when he opened for business in Ogden, Utah, in 1907. After success in the Salt Lake City market he joined the General Film Company, a leading West Coast film distributor. On May 8, 1914, Hodkinson merged eleven film rental businesses to create the first national distributor of films, Paramount Pictures. In fact, he designed the famous mountain peak Paramount logo on a napkin during a lunch meeting with Adolph Zukor. It reminded him of a mountain near his boyhood home in Utah. One of Hodkinson's most famous innovations was the concept of block booking. This meant that exhibitors who wanted a particular movie had to buy a bundled package of features from producers affiliated with Paramount. By 1922 he had left Paramount and formed the W. W. Hodkinson Corporation and had a stake in the movies produced by Cecil B. DeMille.[22]

The next letter from Bessie to J. Q., this one on Searchlight stationery, has an ominous tone. On September 8, 1922, she wrote:

Dear Son:

Your communication and the box of apples received. I want to thank you for both for they were greatly appreciated.

I guess you see by the papers that we are still having trouble but it is just the usual framing up tactics of that contemptible bunch.

—*Mother*[23]

Because of all the negative press, Bessie and Edward were becoming liabilities to the Klan. The "contemptible bunch" was headed by none other than Hiram Wesley Evans.

Evans was a very different man than William Joseph Simmons. Bessie and Edward had gravely underestimated the Texas dentist. One contemporary said he "possessed the determined convictions of Martin Luther, the kindness of Lincoln, and the strategy and generalship of Napoleon." He was also very ambitious.[24]

Evans's first step was to discredit Edward. In September Clarke was in Muncie, Indiana, addressing a Klan rally on law enforcement. After the speech local police acted on a tip and searched Edward's luggage. They found a bottle of liquor and arrested the Imperial Wizard Pro Tem on a violation of the Volstead Act. Edward protested that he had been framed, and he probably was. Indiana Grand Dragon David C. Stephenson was one of Evans's co-conspirators. Clarke was also indicted for violation of Section 215 of the Postal Code for supposedly using the mails in his alleged bond rake-off scheme. Someone had tipped off the Justice Department.[25]

Although Edward was never prosecuted on these charges, he knew more probes into his past were likely in his future and he decided to voluntarily step down from the helm of the Klan. He continued in his capacity in the Propagation Department.

As the Grand Klonvocation drew near, Simmons returned from his leave of absence. He was prepared to resume his Imperial Wizard role at the first great gathering of his Klan. The Evans cabal had other ideas. On the night of November 26, the eve of the opening, Fred Savage, Stephenson, Texas Grand Dragon H. C. McCall, and Arkansas Grand Dragon James Comer met at the Piedmont Hotel to map a strategy. At 3 a.m. Stephenson and Savage went to "KlanKrest," Simmons's lavish home at 1840 Peachtree Street, and woke the colonel. They told him of a conspiracy afoot where Simmons's character would be attacked on the convention floor and gunfire would result. To avoid inevitable tragedy, they advised that Simmons refuse to offer his name up for renomination, instead accepting the post of emperor for life. Stephenson and Savage suggested a temporary Imperial Wizard be selected until a solution to the crisis could be found.

Simmons agreed to the action, and the next day he sat quietly and was awarded his lifetime post. The title of Imperial Wizard went to

Hiram Evans. The new "temporary" wizard would remain in the post for the next seventeen years.[26] Simmons later called that day "a fiendish frame-up . . . successfully put over . . . by the very ones whom I most trusted. Evans's election . . . was unholy in concept, underhanded in method, illegal in fact, and destructive in results."[27] When the colonel realized the extent of the trickery he realized he no longer possessed any power within the Klan. "Not long after Evans got in I noticed a coldness among all the office help. I didn't have any office to go to. I just had to sort of hang around the place even though my title was emperor."[28]

The power base of the Southern Publicity Association was eroding rapidly. On December 23, 1922, J. Q. received a letter in Ellijay.

My Dear Son,

I received the apples and walnuts and think it is very kind of you to remember me away down here all mussed up with business and everything.

I wish I could spend Christmas with you. . . . However, I am leaving on Christmas Day with Dorris for the West and I am just hoping and trusting that she may have a chance, if I can get her out there in time.

—Mother[29]

Bessie, her daughter, and her new husband were on their way to California. Minnie Dorris's health was failing and the hope was that the sunny, warm climate of southern California would help remedy the situation. They would end up in Altadena, California, home to a number of respected tuberculosis facilities. Foremost among them were the Esperanza Sanitorium and the Lavina Sanitarium.[30] Bessie may also have left to escape the intense public scrutiny in Georgia's capital.

By a number of accounts, Bessie left with nearly $800,000 in cash—approximately $10,000,000 in 2014 dollars.[31]

Elizabeth Tyler would never again return to Atlanta.

As 1923 began, Edward remained at the helm of the Klan's Propagation Department. There are a series of communications between Edward and

J. Q. Jett between January 11 and February 9 regarding the formation of a press clipping bureau for the Klan. Edward wanted J. Q. to run the operation from Ellijay. On January 11, Edward wrote: "Dear Quincy, I am seriously thinking of establishing the press clipping bureau which you and I discussed when you were last in Atlanta." Clarke requested a meeting in Atlanta and enclosed a check for $25 to be used to buy clothing for J. Q.'s baby, apologizing for not doing it at Christmas.

On February 9, J. Q. wrote of early results.

Dear Mr. Clarke,

I beg to report to you that the Clipping Bureau is getting results and the members of your organization in other states are responding nicely to our letters asking them to send in clippings. We are averaging getting about seventy-five clippings per day for the past week. Everyone is cooperating with the Bureau in putting it over and collecting all clippings that it is possible to get.

After providing a number of specific details, it was signed:

Yours to Command,

J. Q. Jett

Clipping Bureau[32]

Edward's career with the Klan would not last much longer. In March his past would come back to haunt him again. Evans's investigators turned over evidence to the Justice Department that Clarke was in violation of the Mann Act. The 1910 law prohibited the interstate transport of females for "immoral purposes." Apparently Edward had persuaded a young Houston woman named Laurel Martin to come to New Orleans where she registered in a hotel as Mrs. E. Y. Clarke on February 11, 1921.

Edward was arrested, and five days later Imperial Wizard Hiram Evans cancelled the Propagation Department contract "for the good of the order" and severed all of Clarke's connections with the Klan. Evans announced that all money coming in from membership activities would "henceforth be turned back into the extension of the order."

To avoid prosecution Clarke fled the country. Later he would call the arrest "simply another effort to discredit me, and through discrediting me, damage the Knights of the Ku Klux Klan."[33]

Only William Joseph Simmons now remained of the infamous "Big Three."

Simmons attempted to reassert himself with the Klan faithful, many of whom still respected the Invisible Empire's founder. There were many well-publicized verbal assaults between Evans and the colonel, each accusing the other with treason and disloyalty. In April 1923 Simmons saw an opportunity. When Evans left on an extended business trip he forcibly took possession of the Imperial Palace in a dramatic counter coup.

Evans immediately returned to Atlanta and a complex legal battle ensued. A political cartoon in the *New Orleans Times-Picayune* showed Evans and Simmons violently fighting beneath a Klan robe. The courts temporarily administered the affairs of the Klan. At the heart of the matter was Simmons's ownership of the rituals and regalia of the organization. He had wisely copyrighted the material back in 1915. The conflict had attracted national attention and it needed to be resolved.

An out-of-court settlement was finally reached on May 1, 1923. In return for his copyrights, Simmons received a lump sum payment of $145,000 ($1,800,000 in 2014 dollars). [34] A cartoon in the *Memphis Commercial Appeal* depicted a Klansman labeled "former Imperial Wizard Simmons" happily accepting $145,000 from the Klan Kashier. Simmons is quoted as saying "Thanks awfully, I'll quit" The caption reads, "The Ghost Walks."[35]

He did, indeed, walk. The colonel was forever banished from his Klan.

It had all started on the dark summit of Stone Mountain eight years earlier. Sixteen men on a rented travel bus had grown into an organization of nearly five million members found in every state of the union. It was a fraternity of men bound together by bigotry, hatred, and violence. Its influence now permeated nearly every aspect of American life.

A combination of zeal, ambition, and greed had changed the face of a nation.

CHAPTER 13
End Game

"All the world's a stage, and all the men and women merely players:
They have their exits and their entrances."
—William Shakespeare, *As You Like It*,
Act II, Scene VII

The 1922 Pulitzer Prize for Public Service went to the editorial staff of the *New York World* for articles exposing the operations of the Ku Klux Klan. No names were listed with the prize as the practice of the day did not include bylines. Rollin Kirby won the first-ever Pulitzer for Editorial Cartooning in 1922, but for his work in the "On the Road to Moscow"[1] series and not for his Klan cartoons.

Herbert Bayard Swope lived a spectacular and gregarious life in the days following the Klan series. He continued as executive editor of the *World,* running the paper in his creative, dynamic style. His fame was such that a smiling Swope appeared on the cover of *Time* magazine on January 28, 1924. He grew increasingly dissatisfied with Herbert Pulitzer's management of the paper, however, and resigned in 1928, never to work in journalism again.

He had no financial worries. Swope had become a multi-millionaire from stock tips provided by rich friends. His mansion on Long Island was home to legendary parties attended by the rich and the famous. "Land's End" boasted 20,000 square feet of living space, featuring fifteen bedrooms, fourteen baths, a seven-car garage, and a tennis pavilion, on its 13.35-acre grounds. Guest lists included the Duke and Duchess of Windsor, Harpo Marx, Winston Churchill, Albert Einstein, and

F. Scott Fitzgerald. In fact, it has been said that Fitzgerald used Swope's mansion as the model for Daisy Buchanan's home in *The Great Gatsby*.[2]

Swope lost much of his money in the stock market crash, but he continued his lavish lifestyle. As a journalist he often gambled—took risks—on new stories. As a man he simply loved to gamble. He was fired from an early newspaper job because he got involved in a marathon card game and never showed up to work. Swope began that game with $2 and left with over $6,000. Later in life his poker-playing partners included folks like oil magnate Harry Sinclair and movie mogul Sam Goldwyn. Swope's notes indicate he was an adept player, ending the year 1922 in the black to the tune of $188,758. The biggest poker game in Swope's life took place in Palm Beach, Florida, in 1923. In order to not be disturbed, the two-day game took place in a custom railroad car. Oil millionaire Joshua Cosdon lost over $433,000 in that game, while theatrical producer Flo Ziegfield walked away $294,000 poorer. Swope, the big winner, pocketed $470,300.

Swope's other passion was croquet. "The game gives release to all the evil in you," he said. "It makes you want to cheat and kill . . . It's a good game." His Long Island estate had one of the best courses in the country, complete with obstacles, sand traps, and lighting for night games. Harpo Marx was a regular player. Movie producer Darryl F. Zanuck was known as "the terrible tempered Mr. Bang" for his particular style of play. Swope limited his croquet wagers to $1,000 a game so that money would not get in the way of the fun.[3]

In 1929 Swope joined the board of directors of the RKO movie company, and made an unsuccessful attempt to buy the *New York World* in 1931 when the Pulitzers sold the newspaper. For the rest of his life Swope was known as a social celebrity, a public relations consultant, and a confidante of every president from Wilson to Truman. While working for Bernard Baruch on the United Nations Atomic Energy Commission in 1946, Swope coined the term "Cold War."

A 1931 dinner toast to Swope by Ralph Pulitzer demonstrates the wide affection for this singular character:

> *Now here's to Herbert Bayard Swope.*
> *God save the King. God help the Pope.*

And God protect the President
From this demure, retiring gent.
He taught George Rex to put his crown on,
Queen Mary how to put her gown on,
And David Windsor, Prince of Wales,
To fall from horses and for frails.
Explained just how to outmaneuver
Depressions to our Mr. Hoover;
And for the Pontiff, as a pal,
He's written his encyclical.
His lessons finished to Lenin, he
Gave castor oil to Mussolini;
And after multiple attempts he
Coached Tunney how to K.O. Dempsey;
Instructed Lindbergh how to fly,
And taught Munchhausen how to lie,
Trained Washington to tell the truth,
Perfected batting in Babe Ruth.
He fertilized the many ova
Unjustly claimed by Casanova;
And, last and loftiest feat, inspired
The peerless nerve of Herbert Bayard.[4]

Herbert Bayard Swope died on June 20, 1958, at his beloved Land's End. He was remembered as extroverted, gregarious, self-assured, egocentric, generous, and chronically late. David Sarnoff, Swope's employer at RCA and NBC, once made this comment: "Swope had enough initiative and enough brass so that if you wanted to meet God, he'd arrange it somehow."[5]

The fascinating and eclectic life of Henry Peck Fry continued after the publication of his *Modern Ku Klux Klan* in 1922. Immediately after his discharge from the Army in 1919 he had joined the Infantry Reserve as a captain. In 1923 he transferred to the Chemical Warfare Division of the Officers Reserve Corps, where he was soon promoted to major. He once said of this work, "It behooves every man in the country who is interested in military affairs to give the government as much time in study and training as possible, and help build up an efficient reserve corps for the national defense." Fry remained with the Chemical Warfare Division for twelve years. In April 1935 he was promoted to lieutenant colonel in the Inactive Reserve and then retired. In his 1956 obituary he is correctly referred to as Lieutenant Colonel Fry.

Between January 1922 and the end of 1928 Henry operated a publicity agency called the Independent Publicity Association. He was sponsored in this endeavor by Herbert Bayard Swope, his editor at the *New York World*. Fry's clients were fifteen editors and publishers of leading newspapers across the country. His agency provided articles written against the Klan and other groups bent on religious and racial hatred.

For much of the remainder of his life, Fry worked as a salesman. He sold books, encyclopedias, securities, advertising, and association memberships. He was also involved in the publishing industry.

In the meantime, Henry had developed an intense interest in the field of astrology. He claimed to have predicted the 1929 stock market crash, the death of Charles Lindbergh's baby, and Huey Long's assassination. Fry also prepared horoscopes for 1941 and 1942 for FDR, Wendell Wilkie, Hitler, Mussolini, King George VI, and Winston Churchill. With the aid of these horoscopes, he predicted that Roosevelt would die in office and that Hitler would defeat Great Britain.[6]

Rowland Thomas remained in the newspaper business, but not in New York City. In 1923 he accepted an invitation from an old friend and moved to Arkansas. While working with the education department in the Philippines in 1902, Thomas had made the acquaintance of Fred Heiskell, the secretary to Gov. Luke Wright. In 1923 Heiskell and his brother were the owners of one of the leading newspapers in the South, *The Arkansas Gazette*. Rowland joined the paper as associate editor and worked in that capacity until his death at sixty-five in May 1945.

In 1927 Thomas married a young journalism major from Louisiana State University, Ruth Harris, who was working on the *Gazette* staff. The couple moved to the country outside Little Rock and enjoyed their shared passion of bird watching. Rowland's obituary ended with this tribute:

Arkansas has suffered a great loss in the death of Rowland Thomas but it has profited much by his life. His long range foresight and vision, his ambitions and his tremendous pride in his adopted state will make him a living part of it. Those fortunate enough to have worked with him know of his reputation for facts, his love for truth, and his insistence for perfection.[7]

With its growing numbers, the Klan began to exert itself in the political arena. Representative Phillip Pitt Campbell would pay dearly for his relentless and aggressive questioning of Imperial Wizard Simmons during the House Rules Committee hearings in October 1921. The ten-term Republican from Kansas ran for re-election in November 1922 and lost in the party primary. He wasn't the only one. The *New York Times* ran a story after the November elections that year. The December 10 article contained the following headline, "SHADOW OF KU KLUX KLAN GROWS LARGER IN CONGRESS AND NATION." The sub headline followed, "Seventy-five members of the House reported elected by its vote—Well known legislators defeated." Campbell was one of them. The article continued:

Across the state line from Missouri is Kansas another state where, if reports are true, the "Invisible Empire" has been making great headway. Representative Phillip Campbell, Chairman of the House Committee on Rules, was head of the committee which investigated the Klan last year. He was badly defeated when he stood for re-nomination and will not be in the next Congress.[8]

Orin B. Strong, editor of the Klan-run *Mulberry* (KS) *Independent*, would later confirm that the Klan had joined with organized labor to defeat Campbell, saying many people felt the loss was a result of Campbell's involvement in the investigation of Klan activities.[9]

Campbell remained in the Republican Party and practiced law in Washington, D.C. He died on May 26, 1941. [10]

J. Q. continued to correspond with Bessie and Edward throughout 1924, but little was heard of J. Q. Jett after he left Atlanta and the Southern Publicity Association. The 1930 census listed his occupation as a house painter in Etowah, Tennessee.[11] J. Q. and his wife, Leastie, then returned to their Gilmer County, Georgia, roots and to the town of Ellijay sometime in 1936. There, John Quincy Jett died on October 30, 1937. The November 4 *Ellijay Times Courier* recorded it:

BURIAL SUNDAY FOR J.Q. JETT
WHO DIED FROM RIFLE WOUND

Carrying out his wishes that no funeral services be held, the body of J.Q. Jett who died instantly late Saturday afternoon as the result of a bullet wound in the heart, was laid to rest Sunday in Ellijay Cemetery. Mr. Jett's death was said to have been accidental, and happened while in the act of cleaning a 22-rifle he had borrowed from a neighbor to go hunting that day. Mrs. Jett was in an adjoining room, dressing to accompany Mr. Jett to the neighbor's home when the gun fired, and there was no eyewitness to the accident. The bullet, according to reports, struck him in the right lung and emerged over the heart. A former resident of this county, Mr. Jett and his family had lived for the past several years in Etowah, Tennessee, but came back to Ellijay about a year ago. Known here as a former official in the Ku Klux Klan, Mr. Jett was a man of strong convictions and freely expressed his views on any subject. He is survived by his wife, and 2 children, Mary and Arthur Jett.[12]

J. Q.'s life had ended as mysteriously as he had lived it.

William Joseph Simmons had been banished from the Ku Klux Klan, but he was not finished with the world of fraternal orders. When he left the Klan the colonel said, "Like General Lee at Appomattox, I had neither the men nor the munitions to carry on." He also rationalized that he had only sold insignificant copyrights to Evans, ones which had little to do with the sublime secret and essence of Klankraft. Simmons declared,

"It [Klankraft] is not a commodity of commercial traffic. It can neither be bought or sold . . . When I withdrew from the Klan organization (I can never retire from the REAL Klan), its SOUL departed from it."[13]

Simmons moved to Jacksonville, Florida, and made plans to start a new order. He still had followers in the Klan, and he organized a meeting with disgruntled Klansmen from twenty-five states. The result was an organization known as The Knights of the Flaming Sword. However, in the years since 1915, the colonel's organizational and administrative skills had not improved. The new organization was short lived. By 1926 Simmons had returned to Atlanta to form another ultra-right, ethnocentric society known as the White Band. At the same time he published a melodramatic account of his ordeal with the Klan entitled, *America's Menace, The Enemy Within*. Neither the White Band nor the book attracted much attention.

Simmons returned to his boyhood state of Alabama and spent nearly two decades in relative obscurity in the town of Luverne. He died, penniless, in May 1945 at the age of sixty-five.[14]

In March 1924 Bessie sent a telegram to J. Q. from California.

J.Q. JETT,
BEEN GRAVELY ILL MANY WEEKS...I REGARD
YOU AS MY OWN SON. LOVE TO ALL.

MOTHER.[15]

Bessie had relocated to California to care for her ill daughter, but now she was the one who was sick.

At 7:45 a.m. on September 10, 1924, Bessie died at the age of forty-three. Her Los Angeles County Death Certificate incorrectly listed her birth year as 1887 and her age as thirty-seven. It was perhaps a typographical error. Death came at a home on Strand Street in Hermosa Beach. There is no information on why Bessie was at this beachside house. She and Stephan's home address was 2051 Foothill Boulevard in Altadena.

The cause of death was listed as "apoplexy," an old-fashioned term referring to a stroke or a cerebral hemorrhage. Dr. J. F. Spencer indicated that he had been treating Bessie since September 7 and had last seen her alive on the 9th.

The certificate stated that Bessie was suffering from advancing arteriosclerosis, or hardening of the arteries, the symptoms of which could have caused her to be "gravely ill."

That same day, the *Los Angeles Times* reported the death of Elizabeth Tyler Grow in Altadena, California. It was a very short article, but it did tie Bessie to her Klan connections.[16] She was buried at the nearby Inglewood Park Cemetery as Mary Elizabeth Cornett Tyler Grow.

There is no mention of what happened to Bessie's money.

The National Registry of Historic Places has traced the history of Bessie's Howell Mill Road mansion. On July 7, 1924, two months before Bessie's death, Minnie gave the house to Edward. On her deathbed, Bessie may have wanted the mansion to go to Edward. The original purchase was probably handled through Clarke Realty and Edward's name was likely on the deed.

Clarke quickly defaulted on the mortgage. The home was eventually sold on the courthouse steps of Fulton County for $3,000, a fraction of the property's value, to a C. B. Davis in November 1925. Davis immediately sold a quit claim deed to a M. W. Lamar of Dade County, Florida. C. B. Davis was one of the names listed as owners of Gate City Manufacturing, the company which provided robes and regalia to the Klan. Davis and his wife, Lottie, were widely thought to be aliases for Edward and Bessie. It's possible that Edward repurchased the Howell Mill Road estate at an extremely low price and then sold it for a significant profit.[17]

Minnie's tuberculosis treatments seemed to work. A year after Bessie's death, in November 1925, she married her mother's former husband, Stephen Grow. Documents indicate they were husband and wife until at least 1935. In 1939 Minnie Doris married for a third time to a California rancher named George Frame. He was a much older man who died in 1966. She passed away a year later in 1967 at age seventy and was buried in the same cemetery as her mother.

Edward returned from his self-imposed exile in late 1923, pled guilty to the Mann Act charge, and paid a $5,000 fine. In a last ditch effort to regain control, Clarke called for a National Congress of the Klan to meet in Atlanta on February 26, 1924. The express purpose was to discuss methods of eliminating evils in the order. This, of course, was aimed directly at Hiram Evans. Clarke announced that he expected hundreds of thousands of magnificent men at the conclave. Only 150 showed up.

Instead of working from within the Klan, Edward persuaded that small core of believers to form a new group, the Knights of the Mystic Clan.[18] In a May 16, 1924, letter to J. Q. Edward talked about this new money-making scheme.

> *Dear Quincy:*
>
> *I am sorry you have not been with us the past few days as things are surely getting into fine shape for the building of the big organization which you and I discussed. I have finally gotten together about thirty of the biggest businessmen in Atlanta, and they have agreed to put up an expense fund of $50,000 for the launching of the movement, and I am working night and day on the details of the organization and the literature, and expect to be going full blast by the first of June. I expect I will want you down here about that time. Keep your shirt on your back and expect big things and you won't be disappointed.*

Then Edward injected a bit of levity. Apparently he had a reputation as an idea man and not a worker.

> *I am actually spending six or eight hours per day at the office. What do you think of that?[19]*

The name of the new group was soon changed to the Mystic Kingdom. It is not known if J. Q. became a part of the organization. Edward claimed the Kingdom would "weld together the Protestant White people of the world into a universal movement for the furtherance of the faith and the preservation of racial integrity." He stated a membership of 5,000 and made grandiose promises to build a $1 million maternity hospital in Atlanta and a $2 million narcotics sanitarium in Chicago.

When the Mystic Kingdom began to fail, Clarke saw an opportunity to capitalize on the 1925 Scopes Monkey Trial in Dayton, Tennessee. He formed a new group called the Supreme Kingdom. Its goal was to drive the teaching of evolution out of every school and college in the country. He announced a $5 million fund drive and opened his group to Jews and Catholics. Membership fees went to a separate entity, the Organization Service Company. Edward was president and his latest female companion, Martha Mason, was listed as secretary.

In 1932 E. Y. and his now-wife, Martha, resurfaced in Chicago at the head of the new organization Esskaye (the first letters in Supreme Kingdom).

Clarke finally ran afoul of the law. The Illinois Securities Commission began investigating phony Esskaye contracts. On May 4, 1934, E. Y. Clarke and Martha Mason Clarke were convicted in U.S. District Court on six of seven counts charging use of the mails to defraud. Edward was sentenced to five years in the Atlanta Penitentiary and his wife to two years in a women's prison.[20]

Edward was eventually paroled and next appeared in 1942. World War II required all able-bodied American men to register for the draft. Clarke's card showed his residence then as 5130 S. University Avenue in Chicago's Hyde Park neighborhood. His employer was listed as the Greater American Corporation at 109 N. Dearborn. He was sixty-four years old.[21]

There is one last mention of E. Y. Clarke Jr. He had apparently returned to his conniving and defrauding ways and had violated the terms of his parole from the 1935 conviction. Clarke was being escorted from New York back to the Atlanta Penitentiary on March 25, 1949, when he escaped from his parole supervisor at a Philadelphia train station. Edward was seventy-three years old.[22]

He was never heard from again.

It is difficult to stop a runaway train.

Under the leadership of Hiram Evans, Klan numbers continued to multiply at an unprecedented rate.

With all opponents vanquished, Evans began repairing the Klan's tarnished image. The organization Edward and Bessie created was still in place. He immediately put the individual kleagles on a salary rather than a commission basis. The hope was that a closer screening of candidates would improve the quality of the general membership. Evans also restricted the wearing of robes to regular chapter meetings. In addition, the new Imperial Wizard announced that Klan initiatives would be advanced through political actions. Any Klansman participating in lawless activities would be immediately banished from the organization. Simmons had talked this talk, but he had never taken serious action.

Evans targeted his core constituency and positioned the Klan as a champion of education, temperance, the flag, Protestantism, morality, and charity. The Klan believed in old-time religion, rejected the teaching of evolution, and held that the Bible was the one and only true word of God.

The main target was "Demon Rum." The Eighteenth Amendment had outlawed liquor, but the Volstead Act was woefully inadequate in enforcing the law. Fundamentalist, rural Christians were shocked with Roaring Twenties images of women in short skirts dancing in smoke-filled rooms. This was a reaction to a modern world moving too fast and in all the wrong directions. The Klan came out steadfastly against gambling, prostitution, bootleggers, moonshiners, and wild women. Catholics continued to be painted as un-American and associated with big-city evils. A Klan pamphlet from this time summed up the message:

> *Every criminal, every gambler, every thug, every libertine, every girl ruiner, every home wrecker, every wife beater, every dope peddler, every moonshiner, every crooked politician, every pagan Papist priest, every shyster lawyer, every K. of C., every white slaver, every brothel madam, every Rome controlled newspaper,—is fighting the Klan. Think it over. Which side are you on?*

The Klan also stood squarely behind the public school system, calling it the "cornerstone of good governance and the secret of our prosperity as a nation." They advocated the reading of the Bible in every classroom.[23]

Klan messages of the virtues of motherhood, chastity, temperance, clean motion pictures, and decent literature appealed strongly to women. Many became great allies of the organization, some joining Klan auxiliaries, others endorsing their husband's participation.

The momentum built by Edward and Bessie continued at a never dreamed of pace. By 1925 it is estimated that Klan membership had reached between 3,000,000 and 5,000,000. Of that total nearly 500,000 were women. Bessie's Women's Klan, the WKKK, had finally materialized. A quarter to a third of all eligible men in the United States belonged to the Klan. Six months after Herbert Bayard Swope's appearance on *Time's* cover, Hiram Wesley Evans took his turn on the lead page of the influential news magazine.

The most searing images of this time are photos of over 40,000 robed Klansmen parading down Pennsylvania Avenue in Washington, D.C., on August 8, 1925. Famed newspaperman H. L. Mencken was there to observe:

> *The parade was grander and gaudier by far than anything the wizards had prophesied. It was longer, it was thicker, it was higher in tone. I stood in front of the Treasury for two hours watching the legions pass. They marched in lines of eighteen to twenty, solidly shoulder to shoulder. I retired for refreshment and was gone an hour. When I got back Pennsylvania Ave. was still a mass of white from the Treasury to the foot of Capitol Hill—a full mile of Klansmen.*[24]

Incidents of Klan violence grew along with the increasing membership.

Evans's goal of influencing America through political action gained considerable traction in the early twenties. Klan-friendly governors were elected in twelve states, and Texan Earle Mayfield, called the Klan candidate, was elected in 1922 to the United States Senate. The Invisible Empire controlled the state legislatures in many states, most notably in Indiana, Oklahoma, Oregon, and Texas. Evans's ally in the Simmons coup, D. C. Stephenson, had been rewarded with the title of Grand Dragon of Indiana and twenty-two other northern states. Under his leadership Klan membership in Indiana would exceed 250,000 and control almost every aspect of life in that Midwestern state.[25]

The Klan, and Evans, boasted of influencing the 1924 presidential election in favor of Republican Calvin Coolidge. The Democratic National Convention that year was a highly contentious affair. Evans had two objectives at that convention. He wanted to thwart the nomination of Al Smith and defeat a plank in the party platform condemning Klan violence. He won on both counts. Smith was a big-city Catholic and a vocal critic of Prohibition. Evans's backing went to Klan-friendly Californian William McAdoo.

A chaotic convention nominated compromise candidate John Davis on the 103rd ballot. The Democratic Party was fractured as a result, and many party members fled to liberal third-party candidate Robert La Follette. Conservative Republican Cal Coolidge won in a landslide.

When the Klan violence plank was defeated, 20,000 hooded Klansmen met in a New Jersey field across from the Convention headquarters. The gathering was known as the "Klanbake." Speakers urged violence against blacks and Catholics, and attacked effigies of Al Smith.[26]

The year 1925 would prove to be the high-water mark for the Klan. When the organization called for another march in Washington, D.C., in 1926, only half the members could be mobilized. By 1927 national membership had dwindled to 350,000. By the end of the decade, estimated Klan membership stood at around 5,000.

There are a number of reasons for the precipitous decline. Many Americans were repulsed by growing reports of violence attributed to the Klan. There were also more exposés in newspapers of financial misappropriation among Klan executives. The stock market crash and the onset of the Great Depression dried up dollars once spent on initiation, dues, and regalia. And, there were front-page scandals involving Klan leaders. The most devastating to the Klan image involved Indiana's D. C. Stephenson. The man who once declared "I am the law in Indiana" stood trial in 1925 for murder.

Stephenson, a declared Prohibitionist and a defender of Protestant womanhood, was charged with the abduction, forced intoxication, rape, and subsequent death of Madge Oberholtzer. He had met the young woman, given her enough alcohol to render her unconscious, and savagely raped her on a train bound for Chicago. Among the alleged atrocities was that Stephenson had bitten the woman so many times that one person who saw her described her appearance as if having been "chewed by an animal." Unable to free herself from her abductor, Oberholtzer attempted suicide by swallowing poison. Stephenson had his bodyguards drive the woman to her parents' home. They called for medical help, but she died ten days later. Stephenson was convicted and sentenced to life in prison. He expected his Klan-controlled Indiana governor to commute his sentence. When that did not happen, Stephenson released a list of all public officials in Indiana who were on the Klan payroll. The national moral outrage caused members to disavow the organization on a grand scale.[27]

Hiram Evans remained at the head of the Klan until 1939, when he was succeeded by James A. Colescott. He died in Atlanta in 1966 at the age of eighty-four.

The Klan did not die. Hatred and bigotry never really go away for good. There were still reports of hate-based beatings, of intimidations, and of lynchings throughout the middle decades of the twentieth century, much of it attributed to Klan members. And then, a new threat to white America caused membership to swell once more—the 1954 Supreme Court decision of *Brown v. Board of Education* ended the practice of separate but equal segregation in America and ushered in the modern civil rights movement.

At the time of Rosa Parks's famous arrest, the Klan was alleged to have been involved in the 1956 bombing of Martin Luther King Jr.'s Montgomery home. In 1961 Klansmen were part of mobs that savagely beat Freedom Riders in Anniston, Birmingham, and Montgomery, Alabama. On September 15, 1963, four Klansmen planted a box of dynamite under the steps of the 16th Street Baptist Church in Birmingham. Four young girls died in the explosion. In May 1964 three young civil rights workers, James Chaney, Andrew Goodman, and Michael Schwerner, were brutally abducted and murdered near Philadelphia, Mississippi, by local Klansmen. As African Americans sought civil rights and social equality, the Klan responded with dozens of bombings, arsons, and murders.[28]

The Klan exists to this day. Its numbers are small and the organization is decentralized. The Southern Poverty Law Center, a nonprofit civil rights organization dedicated to fighting hate and bigotry, based in Montgomery, Alabama, estimates Klan members nationally at fewer than 5,000 in 2012.[29]

Would there be a Klan today without Edward Young Clarke and Bessie Tyler? Would twentieth-century history look quite different if the two Atlanta promoters had just stuck with their mainstream clients?

The early 1920s were certainly ripe for the exploitation of hate. The ground was especially fertile then for the growth of an organization based on white fear. Still, there is the "What if?" factor in this story. What if J. Q. Jett had never answered the Colonel's ad? What if Clarke and Tyler decided not to pursue the Klan?

Historian and public relations professor Scott Cutlip made this comment on Clarke and Tyler: "What did flow from their skills and efforts to enrich themselves remains forever a discredit to them and to the vocation of which they were a part. This is a dark side of public relations history."[30]

Edward and Bessie were innovative and groundbreaking communications professionals in many ways. They were exceptional at what they did. The roster of strategies they employed on behalf of the Klan could serve as a PR playbook. Their story in the end is more than a tale of shocking deceit, ambition, and greed. It's a reminder about the importance of morality, ethics, and standards of professionalism, and the power of the choices we make in our work and civic activities.

EPILOGUE

On December 13, 1919, only six weeks after Edward and Bessie's scandalous, alcohol-fueled, partially-clad arrest in downtown Atlanta, a slightly built, dark-haired, five-foot, two-inch tall man quietly entered Boston City Hall. His coat was threadbare, but his bearing was regal. With the aid of a clerk, he filled out paperwork declaring he would do business as the International Security Company. The fee for this transaction was the princely sum of fifty cents. Two weeks later, on the day after Christmas, the man returned. For an additional fifty cents he changed the name of his new venture to the Security Exchange Company.[1]

With that, Charles Ponzi began to build a spectacular financial empire.

Ponzi found in 1920, as had Bessie and Edward, a nation ripe for the picking. The Roaring Twenties would prove to be a decade unlike any other in American history. World War I had changed everything. It had pulled a sleeping giant of a country from its traditional and idealistic roots and thrust it into the bright lights of a bustling, modern world. There was a loosening of age-old moralities and a growing sense of cynicism. There was also a driving desire for immediate gratification and the dream of getting rich quick.

History has always been populated by con men willing to take money from unsuspecting and gullible targets. However, the modern marketing techniques and the emerging communications technologies of the early twentieth century made the swindle possible on a scale never before seen. As such, there are many eerie similarities between the stories of Charles Ponzi, and Clarke and Tyler.

Charles Ponzi possessed a shrewd financial mind and a history of fraudulent activities. An avid stamp collector, he had discovered an investment vehicle called international reply coupons, or IRCs. In 1906 the United States and representatives of sixty-two other countries met in Rome to devise a way to make it easier to send mail across national borders. The IRCs they created could be redeemed for stamps in any country. For example, a coupon purchased for an American dollar in New York yielded a dollar's worth of French stamps in Paris. IRCs worked in 1906, but not in the post–WWI world where many countries struggled with devastated economies and wildly devalued currencies. Ponzi figured he could buy coupons in war-torn Italy and redeem them in the United States,[2] making a tidy profit—shrewd *and* legal.

In theory the plan could have worked, but Charles Ponzi never purchased an IRC with his own money. It would have required capital he did not possess. Instead he began soliciting investors. Each certificate issued stated:

> *The Securities Exchange Company, for and in consideration of the sum of (amount invested) dollars, receipt of which is hereby acknowledged, agrees to pay to the order of (investor's name), upon presentation of this voucher at ninety days from date, the sum of (invested amount plus 50 per cent) at the Company's office, 27 School Street, Room 227, or at any bank.*
>
> The Securities Exchange Company
Per Charles Ponzi[3]

In reality, Ponzi never purchased an IRC for his clients. As word of this incredible fifty percent return spread, people flocked to hand the "investment genius" their money. Ponzi then used that money to pay off the original investors. This worked beautifully as long as the base continued to grow. Ponzi knew it would. He later said, "We are all gamblers. . . . We all crave easy money. And plenty of it. If we didn't, no get-rich-quick scheme could be successful."[4]

This classic Peter-to-Paul scheme grew exponentially. In the early months of 1920 the dollars came in small amounts. In April, Ponzi collected $140,000. In June of that year, when Bessie and Edward signed their contract with Imperial Wizard Simmons, his total was up to $2.5

million. By the end of July, only eight months after Ponzi paid his half dollar registration fee, the Securities Exchange Company had collected nearly $9.6 million ($105 million in 2014 dollars). Ponzi lived a lavish lifestyle funded by his adoring investors.

Ponzi's eventual rise and fall was fueled by public relations and journalism, much as Bessie and Edward's had been. The early days of the scheme relied heavily on word of mouth recommendations. Happy investors told their friends about the venture. Ponzi made sure his personal image showed wealth and success. Soon Boston newspaper reporters filed positive stories about the dapper financier with the impressive mansion and the expensive cars. Each report brought more investors. Bessie and Edward often manipulated the press, using the newspapers as a form of free advertising. As seen in the *New York World*'s coverage of the Klan, even negative stories increased business.

The *Boston Post* was among the papers that praised the little businessman in the early days of 1920. The *Post* was owned and edited by Edwin Atkins Grozier, who had learned the newspaper business through six exhausting years as the personal secretary to Joseph Pulitzer. At age twenty-eight he became city editor of the *World*, and later editor in chief and business manager of the *Evening World* and the *Sunday World*.

Grozier's dream, however, was owning his own newspaper. That opportunity came with the struggling *Boston Post*. The purchase exhausted Edwin's personal savings and the paper teetered on the brink of failure as it was getting back off the ground. But Edwin had learned well from his former employer. He reduced the paper's price from three cents to a penny. Grozier supported the Democratic Party and targeted the surging Irish Catholic population of the city. Grisly crime stories were featured on page one, especially the sensational Lizzie Borden murders. Nearly every week brought a new promotion. The *Post* sponsored a children's fundraiser to purchase three elephants for the zoo; it gave away Ford Model Ts, hired a talent agent to look for beautiful women, and gave an engraved cane to the oldest man in each city in New England. In a "primitive man" stunt, Grozier sent a man named Joe Knowles into the Maine woods, naked and empty handed for sixty days. Throughout those two months the *Post* carried dispatches and drawings from Knowles done with charcoal on birch bark and left at prearranged drop points. When Knowles emerged from the woods wearing deerskin and carrying cave-man tools, 400,000 people lined Boston's Washington Street to greet him. The *Post's* circulation doubled that year. Grozier's newspaper became the leading daily in Boston, surpassing even the formidable *Globe*. In fact, the *Post* even out sold Pulitzer's *World*.[5]

Edwin Grozier tried to emulate his mentor in every way. In the spring of 1920 eighteen- to twenty-hour work days took their toll. Never in robust health, he suffered a complete physical breakdown and was put in intensive care. Who would run the *Post*? Grozier's managing editor was away for the summer. The job fell to the *Post's* assistant publisher and assistant editor, Edwin's thirty-two-year-old son, Richard.

Richard Grozier had been a bit of a disappointment to his hard-driving father. He attended Harvard but had seldom studied, preferring instead the life of a young wealthy partier. Eventually he dropped out. Joseph Pulitzer had a similar experience. Two of his sons had done poorly at Harvard, and Joseph Jr. had been expelled. Richard, on the other hand, *had* observed and learned working under his father. This would be his great opportunity.

He had not succumbed to the frenzy surrounding Charles Ponzi and believed his investment guarantees must have been too good to be true. Grozier immediately put members of the reporting staff on the story.

On July 23, 1920, Ponzi hired a publicity man. With the growing demands of press and public, the move seemed a good one. The man recommended to him was William McMasters. McMasters was a PR professional well versed in the Boston scene. He had worked on the successful mayoral campaigns of John "Honey Fitz" Fitzgerald and James Michael Curley. ("Honey Fitz" was the father of Rose Kennedy and the maternal grandfather of John, Bobby, and Ted Kennedy. Curley was a longtime Massachusetts politician who was succeeded in the U.S. House in 1948 by a young John F. Kennedy.) McMasters had also helped Calvin Coolidge become Massachusetts governor in 1918.[6]

And McMasters had been a reporter for the *Boston Post*.

The move paid immediate dividends. That same day, the 23rd, brought a *Post* reporter for an interview. He spent the day with Ponzi at his office on School Street and at his home in Lexington. The next day's edition featured the following headline:

Doubles the Money Within Three Months
50 Per Cent Interest Paid in 45 Days by Ponzi—
Has Thousands of Investors
Deals in International Coupons Taking Advantage
of Low Rates of Exchange

The article glowed about Ponzi and his success and claimed "authorities have not been able to discover a single illegal thing about it." The story told how the investors "have seen their money doubled, trebled, and quadrupled," and that Ponzi had begun on a shoestring and "is today rated as worth $8,500,000." The story brought new droves of investors to the Security Exchange Company offices.

Richard Grozier released his next salvo. He enlisted the aid of financial genius Clarence Barron, the owner of the *Wall Street Journal* and its parent, Dow Jones & Company. Barron was highly skeptical of Ponzi's operation. On Thursday the young acting publisher delivered his first editorial under the headline, "IT CANNOT LAST." He asked, "Is Mr. Ponzi the wizard of the foreign exchange market . . . or is he running an old game under a new guise?" Richard was careful to avoid libel, as Ponzi was notoriously litigious.

Meanwhile, William McMasters had quickly gained his new employer's confidence. On Sunday, August 1, Ponzi was glowing over the afternoon he had just spent at the Lexington house with a crew of movie men from the Fox Film Company, more publicity presumably set up by McMasters. Earlier that day the *Boston Herald* had run a highly complimentary story.

But the night of July 31, McMasters had phoned Richard Grozier at the *Post*.

After only eight days on the job, William McMasters was ready to turn on his boss. He later said he first started doubting Ponzi's scheme as he accompanied his employer to meetings with investors. The message seemed to change daily, and the PR man sniffed a fraud. He began searching the School Street office looking for evidence of wrongdoing. Grozier was very interested. On Monday, August 2, the *Post's* page one declared:

DECLARES PONZI IS NOW HOPELESSLY INSOLVENT

Publicity Expert Employed by "Wizard" Says He Has Not Sufficient Funds to Meet His Notes— States He Has Sent No Money to Europe nor Received Money from Europe Recently

The story, written under McMasters's byline, provided considerable detail into the Ponzi operation. When asked why he did it, McMasters gave an altruistic response, "As a publicity man, my first duty is to the public." [7]

The final nail in Ponzi's coffin came when *Post* background investigations discovered his prior arrests for fraud in Montreal and Georgia under various aliases. The financial empire crumbled, and Ponzi would spend jail time in state and federal prisons. When released, the federal government deported Ponzi to Italy. He had never obtained U.S. citizenship.

Richard Grozier had earned his stripes. The *Boston Post* received the 1921 Pulitzer Prize.

Lost in the details of Ponzi's downfall was the fact that William McMasters had been paid $6,000 for his story. [8] In 2014 dollars that amount is the equivalent of nearly $65,000. In the light of revelations about the role of Henry Peck Fry in the *World*'s Klan story, should we wonder if McMasters's noble assertion is genuine? Or was he opportunistically profiting from an eroding situation and saving his reputation? There is another possibility. As a former *Post* reporter, was McMasters planted in the Ponzi organization by Grozier?

Don't kill the messenger—the concept is not a new one. The theme has appeared over the centuries in literary works by Shakespeare, Sophocles, and Plutarch. In early history the messenger was an essential communication tool used to deliver important news between cities and governments. They were a conduit, trusted with transmitting the message as it was given. If they were the bearers of bad news, they certainly did not want to be blamed for the details.

In twentieth-century America this was all changing. The lines were becoming fuzzy. The art of communications was increasingly sophisticated and often manipulative, with new modern twists all the time. The emerging disciplines of advertising, marketing, and public relations were developing powerful methods to sell products and ideas to the public. In the days before radio and television, the newspaper played a vital role in these messages, and there was a constant tension in the paper–reader relationship. Was the paper simply a transmitter of carefully crafted self-serving ideas, or was it a public sentinel forever seeking truth? Underlying everything was the motive of increased profits with increased readership.

Edward and Bessie were masters at controlling the message. They were able to mold the Klan into a product palatable to a carefully identified marketplace. Charles Ponzi tapped into the most basic human instinct—greed. As long as he delivered on his promises, people cared little about his methods. In fact, several of the reporters and pressmen of the *Boston Globe* were among his many adoring investors.

And what of the roles of Swope and Grozier? Had they merely reported stories or did they have a hand in creating them? Were they like Roman tribunes guarding the rights of the public, or were they businessmen watching the bottom line? Or both?

In the early 1960s communications visionary Marshall McLuhan sounded a warning in his book *Understanding Media*. In it he presented his famous "the medium is the message." McLuhan observed a blurring between the medium and the message, noting how a medium influences how a message is ultimately perceived. He said, "The content of a medium is like a juicy piece of meat carried by the burglar to distract the watchdog of the mind." [9]

History tells us there will always be people quite willing to relieve others of their nest eggs. Seventy years after Charles Ponzi's arrest, asset manager Bernie Madoff recreated the infamous scheme to perpetrate the largest financial fraud in U.S. history. So skillful was Madoff that he was able to dupe his investors for nearly twenty-five years. The amount missing from client accounts totaled nearly 65 billion dollars.

With new technologies come greater opportunities to communicate, to persuade...and to mislead. Beneath the shiny red fruit may very well be the barbed hook Vance Packard warned us about. If there is a lesson to be learned it is that we need to consider each message carefully—as well as its messenger.

NOTES

Prologue

1. United States Weather Bureau Archives, 25 November 1915.
2. *Atlanta Constitution,* 25 November 1915.
3. Scott M. Cutlip, *The Unseen Power: Public Relations, a History* (Hinsdale, NJ: Routledge, 1994), 372.
4. L.A. Herrmann, "Geology of the Stone Mountain–Lithonia District, Georgia," *Georgia Geological Survey Bulletin* 61.
5. "Land & Resources, Stone Mountain," New Georgia Encyclopedia, http://www.georgiaencyclopedia.org.
6. "Attractions," Stone Mountain Park, http://www.stonemountainpark.com.
7. "Park History," Stone Mountain Memorial Association, http://www.stonemountainpark.org.
8. Cutlip, 376.

Chapter 1: True Believer

1. Charles O. Jackson, "William J. Simmons: A Career in KuKluxism," *Georgia Historical Quarterly,* vol. 50 (December 1966): 352.
2. *New York World,* 1897.
3. Donald A. Ritchie, *American History: The Modern Era Since 1865* (New York: Glencoe/McGraw Hill, 1997), 376–378.
4. Patrick McSherry, "A Brief History of the 1st Alabama Volunteer Infantry," The Spanish American War Centennial Website, http://www.spanamwar.com/1stAlabama.html.
5. Cutlip, 374.
6. Charles Elliott, *A History of the Great Secession from the Methodist Episcopal Church in the year 1845* (Cincinnati: Swormstedt and Poe, 1855).
7. Gross Alexander, *A History of the Methodist Church South in the United States* (Nashville: Publishing House of the M.E. Church, South, 1907), 110.
8. Ibid., 133.

9. David M. Chalmers, *Hooded Americanism: The First Century of the Ku Klux Klan 1865 to Present* (Garden City, NY: Doubleday & Co. Inc., 1965), 29.
10. Charles O. Jackson, 352.
11. Chalmers, 28.
12. Michael Newton, *The Ku Klux Klan: History, Organization, Language, Influence and Activities of America's Most Notorious Secret Society* (Jefferson City, NC: McFarland & Co. Inc., 2007), 6.
13. Ibid., 7.
14. Ibid., 14.
15. Ibid., 8.
16. Ibid., 9.
17. Jeffrey D. Wert, *Custer: The Controversial Life of George Armstrong Custer* (New York Simon and Shuster, 1996), 295.
18. Alvin Schmidt, *The Greenwood Encyclopedia of American Institutions: Fraternal Organizations* (Westport, CT: Greenwood Press, 1980), 3.
19. Ibid., 24–363.
20. Alexis De Tocqueville, *Democracy in America* (London: Saunders and Otley, 1838), 106.
21. Schmidt, 4.
22. Ibid., 16–17.
23. Ibid., 355.
24. "Woodmen Group," The Phoenixmasonry Masonic Museum and Library, http://www.phoenixmasonry.org./masonicmuseum/fraternalism/woodmen.htm.
25. Newton, 13.
26. Ibid.
27. Kenneth T. Jackson, *The Ku Klux Klan in the City, 1915–1930* (New York: Concord University Press, 1967), 6.
28. Newton, 13.
29. Steve Oney, *And the Dead Shall Rise* (New York: Pantheon Books, 2003), 3.
30. Ibid., 6.
31. Leonard Dinnerstein, *The Leo Frank Case* (New York: Columbia University Press, 1968), 2.
32. Oney, 10.
33. Ibid., 467.
34. Dinnerstein, 126.
35. Ibid., 139–140.
36. Ibid., 143.
37. Cutlip, 375.
38. Richard Schickel, *Griffith: An American Life* (New York: Simon and Shuster, 1984), 17–19.
39. David Wark Griffith, *The Man Who Invented Hollywood: The Autobiography of D. W. Griffith,* Edited by James Hart (Louisville: Touchstone Publishing Co., 1972), 24.

40. Schickel, 20–23.
41. Ibid., 24.
42. Ibid., 31.
43. Griffith, 49.
44. Schickel, 98.
45. Frank Capra in Griffith Foreword, vii, viii.
46. Griffith, 94.
47. Ibid., 74.
48. Edward Wagenknecht and Anthony Slide, *The Films of D. W. Griffith* (New York: Crown Publishers, Inc., 1975), 1.
49. Schickel, 192.
50. Ibid., 15.
51. Griffith, 89.
52. Wagenknecht, 60.
53. *Atlanta Journal*, 7 December 1915.
54. Cutlip, 377.
55. Robert L. Duffus, "Salesmen of Hate: The Ku Klux Klan," *World's Work*, vol.42 (October 1923): 33.

Chapter 2: Flim-Flam Man

1. Meredith Willson, *The Music Man*, opening scene.
2. Edgar I. Fuller, *The Visible of the Invisible Empire: The Maelstrom* (Denver: Maelstrom Publishing Co., 1925), 16.
3. Philip B. Kunhardt, Jr., *P. T. Barnum: America's Greatest Showman* (New York: Alfred A. Knopf Inc., 1995), vi.
4. Ibid., 4.
5. Ibid., 10–11.
6. Ibid., 20.
7. Ibid., 34.
8. Ibid., 53.
9. Cutlip, 379.
10. Megan Kate Nelson, *Trembling Earth: A Cultural History of the Okefenokee Swamp* (Athens, GA: University of Georgia Press, 2005), 80.
11. Tim Jeal, *Stanley: The Impossible Life of Africa's Greatest Explorer* (New Haven, CT: Yale University Press, 2007), 31.
12. Ibid., 46–48.
13. Ibid., 69–76.
14. Ibid., 99.
15. Ibid., 116.
16. Nelson, 82.
17. Ibid., 2.
18. Okefenokee Swamp Home Page, http://www.okefenokee.com.

19. Nelson, 83.
20. Ibid., 83–86.
21. Ibid., 86.
22. *Atlanta Constitution*, 7 September 1876.
23. Chalmers, 31.
24. Cutlip, 379.
25. *Atlanta Constitution*, 6 December 1903.
26. Fuller, 16.
27. Duffus, 34.
28. Cutlip, 380.
29. *Atlanta Constitution*, 22 April 1910.
30. Cutlip, 380.
31. *Atlanta Constitution*, November 1915.
32. Ibid.
33. Cutlip, 380.

Chapter 3: On Her Own

1. United States Census, 1890.
2. Grey House Publishing, *Working Americans: 1880–1999*, Vol. 1, *The Working Class* (Millerton, NY: Grey House Publishing, 2000), 22.
3. "Education," New Georgia Encyclopedia, http://www.georgiaencyclopedia.org/Education.
4. Department of Education for Georgia, *1898 Annual Report*.
5. U.S. Census, 1900.
6. Cutlip, 379.
7. U.S. Census, 1900.
8. Eastern Cherokee Claim #27076, 29 June 1907.
9. Chalmers, 31.
10. *Atlanta Constitution*, 17 July 1913.
11. Ibid.
12. Duffus, 35.
13. Annette K. Dorey, *Better Baby Contests: The Scientific Quest for Perfect Childhood Health in the Early Twentieth Century* (Jefferson, NC: McFarland & Co., 1999), 11.
14. Ibid., 13.
15. Ibid., 31.
16. Ibid., 25.
17. Ibid., 111.
18. David Starr Jordan, *The Blood of the Nation* (Boston: American Unitarian Association, 1902).
19. Dorey, 92.

Chapter 4: An Association

1. Fuller, 18.
2. Cutlip, 380.
3. *New York World*, 19 September 1921.
4. K.S. Miller, "U.S. Public Relations History: Knowledge and Limitations," *Communications Yearbook*, vol. 23: 381–420.
5. "Dr. James Wideman Lee, Sr.," Find a Grave, http://www.findagrave.com.
6. Ivy L. Lee Papers, Princeton University Digital Library, http://pudl.princeton.edu.
7. James Sage Jenkins, *Atlanta in the Age of Pericles* (Lithonia, GA: Chimney Hill Press, 1995), 68–70.
8. John N. Ingham, "Ivy Lee," *Biographical Dictionary of American Business Leaders* (Westport, CT: Greenwood Publishing Group, 1983).
9. George Creel, *Rebel at Large: Recollections of Fifty Crowded Years* (New York: G. P. Putnam and Sons, 1947), 195–196.
10. Thomas Fleming, *The Illusion of Victory: America in World War 1* (New York: Basic Books, 2003), 117.
11. Cutlip, 381.
12. Ibid., 381.
13. Ernest Hurst, ed., *The Anti-Saloon League Year Book 1919: An Encyclopedia of Facts and Figures Dealing with the Liquor Traffic and Temperance Reform* (Columbus, Ohio: The Anti-Saloon League of America, 1919).
14. Anti-Saloon League Museum, Westerville (Ohio) Public Library, http://www.wpl.lib.oh.us/AntiSaloon/.
15. "American Issue Publishing Company," Alcohol: Problems and Solutions, http://www2.potsdam.edu/hansondj/Controversies/American-Issue-Publishing-Company.html#.Ut1ZpBDnaM8.
16. Cutlip, 381.
17. Ibid., 405.

Chapter 5: Contract with the Devil

1. Duffus, 33.
2. Cutlip, 377–378.
3. Duffus, 35.
4. Katherine M. Blee, *Women in the Klan: Racism and Gender in the 1920s* (Berkeley: University of California Press, 1991), 20.
5. United States Congress House Committee on Rules, *Hearings before the Committee on Rules on the Ku Klux Klan, 1921* (New York: Arno Press, 1969), Exhibit E, 111.
6. Cutlip, 381.

7. Duffus, 36.
8. Henry Peck Fry, *The Modern Ku Klux Klan* (Boston: Small, Maynard & Company, 1922), 23
9. "Direct Selling Methods: Single Level and Multilevel Marketing," More Business, http://www.morebusiness.com.

Chapter 6: Fertile Ground

1. "Jim Crow Laws," University of Dayton, http://www.academic.udayton.edu/race/02rights/jcrow02.html.
2. "What Was Jim Crow?" Ferris State University, http://www.Ferris.edu/Jim-Crow.
3. "Plessy v. Ferguson," Infoplease, http://www.infoplease.com.
4. "Great Migration," eNotes, http://www.enotes.com/topic/greatmigration.
5. *Chicago Defender*, 13 January 1917.
6. William H. Frey, "The Great Migration: Black Americans Return to the South 1965–2000," The Brookings Institution (May 2004): 1–3.
7. Campbell Gibson, "Population of the 100 Largest Cities and other Urban Places in the United States: 1790–1990," U.S. Bureau of the Census—Population Division (June 1998).
8. James Gilbertlove, "African Americans and the American Labor Movement," *Prologue* (Summer 1997, vol. 29).
9. Geoffrey C. Ward, *Unforgivable Blackness* (New York: Knopf Publishing, 2004), 3.
10. Ibid., 6.
11. Ibid., 182.
12. Ibid., 51.
13. Ibid., 121–127.
14. Ibid., 133.
15. John Ridley, "A True Champion vs. the Great White Hope," National Public Radio, 2 July 2010, http://www.npr.org/templates/story/story.php?storyId=128245468.
16. Janne Romppaninen, "Time Tunnel: James J. Jeffries—The Forgotten Grizzly Bear," East Side Boxing, 29 June 2004, http://www.eastsideboxing.com/news.
17. Ward, 205–212.
18. Ibid., 214.
19. Ibid., 216.
20. Ibid., 216–217.
21. James W. Loewen, *Lies My Teacher Told Me* (New York: Touchstone Press, 1996), 32
22. Ibid., 22.
23. Ibid., 26–27.

24. Ibid., 28.

25. Peter Perl, "Race Riot of 1919 Gave Glimpse of Future Struggles," *Washington Post*, 1 March 1999, A1.

26. Richard Wormser, "The Rise and Fall of Jim Crow," PBS, http://www.pbs.org/wnet/jimcrow/stories_events_red.html.

27. *Arkansas Gazette*, 3 October 1919.

28. O.A. Rogers, Jr., "Sharecropping," *Arkansas Historical Quarterly* (Summer 1960).

29. "Elaine Massacre," Encyclopedia of Arkansas, http://www.encyclopediaofarkansas.net.

30. Wormser.

31. *New York Times*, 3 October 1919.

32. "Chinese Immigrants and the Building of the Transcontinental Railroad," Digital History, http://www.digitalhistory.uh.edu/voices/china1.cfm.

33. "The Chinese Exclusion (1882): Brief Overview," Virtual Americana, http://www.lehigh.edu/~ineng/VirtualAmericana/chineseimmigrationact.html.

34. U.S. Census, 1920.

35. Josephine Ross, *The Tudors: England's Golden Age* (New York: Putnam, 1979).

36. "Anti-Catholicism in the United States," Wikipedia, http://en.wikipedia.org/wiki/anticatholicism_in_the_united_states.

37. Edward A. Fitzpatrick, "Miniatures in Georgetown, 1634 to 1934," *The Journal of Higher Education* (January 1936).

38. "Anti-Catholicism in the United States."

39. Edwin Hooey, "Terror in New York, 1741," *American Heritage* (June 1974).

40. R. F. Weigley, et al., *Philadelphia: A 300 Year History* (New York: W. W. Norton & Co., 1982).

41. Ray Allen Billington, *The Protestant Crusade, 1800–1860: A Study of the Origins of American Nativism* (Quadrangle Paperbacks, 1938).

42. Bush, Bryan S., "Bloody Monday Riots: August 6, 1855," Bryan S. Bush Books, http://www.bryansbush.com/hub.php?page=articles&layer=a0709.

43. Donald L. Kinzer, *Episode in Anti-Catholicism: The American Protective Association* (Seattle: University of Washington Press, 1964).

Chapter 7: Power Play

1. Kenneth T. Jackson, 10.

2. Duffus, 34.

3. House Committee, *Hearings on the Ku Klux Klan*, 133.

4. Cutlip, 407.

5. Duffus, 30.

6. House Committee, *Hearings on the Ku Klux Klan*, 174.

7. Chalmers, 32–33.

8. Cutlip, 385.
9. Fuller, 16.
10. Ibid.
11. *New York Herald*, 10 January 1921.
12. Ibid., 11 January 1921.
13. Ibid., 12 January 1921.
14. Ibid., 13 January 1921.
15. Ibid., 14 January 1921.
16. Cutlip, 386.
17. Ibid., 389.
18. House Committee, *Hearings on the Ku Klux Klan*, 29.
19. Ibid., 29.
20. Ibid., 28.
21. Cutlip, 386.
22. Ibid., 387.
23. Ibid., 388.
24. *Literary Digest*, April 1922.
25. Cutlip, 392.
26. House Committee, *Hearings on the Ku Klux Klan*, 152.
27. Ibid., 153.
28. Charles O. Jackson, 359.
29. Ibid.
30. Cutlip, 399.
31. Ibid., 400.
32. Ibid., 395.
33. Ibid., 398–399.
34. Ibid., 401.
35. "Mary Elizabeth Tyler House," National Register of Historic Places, U.S. Dept. of the Interior, Washington, DC.

Chapter 8: The Whistle

1. Fry, *Modern Ku Klux Klan*, 8.
2. Ibid., 3.
3. John Allison, ed., *Notable Men of Tennessee, Vol. 1* (Atlanta: Southern Historical Association, 1905).
4. Henry Peck Fry, *The Voice of the Third Generation: A Discussion of the Race Question for the Benefit of Those Who Believe that the United States is a White Man's Country and Should be Governed by White Men* (Chattanooga, TN: Published by the author, 1906), 5.
5. Ibid., 6.
6. Ibid., 7.
7. Ibid., 8.

8. Ibid., 28.
9. "Leonard Wood," Arlington National Cemetery, http://www.arlingtoncem-etery.net/lwood.htm.
10. Henry Peck Fry file, Virginia Military Institute Archives, Lexington, VA.
11. Fry, *Modern Ku Klux Klan*, 8.
12. Ibid., 4.
13. Ibid., 9.
14. Ibid., 5.
15. Ibid., 6.
16. Ibid., 7.
17. Ibid., 7.

Chapter 9: The World

1. "The Year 1921," The People History, http://www.thepeoplehistory.com/1921.html.
2. Susan Zannos. *Joseph Pulitzer and the Story Behind the Pulitzer Prize* (Bear, DE: Mitchell Lane Publishers, 2004), 13.
3. Nancy Whitelaw, *Joseph Pulitzer and the New York World* (Greensboro, NC: Morgan Reynolds Inc., 2000), 11.
4. Ibid., 11.
5. Ibid., 12.
6. Zannos, 17.
7. Whitelaw, 18.
8. Ibid., 21.
9. Ibid., 27.
10. Ibid., 30–32.
11. Ibid., 32.
12. Ibid., 34–36.
13. Ibid., 102.
14. Ibid., 65.
15. Ibid., 69–73.
16. Ibid., 80.
17. Ibid., 82.
18. John K. Hutchens and George Oppenheimer, eds., *The Best in the World: A Selection of News and Feature Stories, Editorials, Humor, Poems, and Reviews from 1921–1928* (New York: The Viking Press, 1973), xix.
19. Andrew T. Crosland, "Swope, Herbert Bayard," American National Biography, http://www.anb.org.
20. Rowell & Ayers, *American Newspaper Directory, 1869–1922*, 669.
21. Roy J. Harris, *Pulitzer's Gold: Behind the Prize for Public Service Journalism* (Columbia, MO: University of Missouri Press, 2007), 132.
22. Crosland.

23. Ibid.
24. Henry Peck Fry file.
25. *Alexandria Virginia Gazette*, 11 February 1956.
26. Broooke Kroeger, *Nellie Bly: Daredevil, Reporter, Feminist* (New York: Times Books, 1994), 4.
27. Ibid., 44.
28. Ibid., 70.
29. Ibid., 75.
30. Ibid., 85.
31. Ibid., 85.
32. Ibid., 89.
33. Ibid., 93.
34. Ibid., 97.
35. Ibid., 101.
36. Ibid., 143.
37. Ibid., 172.
38. Ibid., xiii.
39. Ibid., 187.
40. Annotated Code of Tennessee (1896), Article VI, 1631.
41. Ibid., 1437.
42. American Bar Association, Rules of Professional Conduct, 4.1: Truthfulness in Statements to Others.
43. Hutchens, xx.
44. *Collier's Magazine*, 11 February 1905.
45. Ritchie, 383.
46. Ibid., 381.
47. Ibid., 380.
48. Ibid., 377.
49. Paul Boyer, et al., *The Enduring Vision: A History of the American People, Vol. 2: From 1865* (Boston: Houghton Mifflin Company, 1998), 471.
50. Harvard College, *Class of 1901, Twenty-Fifth Anniversary Report, 1901–1926* (Cambridge, MA: The Riverside Press, 1926).
51. Rowland Thomas, *The Little Gods: A Masque of the Far East* (Boston: Little, Brown, and Company, 1909), preface.
52. "Collier's Weekly," Spartacus Educational, http://www.spartacus.schoolnet.co.uk/USAcolliers.htm.
53. *Collier's*, 11 February 1905.
54. United States Passport Applications, Rowland Thomas, June 1919 and May 1920.
55. *New York World*, 6 September 1921.
56. *New York World*, 7 September 1921.
57. The Pulitzer Prizes, http://www.pulitzer.org.
58. *New York World*, 8 September 1921.
59. Ibid., 9 September 1921.

60. Ibid., 10 September 1921.

Chapter 10: Damage Control

1. Alice Rains Trulock, *In the Hands of Providence: Joshua Chamberlain & the American Civil War* (Chapel Hill, NC: The University of North Carolina Press, 1992), 9.
2. Ibid., 133.
3. Ibid., 8.
4. Ibid. 147.
5. Fry, *Modern Ku Klux Klan*, 108.
6. Ibid., 109.
7. *New York Times*, 11 September 1921.
8. Cutlip, 381.
9. *New York Times*, 11 September 1921.
10. *New York World*, 11 September 1921.
11. *New York Times*, 11 September 1921.
12. Ibid.
13. *New York World*, 11 September 1921.
14. *New York Times*, 12 September 1921.
15. *New York World*, 12 September 1921.
16. *New York Times*, 13 September 1921.
17. *New York World*, 13 September 1921.
18. Cutlip, 403.
19. *New York World*, 15 September 1921.
20. *New York American*, 15 September 1921.
21. Ibid.
22. Ibid., 16 September 1921.
23. Ibid.
24. *New York World*, 17 September 1921.
25. *New York American*, 17 September 1921.
26. *New York World*, 18 September 1921.
27. *New York American*, 18 September 1921.
28. *New York World*, 19 September 1921.
29. Ibid., 20 September 1921.
30. Cutlip, 405.
31. *New York World*, 21 September 1921.
32. Ibid., 25 September 1921.
33. Fry, *Modern Ku Klux Klan*, 111.
34. Cutlip, 406.
35. Ibid., 405.
36. *New York World*, 20–28 September 1921.
37. Ibid., 29 September 1921.

38. *New York American*, 19 September 1921.
39. Ibid., 20 September 1921.
40. Ibid., 21–30 September 1921.
41. Ibid., 25 September 1921.
42. *New York World*, 27 September 1921.
43. Ibid., 1 October 1921.
44. Ibid.
45. J. Q. Jett Papers, Hargrett Rare Book & Manuscript Library, University of Georgia Library, Athens, GA, 11 October 1921.

Chapter 11: Shock Waves

1. House Committee, *Hearings on the Ku Klux Klan*, 11 October 1921, opening statement.
2. "About the Committee on Rules," House of Representatives Committee on Rules, http://www.rules.house.gov.
3. Biographical Directory of the United States Congress, 1774–present, http://bioguide.congress.gov.
4. House Committee, *Hearings on the Ku Klux Klan*, 11 October 1921.
5. *New York Times*, 12 October 1921.
6. Ibid., 13 October 1921.
7. Fuller, 21.
8. Chalmers, 37.
9. *Le Petit Journal* (Montreal), 10 June 1934.
10. "Upshaw, William David," Wikipedia, http://en.wikipedia.org/wiki/William_D._Upshaw.
11. Fuller, 53.
12. House Committee, *Hearings on the Ku Klux Klan*, 12 October 1921.
13. Ibid., 13 October 1921.

Chapter 12: Flight

1. House Committee, *Hearings on the Ku Klux Klan*, 17 October 1921.
2. H.J. Res 201 (11 October 1921).
3. Fuller, 53.
4. Schmidt, 3.
5. Chalmers, 38.
6. Cutlip, 407.
7. *New York Times*, 3 December 1921.
8. Cutlip, 408.
9. *New York Times*, 3 December 1921.

10. Ibid.

11. Ibid., 15 December 1921.

12. Cutlip, 408.

13. Ibid.

14. *New York Times*, 10 June 1922.

15. Cutlip, 408.

16. Duffus, 38.

17. Kenneth T. Jackson, 14.

18. Blee, 22.

19. *New York Times*, 17 July 1922.

20. J. Q. Jett Papers, 3 August 1922.

21. *New York Times*, 20 August 1922.

22. J.A. Aberdeen, *Hollywood Renegades: The Society of Independent Motion Picture Producers* (Los Angeles: Cobblestone Entertainment), 1999.

23. J. Q. Jett Papers, 8 September 1922.

24. Kenneth T. Jackson, 14.

25. Cutlip, 409.

26. Kenneth T. Jackson, 14.

27. Charles O. Jackson, 361.

28. Kenneth T. Jackson, 14.

29. J. Q. Jett Papers, 23 December 1922.

30. Altadena Public Library, Altadena, CA.

31. Fuller, 18.

32. J. Q. Jett Papers, 9 February 1923.

33. Cutlip, 409.

34. Charles O. Jackson, 362–363.

35. Chalmers, 132.

Chapter 13: End Game

1. "1922 Winners," The Pulitzer Prizes, http://www.pulitzer.org/awards/1922.

2. Crosland.

3. Byron Liggett, "Press, Politics, and Poker—Herbert Bayard Swope," Poker Player, 2005, http://www.pokerplayernewspaper.com.

4. E. J. Kahn, *The World of Swope* (New York: Simon and Schuster, 1965), 6.

5. Crosland.

6. Henry Peck Fry file, Virginia Military Institute Archives.

7. *Arkansas Gazette*, May 1945.

8. *New York Times*, 10 December 1922.

9. Lila Lee Jones, "The Ku Klux Klan in Eastern Kansas during the 1920s," *Emporia State Research Studies*, vol. 23, no. 3 (Winter 1975).

10. Biographical Directory of the U.S. Congress.

11. U.S. Census, 1930.

12. *Ellijay* (Georgia) *Times Courier*, 4 November 1937.
13. Charles O. Jackson, 363.
14. Ibid.
15. J. Q. Jett Papers, March 1924.
16. *Los Angeles Times*, 10 September 1924.
17. National Registry of Historic Places.
18. Cutlip, 411.
19. J. Q. Jett Papers, 16 May 1924.
20. Cutlip, 411.
21. United States Draft Registration, E. Y. Clarke, 1942.
22. Cutlip, 411.
23. Kenneth T. Jackson, 17–19.
24. *New York Sun*, 8 August 1925.
25. "Rise and Fall of D. C. Stephenson," Ohio State University Department of History, http://ehistory.osu.edu.
26. "Democratic Convention of 1924," Digital History, http://www.digitalhistory.uh.edu.
27. "The Rise and Fall of D. C. Stephenson."
28. Klanwatch Project, *Ku Klux Klan: A History of Racism and Violence, 6ᵗʰ Ed.* (Montgomery, AL: Southern Poverty Law Center, 2011).
29. Southern Poverty Law Center.
30. Cutlip, 412.

Epilogue

1. Mitchell Zuckoff, *Ponzi's Scheme: The True Story of a Financial Legend* (New York: Random House, 2005), 106.
2. Harris, 125.
3. Zuckoff, 107.
4. Ibid., 108.
5. Ibid., 36–43.
6. Ibid., 174.
7. Ibid., 227–229.
8. Harris, 130.
9. Marshall McLuhan, *Understanding Media: The Extensions of Man* (New York: McGraw Hill, 1964), 18.

BIBLIOGRAPHY

"1922 Winners." The Pulitzer Prizes. http://www.pulitzer.org/awards/1922.

Aberdeen, J. A. *Hollywood Renegades: The Society of Independent Motion Picture Producers.* Los Angeles: Cobblestone Entertainment, 1999.

"About the Committee on Rules." House of Representatives Committee on Rules. http://www.rules.house.gov.

Alexander, Gross. *A History of the Methodist Church South in the United States.* Nashville: Publishing House of the M.E. Church, South, 1907.

Alexandria (Virginia) Gazette. 11 February 1956.

Allison, John, ed. *Notable Men of Tennessee, Vol. 1.* Atlanta: Southern Historical Association, 1905.

Altadena Public Library, Altadena, CA.

American Bar Association, Rules of Professional Conduct, 4.1: Truthfulness in Statements to Others.

"American Issue Publishing Company." Alcohol: Problems and Solutions. http://www2.potsdam.edu/hansondj/Controversies/American-Issue-Publishing-Company.html#.Ut1ZpBDnaM8.

Anbinder, Tyler. *Nativism and Slavery: The Northern Know Nothings and the Politics of the 1850s.* Oxford: Oxford University Press, 1992.

"Anti-Catholicism in the United States." Wikipedia. htttp://en.wikipedia.org/wiki/anti-catholicism_in_the_united_states.

Anti-Saloon League Museum. Westerville (Ohio) Public Library. http://www.wpl.lib.oh.us/AntiSaloon/.

Annotated Code of Tennessee (1896), Article VI.

Arkansas Gazette.

Atlanta Constitution.

"Attractions." Stone Mountain Park. http://www.stonemountainpark.com.

Billington, Ray Allen. *The Protestant Crusade, 1800–1860: A Study of the Origins of American Nativism.* Quadrangle Paperbacks, 1938.

Biographical Directory of the United States Congress, 1774–present. http://bioguide.congress.gov.

Blee, Katherine M. *Women in the Klan: Racism and Gender in the 1920s.* Berkeley: University of California Press, 1991.

Boyer, Paul S., et al. *The Enduring Vision: A History of the American People, Vol. 2: From 1865.* Boston: Houghton Mifflin Company, 1998.

Bush, Bryan S. "Bloody Monday Riots: August 6, 1855." Bryan S. Bush Books. http://www.bryansbush.com/hub.php?page=articles&layer=a0709.

Chalmers, David M. *Hooded Americanism: The First Century of the Ku Klux Klan 1865 to Present.* Garden City, NY: Doubleday & Co. Inc., 1965.

Chicago Defender, 13 January 1917.

"The Chinese Exclusion (1882): Brief Overview." Virtual Americana. http://www.lehigh.edu/~ineng/VirtualAmericana/chineseimmigrationact.html.

"Chinese Immigrants and the Building of the Transcontinental Railroad." Digital History. http://www.digitalhistory.uh.edu/voices/china1.cfm.

Collier's Magazine, 11 February 1905.

"Collier's Weekly." Spartacus Educational. http://www.spartacus.schoolnet.co.uk/USAcolliers.htm.

Creel, George. *Rebel at Large: Recollections of Fifty Crowded Years.* New York: G. P. Putnam and Sons, 1947.

Crosland, Andrew T. "Swope, Herbert Bayard." American National Biography. http://www.anb.org.

Cutlip, Scott M. "Clarke and Tyler: Builders of the Ku Klux Klan." In *The Unseen Power: Public Relations: a History.* Hinsdale, NJ: Routledge, 1994.

"Democratic Convention of 1924." Digital History. http://www.digitalhistory.uh.edu.

Department of Education for Georgia. *1898 Annual Report.*

De Tocqueville, Alexis. *Democracy in America.* London: Saunders and Otley, 1838.

Dinnerstein, Leonard. *The Leo Frank Case*. New York: Columbia University Press, 1968.

"Direct Selling Methods: Single Level and Multilevel Marketing." More Business. http://www.morebusiness.com.

Dorey, Annette K. Vance. *Better Baby Contests: The Scientific Quest for Perfect Childhood Health in the Early Twentieth Century*. Jefferson, NC: McFarland & Co., 1999.

Duffus, Robert L. "Salesmen of Hate: The Ku Klux Klan." *World's Work*, vol. 42 (October 1923): 461–469.

Eastern Cherokee Claim #27076, Mary Elizabeth Carroll (nee Cornett), 29 June 1907.

"Education." New Georgia Encyclopedia. http://www.georgiaencyclopedia.org/Education.

"Elaine Massacre." Encyclopedia of Arkansas. http://www.encyclopediaofarkansas.net.

Ellijay (Georgia) *Times Courier.* 4 November 1937.

Elliott, Charles. *A History of the Great Secession from the Methodist Episcopal Church in the year 1845*. Cincinnati: Swormstedt and Poe, 1855.

Fitzpatrick, Edward A. "Miniatures in Georgetown, 1634 to 1934." *The Journal of Higher Education* (January 1936).

Fleming, Thomas. *The Illusion of Victory: America in World War 1*. New York: Basic Books, 2003.

Frey, William H. "The Great Migration: Black Americans Return to the South 1965–2000." The Brookings Institution (May 2004): 1–3.

Fry, Henry Peck. *The Voice of the Third Generation: A Discussion of the Race Question for the Benefit of Those Who Believe that the United States is a White Man's Country and Should be Governed by White Men*. Chattanooga, TN: Published by the author, 1906.

Fry, Henry Peck. *The Modern Ku Klux Klan*. Boston: Small, Maynard & Company, 1922.

Fuller, Edgar I. *The Visible of the Invisible Empire: The Maelstrom*. Denver: Maelstrom Publishing Co., 1925.

Gibson, Campbell. "Population of the 100 Largest Cities and other Urban Places in the United States: 1790–1990." U.S. Bureau of the Census—Population Division (June 1998).

Gilbertlove, James. "African Americans and the American Labor Movement." *Prologue* (Summer 1997, vol. 29).

"Great Migration." eNotes. http://www.enotes.com/topic/greatmigration.

Grey House Publishing. *Working Americans: 1880–1999.* Vol. 1, *The Working Class.* Millerton, NY: Grey House Publishing, 2000.

Griffith, David Wark. *The Man Who Invented Hollywood: The Autobiography of D. W. Griffith.* Edited by James Hart. Louisville: Touchstone Publishing Co., 1972.

Harris, Roy J. *Pulitzer's Gold: Behind the Prize for Public Service Journalism.* Columbia, MO: University of Missouri Press, 2007.

Harvard College. *Class of 1901, Twenty-Fifth Anniversary Report, 1901–1926.* Cambridge, MA: The Riverside Press, 1926.

Harvard College. *Class of 1901, Eleventh Report, 1943–1946.* Boston: C.A. Peters, 1946.

Henry Peck Fry file. Virginia Military Institute Archives. Lexington, VA.

Herrmann, L.A. "Geology of the Stone Mountain—Lithonia District, Georgia." *Georgia Geological Survey Bulletin* 61.

H.J. Res. 201 (11 October 1921).

Hooey, Edwin. "Terror in New York, 1741." *American Heritage* (June 1974).

Hurst, Ernest, ed. *The Anti-Saloon League Year Book 1919: An Encyclopedia of Facts and Figures Dealing with the Liquor Traffic and Temperance Reform.* Columbus, Ohio: The Anti-Saloon League of America, 1919.

Hutchens, John K., and Oppenheimer, George, eds. *The Best in the World: A Selection of News and Feature Stories, Editorials, Humor, Poems, and Reviews from 1921–1928.* New York: The Viking Press, 1973.

Ingham, John N. "Ivy Lee." *Biographical Dictionary of American Business Leaders.* Westport, CT: Greenwood Publishing Group, 1983.

Ivy L. Lee Papers. Princeton University Digital Library. http://pudl.princeton.edu.

Jackson, Charles O. "William J. Simmons: A Career in KuKluxism," *Georgia Historical Quarterly*, vol. 50 (December 1966): 351–365.

Jackson, Kenneth T. *The Ku Klux Klan in the City, 1915–1930.* New York: Concord University Press, 1967.

Jeal, Tim. *Stanley: The Impossible Life of Africa's Greatest Explorer.* New Haven, CT: Yale University Press, 2007.

Jenkins, James Sage. *Atlanta in the Age of Pericles.* Lithonia, GA: Chimney Hill Press,

1995.

"Jim Crow Laws." University of Dayton. http://www.academic.udayton.edu/race/02rights/jcrow02.html.

Jones, Lila Lee. "The Ku Klux Klan in Eastern Kansas during the 1920s." *Emporia State Research Studies*, vol. 23, no. 3 (Winter 1975).

Jordan, David Starr. *The Blood of the Nation*. Boston: American Unitarian Association, 1902.

J. Q. Jett Papers, Hargrett Rare Book & Manuscript Library, University of Georgia Library, Athens, GA.

Kahn, E. J. *The World of Swope*. New York: Simon and Schuster, 1965.

Kinzer, Donald L. *Episode in Anti-Catholicism: The American Protective Association*. Seattle: University of Washington Press, 1964.

Kroeger, Brooke. *Nellie Bly: Daredevil, Reporter, Feminist*. New York: Times Books, 1994.

Klanwatch Project. *Ku Klux Klan: A History of Racism and Violence, 6th Ed*. Montgomery, AL: Southern Poverty Law Center, 2011.

Kunhardt, Philip B. Jr. *P. T. Barnum: America's Greatest Showman*. New York: Alfred A. Knopf Inc., 1995.

"Land & Resources, Stone Mountain." New Georgia Encyclopedia. http://www.georgiaencyclopedia.org.

Lawrance, Gary. "Herbert Bayard Swope of Land's End." Mansions of the Guilded Age. http://garylawrance.blogspot.com/2011/04/herbert-bayard-swope-of-lands-end.html.

"Lee, Dr. James Wideman Sr." Find a Grave. http://www.findagrave.com.

"Leonard Wood." Arlington National Cemetery. http://www.arlingtoncemetery.net/lwood.htm.

Lewis, Alfred Allan. *Man of the World: Herbert Bayard Swope: A Charmed Life of Pulitzer Prizes, Poker, and Politics*. Indianapolis/New York: The Bobbs-Merrill Company, 1978.

Liggett, Byron. "Press, Politics, and Poker—Herbert Bayard Swope." Poker Player, 2005. http://www.pokerplayernewspaper.com.

Loewen, James W. *Lies My Teacher Told Me*. New York: Touchstone Press, 1996.

"Mary Elizabeth Tyler House." National Register of Historic Places, U.S. Dept. of the Interior, Washington, DC.

McLuhan, Marshall. *Understanding Media: The Extensions of Man.* New York: McGraw Hill, 1964.

McSherry, Patrick. "A Brief History of the 1st Alabama Volunteer Infantry." The Spanish American War Centennial Website. http://www.spanamwar.com/1stAlabama.html.

Mencken, H. L. *New York Sun,* 8 August 1925.

Miller, K. S. "U.S. Public Relations History: Knowledge and Limitations." *Communications Yearbook*, vol. 23: 381–420.

Nelson, Megan Kate. *Trembling Earth: A Cultural History of the Okefenokee Swamp.* Athens, GA: University of Georgia Press, 2005.

Newton, Michael. *The Ku Klux Klan: History, Organization, Language, Influence and Activities of America's Most Notorious Secret Society.* Jefferson City, NC: McFarland & Co. Inc., 2007.

New York American.

New York Herald.

New York Times.

New York World.

Okefenokee Swamp Home Page. http://www.okefenokee.com.

Oney, Steve. *And the Dead Shall Rise.* New York: Pantheon Books, 2003.

"Park History." Stone Mountain Memorial Association. http://www.stonemountainpark.org.

Perl, Peter. "Race Riot of 1919 Gave Glimpse of Future Struggles." *Washington Post*, 1 March 1999.

Le Petit Journal (Montreal), 10 June 1934.

"Plessy v. Ferguson." Infoplease. http://www.infoplease.com/plessy.

Ridley, John. "A True Champion vs. the Great White Hope." National Public Radio, 2 July 2010. http://www.npr.org/templates/story/story.php?storyId=128245468.

"Rise and Fall of D. C. Stephenson." Ohio State University Department of History. http://ehistory.osu.edu.

Ritchie, Donald A. *American History: The Modern Era Since 1865.* New York: Glencoe/McGraw Hill, 1997.

Rogers, O. A. Jr. "Sharecropping." *Arkansas Historical Quarterly* (Summer 1960).

Romppaninen, Janne. "Time Tunnel: James J. Jeffries—The Forgotten Grizzly Bear." East Side Boxing, 29 June 2004. http://www.eastsideboxing.com/news.

Ross, Josephine. *The Tudors: England's Golden Age.* New York: Putnam, 1979.

Rowell & Ayers. *American Newspaper Directory, 1869–1922,* 669.

Schickel, Richard. *D. W. Griffith: An American Life.* New York: Simon and Shuster, 1984.

Schlesinger, Arthur M. "Biography of a Nation of Joiners." *American Historical Review,* vol. 50 (October 1944): 1–25.

Schmidt, Alvin. *The Greenwood Encyclopedia of American Institutions: Fraternal Organizations.* Westport, CT: Greenwood Press, 1980.

Shaara, Michael. *The Killer Angels.* New York: Ballantine Publishing Group, 2003.

Shotwell, John M. "Crystallizing Public Hatred: Ku Klux Klan Public Relations in the early 1920s." Unpublished master's thesis, University of Wisconsin–Madison, 1974.

Southern Poverty Law Center, Montgomery, AL.

Stevens, Albert C. *Cyclopedia of Fraternities: A Compilation of Existing Authentic Information and the Results of Original Investigation as to the Origin, Derivation, Founders, Development, Aims, Emblems, Character, and Personnel of More Than Six Hundred Secret Societies in the United States.* New York: E. B. Treat and Company, 1907.

Thomas, Rowland. *The Little Gods: A Masque of the Far East.* Boston: Little, Brown, and Company, 1909.

Trulock, Alice Rains. *In the Hands of Providence: Joshua Chamberlain & the American Civil War.* Chapel Hill, NC: The University of North Carolina Press, 1992.

United States Census, Washington, D.C.

United States Congress House Committee on Rules. *Hearings before the Committee on Rules on the Ku Klux Klan, 1921.* New York: Arno Press, 1969.

United States Draft Registration, E. Y. Clarke, 1942.

United States Passport Applications, Rowland Thomas, June 1919 and May 1920.

United States Weather Bureau Archives (NOAA).

"Upshaw, William David." Wikipedia. http://en.wikipedia.org/wiki/William_D._Upshaw.

Wagenknecht, Edward and Slide, Anthony. *The Films of D. W. Griffith.* New York: Crown Publishers, Inc., 1975.

Ward, Geoffrey C. *Unforgivable Blackness.* New York: Knopf Publishing, 2004.

Weigley, R. F. et al. *Philadelphia: A 300 Year History.* New York: W. W. Norton & Co., 1982.

Wert, Jeffrey D. *Custer: The Controversial Life of George Armstrong Custer.* New York Simon and Shuster, 1996.

"What Was Jim Crow?" Ferris State University. http://www.Ferris.edu/JimCrow.

Whitelaw, Nancy. *Joseph Pulitzer and the New York World.* Greensboro, NC: Morgan Reynolds Inc., 2000.

Willson, Meredith. *The Music Man.* First stage performance 19 December 1957; film, 1962.

"Woodmen Group." The Phoenixmasonry Masonic Museum and Library. http://www. phoenixmasonry.org./masonicmuseum/fraternalism/woodmen.htm.

Wormser, Richard. "The Rise and Fall of Jim Crow." PBS. http://www.pbs.org/wnet/jim-crow/stories_events_red.html.

"The Year 1921." The People History. http://www.thepeoplehistory.com/1921.html.

Zannos, Susan. *Joseph Pulitzer and the Story Behind the Pulitzer Prize.* Bear, DE: Mitchell Lane Publishers, 2004.

Zuckoff, Mitchell. *Ponzi's Scheme: The True Story of a Financial Legend.* New York: Random House, 2005.

ACKNOWLEDGMENTS

Although an author writes alone, he is ultimately dependent on many people. I want to thank all those whose contributions were vital in the completion of *For the Kingdom and the Power*.

First, there are the research librarians and archivists. Their technical expertise and unbridled enthusiasm make them a joy to work with. I want to thank Pam Richards of the Altadena, California, Public Library. She was the key to unlocking the early years of Bessie Tyler. Glenda Garland of the Gilmer County Library in Ellijay, Georgia, provided vital material on J. Q. Jett. Carol Bishop of the Hargrett Rare Book & Manuscript Library at the University of Georgia Libraries helped bring the J. Q. Jett Papers to light. Maira Liriano of the New York Public Library was a wealth of information on Rowland Thomas, Herbert Bayard Swope, and New York City journalism in the early twentieth century. Mary Laura Kludy, archivist at the Virginia Military Institute in Lexington, Virginia, supplied new and exciting information on Henry Peck Fry's role in this story. Michelle Carver of the Center for Research Libraries in Chicago helped access the *New York World*'s 1921 Pulitzer Winning investigative series. Finally, I want to thank the wonderful staff of the Wilmette, Illinois, Public Library. Their assistance in this project was essential.

There are others I want to acknowledge. Dr. Joseph C. Morton taught me American history at Northeastern Illinois University. He was a mentor, historian, author, and, most importantly, a friend. My teaching colleague, Anne McGivern, provided her considerable editing skills and was an excellent sounding board in the early days of the project. Friend and attorney Joe Shipley provided important legal information for the discussion on Henry Peck Fry's motives. John Touhy played a big role in changing *For the Kingdom and the Power* from its original form as a screenplay into a book. And finally I want to thank friend Jim Grutsch for his unflagging enthusiasm for the story of Edward and Bessie.

A while back I made a last-second decision to attend the Printers Row Lit Fest in downtown Chicago. It was there I met my publisher, Sharon Woodhouse. She was instantly interested in my story and put her complete support behind the project. I cannot thank Sharon enough for her publishing expertise and support.

I want to thank my late parents, Harvey and Harriet Laackman. I know Mom and Dad are very proud. My brother, Blair, has always been there for me, and I cherish his love and support. We have come a long way from that tiny speck of a farm and the one-room country schoolhouse in Northwest Iowa.

And, of course, there would be no book without Natalie, Andrew, and Christopher. It all begins at home.

INDEX

ABOUT THE AUTHOR

Born in Iowa and raised in western Michigan, Dale W. Laackman is an award-winning television producer, director, and writer turned historian and author.

Laackman's education includes a B.A. in Advertising from Michigan State University and an M.A. in Television and Film from the University of Michigan. During a 20-year career in broadcasting he worked at various television stations in the Midwest before joining national producer and syndicator Tribune Entertainment Company in Chicago. Mr. Laackman also earned a B.A. in History with a minor in Education from Northeastern Illinois University. He has since taught college courses in Broadcast Journalism as well as middle school World and American History.

The author lives in suburban Chicago with his wife and two sons. *For the Kingdom and the Power: The Big Money Swindle That Spread Hate Across America* is his first book.